The divided economy of Mandatory Palestine

Adopting a systematic, yet non-technical, approach, Jacob M book is the first to analyze the divided economy of Mandatory Pa from the viewpoints of modern economic history and develo economics. While the existing literature has typically focused Jewish economy, this book explores the economic activity of both and Jews in the complex political arena of the period. Draw recently constructed national income accounts for Arabs, Jews, : country as a whole, the book offers new quantitative evidence an pretations concerning key topics such as Palestine's land, capi labor markets, the demographic and socio-economic traits of Ar Jews, their economic performance and bilateral relations, and th cal economy of the country's public sectors. These topics are e: comparatively within the context of the "dual economy" postula distinguishing developmental disparities of a general "dualistic from specific ethno-national political factors. A concluding reviews the complex and uneasy record of Arab–Jewish econ existence over the last three-quarters of a century in the Mandatory Palestine, composed of present-day Israel, the W and the Gaza Strip. The book promises to make a significant tion to the economic history of the modern Middle East a understanding of the Arab-Israeli conflict. The concentratic data will provide a valuable resource for future research.

JACOB METZER is Alexander Brody Professor of Economic the Department of Economics at the Hebrew University of Through most of his career he has worked on the economic l development of Mandatory Palestine and Israel. Besides widely in scholarly journals he has written (in Hebrew) two b field: *National Capital for a National Home* (1979) and *The Je Arab Economy in Mandatory Palestine: Product, Employment* (with Oded Kaplan, 1990).

Cambridge Middle East Studies 11

Cambridge Middle East Studies has been established to publish
books on the nineteenth- and twentieth-century Middle East and
North Africa. The aim of the series is to provide new and original
interpretations of aspects of Middle Eastern societies and their
histories. To achieve disciplinary diversity, books will be solicited from
authors writing in a wide range of fields including history, sociology,
anthropology, political science and political economy. The emphasis
will be on producing books offering an original approach along
theoretical and empirical lines. The series is intended for students and
academics, but the more accessible and wide-ranging studies will also
appeal to the interested general reader.

A list of books in the series can be found after the index

The divided economy of
Mandatory Palestine

Jacob Metzer

CAMBRIDGE
UNIVERSITY PRESS

PUBLISHED BY THE PRESS SYNDICATE OF THE UNIVERSITY OF CAMBRIDGE
The Pitt Building, Trumpington Street, Cambridge CB2 1RP, United Kingdom

CAMBRIDGE UNIVERSITY PRESS
The Edinburgh Building, Cambridge CB2 2RU, United Kingdom
hHp://www.cup.cam.ac.uk
40 West 20th Street, New York, NY 10011–4211, USA
hHp://www.cup.org
10 Stamford Road, Oakleigh, Melbourne 3166, Australia

First published 1998

Printed in the United Kingdom at the University Press, Cambridge

Typeset in 10/12 Monotype Plantin   [SE]

A catalogue record for this book is available from the British Library

Library of Congress cataloguing in publication data

Metzer, Jacob.
    The divided economy of Mandatory Palestine / Jacob Metzer.
        p.   cm. – (Cambridge Middle East studies)
    Includes bibliographical references and index.
    ISBN 0-521-46550-8 (hardbound)
    1. Palestine – Economic conditions.   2. Jews – Palestine – Economic
conditions.   3. Palestinian Arabs – Economic conditions.
    I. Title.   II. Series.
HC415.25.M468   1998
330.95694–dc21   97-38678 CIP

ISBN 0 521 46550 8 hardback

To the memory of Yoram Ben-Porath,
colleague and friend

Contents

Figures

Tables

Preface

After World War I Palestine rapidly turned from being a loosely defined geographical area within the defunct Ottoman empire into a well-delineated territorial and administrative entity, unified by the British Mandate and its modern government. Several major developments took place under the British rule: on the one hand, Jewish immigration grew substantially, Zionist land acquisition expanded, and a thriving Jewish national community, run by self-established and officially recognized autonomous institutions, was taking form. On the other hand, partly in response to the Zionist "nation-building" aspirations and settlement, the period saw the crystallization of the Palestinian-Arab national movement and the intensification of the ethno-national conflict (which is still very much with us) between Arabs and Jews over territory, political domination, and self-determination. It follows that although the Mandate period lasted less than thirty years, it constitutes a highly significant and formative era in the history of modern Palestine.

Scholars have long been attracted to this fascinating and important chapter in the history of the country and its peoples. A large number of studies on Mandatory Palestine have appeared, addressing, among other topics, the economic scene which was a major component of the story. But since most of the scholarly work in the field was done by political historians, political scientists, and sociologists, economic issues were generally treated as part of the political and socio-political context. In this literature attention was therefore given mainly to the economic policies of the government, to their effects on Arabs and Jews, and to the political motivations and implications of the economic relations (or lack thereof) between the two peoples, specifically, their interactions in the land and labor markets.

In the past three decades, however, partly drawing on important economic treatises by contemporaries (such as Bonne, 1938; Himadeh, 1938; Grunenbaum, 1941; Abramowitz and Guelfat, 1944; Nathan, Gass, and Creamer, 1946; Horowitz, 1948), a thin but steady stream of findings on various economic features of Mandatory Palestine has been produced by modern economists and by quantitatively oriented economic historians. One of the early products of this research was the pioneering work by Szereszewski (1968), who constructed estimates of annual series of production, investment, capital stock, and employment for the Jewish sector in 1922–47. These estimates laid the quantitative foundations for later studies on a number of structural and operational attributes of Jewish economic life and growth performance (see for example, Giladi, 1973; Gross and Metzer, 1978; Halevi, 1983; Beenstock, Metzer, and Ziv, 1995).

Another fruitful line of research concentrated on quantitatively documenting and systematically examining the allocational and distributional characteristics of government economic policies (Metzer, 1982; Gross, 1984b). A third line consisted of monographic studies addressing specific topics such as the economy of World War II (Gross and Metzer, 1993) and the land tenure regime in the rural Arab community (Firestone, 1981, 1990).

In general, though, the lack of an appropriate database recording Arab economic activity (except for the estimates made by Gaathon [1941, 1978] for 1936 and by Loftus [1946, 1948] for 1944 and 1945) has severely limited the options for a thorough examination of the economic structure and development of the Arab community, leaving a major component of Mandatory Palestine's economy relatively unexplored. In part, this constraint was removed by our construction of annual output and value-added estimates, by industry, for the Arab sector within a complete system of national-income accounts for Mandatory Palestine (Metzer and Kaplan, 1990). These accounts are presented in the detailed data appendix (part A) to this volume.

Relying on these newly constructed national income accounts, which are essential building blocks for the analysis that follows, and drawing on other source material and previous studies (my own and those of others), this book offers a first thematically designed account of the ethno-nationally divided economy of Mandatory Palestine by a "professional" economic historian, equipped with the "tool-kits" and methodologies of modern historical and development economics. It presents, in a comparative international framework (when possible), rich demographic and socio-economic material and new quantitative documentation and interpretations of Arab, Jewish, and government economic activity, while examining the major components of Palestine's economic structure and change within the complex political context of the Mandate era.

Chapter 1 sets the stage for the entire book. The opening section introduces the subject matter and discusses the conceptual and empirical justification for considering Mandatory Palestine an economy divided between Arabs and Jews, and for adopting the "dual economy" postulate as an organizing theme for its analysis. The second section of this chapter presents a comparative bird's-eye view of the two ethno-national sectors' economic structure, their record of economic activity and growth, and bilateral economic relations; it also serves to identify the issues to be dealt with in more detail in the rest of the book.

Chapters 2 and 3 are devoted to the human factor in the country's economic life. Chapter 2 examines, in a broad comparative context, the demographic and socio-economic traits of Palestine's Arabs and Jews as affected by, and effecting their, disparate states of development and ethno-national split. In chapter 3, the quantitative dimensions and the demographic and socio-economic characteristics of Palestine's Jewish immigrants are treated in greater depth.

The production side of Palestine's economy is taken up in the next two chapters. Chapter 4 provides some orders of magnitude concerning the primary factors of production: land, capital, and labor. We examine, from an economist's viewpoint, the political, demographic, and economic mechanisms underlying the structural characteristics and operation of the markets for these factors (which, more than anything else, typify Palestine's ethno-national economic dualism), and offer interpretive assessments of their distributional, allocative, and growth implications.

Chapter 5 concentrates on the dynamics of production and trade, distinguishing between the inter-war years and the extreme changes brought about by World War II. The first section reviews the sources and patterns of Arab and Jewish output and productivity growth in the aggregate, across and within industries. Emphasis here is on the developmentally distinct compositions of production and employment by industry in the two ethno-national sectors and on the attributes of structure and change in their respective agricultural and manufacturing industries. The second section documents and discusses Palestine's external trade. First, the patterns and composition of the country's merchandise trade are examined vis-à-vis those of inter-war world trade; next, the volume and structure of Arab and Jewish foreign and bilateral trade are dealt with, along with an assessment of their weights in the two sectors' respective economic activity.

Chapter 6 is devoted to the public sectors. The first section begins by discussing the general economic policies of the government in a broad (colonial and Palestine-specific) context. It then moves on to a comparative examination of the distributional effects of the government's fiscal system on Arabs and Jews, and to the attitudes of contemporaries toward its underpinnings and consequences. The second section surveys the outlays of the Jewish non-governmental public sectors, and the third section deals with some questions concerning the public-private mix in the Jewish economy, which distinguished it from the Arab counterpart.

Chapter 7 winds up the main body of the volume with a postscript that puts the economic story of Mandatory Palestine in historical perspectives. It addresses a number of issues stemming from the literature's long-debated comparisons between the economy of Mandatory Palestine and those of typical (African) settlement colonies, and comparatively reviews the main attributes of the complex and uneasy record of Arab-Jewish economic coexistence, over the past three-quarters of a century, in the area of Mandatory Palestine, composed of present-day Israel, the West Bank, and the Gaza Strip.

As it is a scholarly piece of economic history, most readers should see the main value of the book in the findings it reports and in the interpretations it offers concerning economic life in Mandatory Palestine and, in addition, in the reference and source material that its data appendixes provide. However, although largely resting on economic reasoning and analysis, the book is written and presented in a non-technical fashion, aimed at communicating with a wide audience of scholars, students, and interested laypersons, not narrowly confined to economic history "specialists." Besides the "inner circle" of readers interested in the economic, social, and political history of Palestine, and in the evolution of the Israeli-Palestinian relations, this book may find a more general readership as well. It should include, among others, those who are interested in the history of the modern Middle East; students of the economics of development, growth, and migration at large; and readers concerned with general problems of economic coexistence and ethno-national divides.

Acknowledgments

My research journey into various facets of the economy and the political economy of Mandatory Palestine has been a long one, spanning more than two decades. During this time I have benefited from more support, assistance, and constructive criticism than can be properly acknowledged here. But I would like, at least, to thank those institutions and individuals whose contributions were highly significant to my work.

Most of my research in the field was carried out under the auspices of the Maurice Falk Institute for Economic Research in Israel, whose directors and staff provided me with essential financial, academic, and technical support. Additional financial support was rendered over the years by grants received from the Israel Science Foundation administered by the Israel Academy of Sciences and Humanities, the Israel Foundation Trustees, and the Charles H. Revson Foundation of New York via the Jerusalem Institute for Israel Studies.

Nachum Gross, initially my teacher, and later my colleague at the Hebrew University, and at times research partner and co-author, introduced me to this area of inquiry in the mid-1970s and has been a constant source of encouragement and useful criticism ever since. Haim Barkai, Nadav Halevi, Ephraim Kleiman, and Ruth Klinov of the Hebrew University, Stanley Engerman of the University of Rochester, and Joel Mokyr of Northwestern University made helpful comments on various parts of my work produced in the course of time. Hagit Lavsky (then a graduate student and now a faculty member at the Hebrew University) provided invaluable research assistance while I was making my first steps in the field. Oded Kaplan (at the time researcher at the Falk Institute) has been a devoted research associate in constructing Palestine's national income accounts, and Michael Beenstock of the Hebrew University (with the assistance of Sanny Ziv) collaborated with me in a recent econometric exploration of the Mandatory Jewish economy, which was partly based on these accounts.

This book, which builds (among other sources) on many of my accumulated research findings and quantitative evidence, was transformed from a general idea into a concrete project during my stay as visiting fellow at St. Antony's College, Oxford in 1992/93. Roger Owen of Harvard University (then director of the Middle East Centre at St. Antony's College, Oxford University) was very supportive; he generated the needed stimulus to get things started, and at a later stage provided insightful comments on an early draft of the first chapter. Useful comments on various chapter drafts were offered also by Peter Temin of MIT and Gur Ofer of the Hebrew University. Nachum Gross was, as always, extremely helpful. He read the entire manuscript with great care and made very important suggestions. I benefited immensely from all the comments and suggestions that were generously offered to me, including those I could not accept.

In 1993 I was granted a fellowship to pursue my project at the Woodrow Wilson International Center for Scholars in Washington, DC. The exceptionally hospitable and inspiring environment provided by the center's director, fellows, and staff, and the excellent research facilities and assistance made available, enabled me to get a substantial portion of the work done there.

The writing of the book was completed back home in Jerusalem. The Hebrew University provided generous support at the final stages of preparing the manuscript, and the directors of the Falk Institute were again very helpful, particularly in allowing me to benefit from Maggie Eisenstaedt's dedication and skills. She performed her usual indispensable task of turning a raw draft into a proper manuscript (text, tables, and figures). Marigold Acland, Middle East Studies editor at Cambridge University Press, was instrumental in efficiently leading the book from its inception through its acceptance for publication by CUP to the final stages of production and Mary Starkey was an efficient and cooperative copy-editor. I thank them all.

This book is dedicated to the memory of Yoram Ben-Porath, professor of economics at the Hebrew University, director of the Falk Institute for Economic Research, and later rector and president of the Hebrew University. Yoram was an economist of broad vision who, in the grand tradition of Simon Kuznets and T. W. Schultz, attempted throughout his professional career to advance our understanding of the interplay between economic development and growth and manifestations of human behavior in such areas as childbearing, acquisition of education, immigration, and labor supply. Making Israel the focus of the empirical facet of his work, he was also a pioneer in the study of the economic life of Israeli Arabs, unveiling the economic aspects and implications of the complex politics involved. His exemplary studies, his friendship, and his continuously expressed interest in my work inspired me greatly.

On October 18, 1992, Yoram Ben-Porath, his wife Yael, and their son Yahli were killed in a car accident. The loss caused by this tragedy remains with us.

A note on numbers

Due to the rounding of numbers, some totals (or other calculated numbers) in the tables may differ slightly from the summation of (or derivations involving) their quoted components.

1   Palestine's economic structure and performance: introduction and overview

One country – one economy, or two peoples – two economies?

Any student of Palestine's economic history is inevitably confronted with the need to characterize the country's economy during the three decades of British rule (1919–48). At the heart of the matter lies the question whether Palestine should be viewed as a single economy or as a segmented entity, composed of two ethno-national economies, one Arab and one Jewish, coexisting under a single administrative aegis of the Mandate government.

In the uneasy history of Arab-Jewish coexistence in adversity, each of these two viewpoints had distinct and explicitly acknowledged political connotations. The "single economy" approach, adopted mainly by Arabs, was consistent with their political views and objectives, whereby Palestine was a single entity in which Jews, while entitled to individual rights, were by no means supposed to have any separate collective standing, let alone autonomy. The Jewish-Zionist position adopted the notion of a separate Jewish economy and promoted it both as a plan of action, while striving to form an autonomous body politic based on the "National Home" postulate, and as a factually justifiable distinction for reference and analysis (Metzer, 1982).

Another aspect of the debate, which has kept it alive in the scholarly literature, has to do with some methodological ambiguities as to what exactly constitutes an "economy," and what are the practical implications of that concept. These unresolved issues have led to two broadly defined schools of thought. One approach views the unified economic administration of the Mandatory government and the economic relations between Arabs and Jews as dominating attributes warranting the treatment of Palestine as a single economy. According to this school of thought, the socio-economic differences between the two peoples, while affecting the specific structure of the overall economy, are not sufficient evidence of ethno-national economic separation. The other approach regards the array of observed dissimilarities between Arabs

1

and Jews as the decisive factor in modeling the country's "two-economies" fabric.[1]

In view of the vagueness of terms and diversity of viewpoints, it is worthwhile to delve a bit further into specifics. This is done in the following discussion, which elaborates on the conceptual and empirical parameters that ought to be considered before choosing a framework for the presentation and interpretation of facts and findings.

Conceptually, an economy could be defined as a locus of economic activities and transactions in the areas of production, distribution, or consumption, which is set apart from the rest of the "economic world" by various barriers to completely free and frictionless movement, in and out of that locus, of people, capital, or final goods and services (or of any combination of the three). These barriers may be determined by fundamentally objective factors, such as geographical conditions or the quality and cost of transport and information; they may be generated by more subjective policies and regulations; or they may simply reflect such elusive qualities as mental and social affinity to certain locations, customs, and traditions that form group self-identity and determination which may involve, among others, exclusionary attitudes toward the "other." Thus, in addition to the familiar regional, state, and national economies, one may discern distinct "economies," when appropriate, in religious, ethnic, or socio-economic terms, both within and across regions or countries.

Moreover, a given set of barriers may distinguish recognizable groups of people, specific modes of economic conduct, particular regions, or even entire countries as constituting distinct economies with respect to certain aspects of economic life, while remaining indistinguishable from a larger economic realm with respect to some other aspects. Observe, for example, a traditional rural economy in a developing country, one that is well defined by its modes of production and distribution and by its form of land tenure and utilization. The denizens of this rural economy may be indistinguishable from the urban population of the country with respect to, say, taxation or the provision of social services. Another case in point is the membership of individual nation states, with well-defined national economies, in supra-national economic structures (e.g., the EU).

Three major implications arise from these general observations. First and foremost they imply that the search for an "economy," which may by its very nature be a multi-dimensional frame of reference, cannot rely on an *a priori* definition or on a unified set of characteristics. Hence, the

---

[1] For a detailed discussion and summary of the literature dealing with the nature of Palestine's economy in the Mandate period see Owen (1982, 1988) and Kamen (1991), chap. 4.

question whether a certain community, location, or otherwise-defined locus of economic activity should be treated as a distinct economic unit is primarily a practical – even *ad hoc* – one. Its resolution hinges on the nature of the available data and on a cost-benefit-type assessment of the insights to be gained or lost by choosing a disaggregated versus a consolidated approach to the issues under consideration.

The second implication is that once an entity is deemed to be an "economy," that title need not necessarily be considered an all-embracing concept. Therefore, in dealing with the entire scope of a community's economic life, consideration should also be given to the possibility of its belonging to a number of "economies."

The third implication, which follows naturally from the first two, is the clear distinction between an entity's typical characteristics in the economic sphere, on the one hand, and the notion of its economic isolation or complete segregation from the broader economic surroundings, on the other. Note that while the former could justify the treatment of a community as a separate economy, the latter is neither required as a condition for economic segmentation, nor is it commonly observed.

Equipped with these general criteria, let us turn to the specific arena of Mandatory Palestine.

The peace agreements that ended World War I officially designated Palestine as a distinct entity, under British Mandate, in the newly emerging Middle East of the post-Ottoman era. Britain drew the final borders of the Mandate for Palestine in late 1922 (when Trans-Jordan was separated from it) and moved swiftly to consolidate the area west of the Jordan river into an administratively homogeneous unit.[2]

The Mandatory government provided the inhabitants of the country with an official "state" identity and citizenship, and created a unified civil administration with the following attributes: a well-defined legal structure enforced by state police and courts; a centrally designed and administered fiscal system; an integrated monetary regime, operated by the Palestine Currency Board in London; and, from 1927 on, a state currency (the Palestine pound). These institutional rules and means applied equally to all the inhabitants of the country, irrespective of ethno-national affiliation. As such, they constituted a common framework for the conduct of civil affairs, for internal economic activity and for external trade. If we add the modern transportation and communication infrastructure built and operated by the government (Reichman, 1971; Biger,

---

[2] For information and illuminating discussions of the administrative and institutional aspects of the Mandatory government see, among others, *Report* (1925); *Survey* (1946), vols. I, II; *Memorandum* (1947); Biger (1983); Makover (1988); and Reuveny (1993).

1983; Gross, 1984b), there are grounds to argue that, besides contributing to Palestine's administrative integrity, the Mandatory government provided a solid institutional and operational foundation for the formation of a single economy (Owen, 1988).

But Britain's task as the League of Nations' Mandatory for Palestine was more complex than that. While legal and administrative equality in the treatment of the country's population was an unequivocal obligation, the Mandate carried an explicit commitment to the promotion of a Jewish National Home, as clearly embedded in its wording.[3]

The Mandatory shall be responsible for placing the country under such political, administrative and economic conditions as will secure the establishment of the Jewish national home, as laid down in the preamble, and the development of self-governing institutions, and also for safeguarding the civil and religious rights of all the inhabitants of Palestine, irrespective of race and religion. (Article 2)

The terms of the Mandate go into some detail in specifying the means and policies to be employed in realizing the National Home objective, laying special emphasis on the functions of an officially recognized Jewish Agency as

a public body for the purpose of advising and cooperating with the Administration of Palestine in such economic, social and other matters as may affect the establishment of the Jewish national home and the interests of the Jewish population in Palestine, and, subject always to the control of the administration, to assist and take part in the development of the country. (Article 4)

Specifically, the Mandatory was expected to cooperate with the Jewish Agency in settling immigrating Jews – whose influx was to be facilitated by the government – "on the land and waste lands not required for public purpose" (Article 6). The Mandatory administration was also advised to

arrange with the Jewish agency . . . to construct or operate, upon fair and equitable terms, any public works, services and utilities, and to develop any of the natural resources of the country, in so far as these matters are not directly undertaken by the Administration. (Article 11)

The embodiment in the Mandate of these two sets of policy guidelines, namely equal treatment of all the country's inhabitants and cooperation with the Jewish community and its representative bodies in establishing a Jewish National Home, highlighted the dual – and quite asymmetric – role that Britain had undertaken. The political impossibility of executing this double-edged policy, given the diametrically opposed objectives of the Arabs and the Jews, and the attempts made by the British government

---

[3] The text of the Mandate is reprinted in *Survey* (1946), vol. I, pp. 4–11; the following quotations are taken from there.

to modify it by distancing itself from the National Home postulate, are well-known features of the history of Mandatory Palestine, and need not be dwelt upon here.

For our purposes, however, it is important to emphasize that the distinct position of the Jewish community and its institutions, upheld by a government that was also attempting to equalize the *communal* (not merely the individual) treatment of Arabs and Jews, certainly contributed to the division of economic life along ethno-national lines (*Memorandum*, 1947; Owen, 1982; Metzer, 1982; Smith, 1993). Reference here is to the officially recognized national institutions of World Jewry (the World Zionist Organization and, from 1929 on, the Jewish Agency) and to the executive body (*va'ad leumi*) of the elected assembly (*assefat ha-nivharim*) of Palestine's "statutory Jewish community" (the *yishuv*).[4] Their official standing enabled these institutions to use their financial independence (secured mainly by Jewish unilateral transfers from abroad) to develop into a quasi-governmental public sector within the Jewish community, dedicated to the pursuit of the Zionist goals.

The activities of the national and communal institutions were mainly economic and socio-economic: acquisition of land, which was then turned into a publicly owned "national asset"; investment in agricultural settlements and other "nation-building" projects; and the provision of education, health, and welfare services to the Jewish community. In performing these functions, as was fully realized by the Mandatory government itself, these institutions provided the inputs needed for the development of a cohesive and self-reliant Jewish community, and consolidated its position as a viable economic entity (*Memorandum*, 1947; Gross and Metzer, 1978; and chapter 6).

The government, for its part, sought (*inter alia*) to compensate for the lack of comparably developed mechanisms in the Arab community. These considerations were particularly noticeable in the area of education, where government schools served the Arab population almost exclusively (*Survey*, 1946, vol. II, chap. XVI; Metzer, 1982; Biger, 1983). Consequently, the provision of public services, insofar as they were ethnically earmarked, added another dimension to the Arab-Jewish division and contributed to the socio-economic divergence between the two peoples (see chapter 6 for a more detailed discussion of the political economy of public economics in Mandatory Palestine).

---

[4] Note that while over 95 percent of the Jewish inhabitants of Palestine belonged to the "statutory Jewish" national community, certain separate, ultra-orthodox groups, notably "*Agudat Israel*," excluded themselves from the organized *yishuv* (at least partly), and were recognized by the government as a religiously distinct community (see *Survey*, 1946, vol. II, chap. XXII).

All this leads to the conclusion that the diverse measures employed by the government in exercising its double role, and their (implicit or explicit) consequences, in no way prevents the postulate of two distinct economic entities, functioning within the unified Mandatory administration, from being a sound option for the analysis of Palestine's economic structure and development. In probing the usefulness of this option, *vis-à-vis* the "single economy" approach, let us now explore some of the institutional and socio-economic characteristics of the two communities.

On the Jewish side, the General Federation of Jewish Labor in Eretz-Israel (the *Histadrut*) emerged, in addition to the national institutions, as instrumental in shaping the autonomous structure of the *yishuv*. The *Histadrut* was founded in 1920 for the purpose of promoting the national and socio-economic objectives of the working class – which proclaimed itself the driving force of the Jewish "nation-building" endeavor – and of catering to the needs of the workers. The *Histadrut* rapidly evolved into a major multifunction organization. It incorporated 55 percent of Palestine's Jewish employees by 1923, and its membership reached a long-run stable proportion of 75 percent in 1931.[5] *Histadrut* members were enrolled in its centrally controlled federation of trade unions; they were provided with employment services by its labor exchanges; with health, social, and cultural services by its sick fund (*Kupat Holim*) and other institutions; and were also made owners of its conglomeration of production and marketing enterprises. In occupying such a central place in Jewish life, the *Histadrut* obviously complemented the national and communal institutions in establishing the *yishuv* as an autonomous socio-economic entity.

It should be stressed, though, that while concentrating on the promotion of the interests of Jewish labor – for instance, in struggling to achieve ethno-national segregation of employment – several attempts were made by the *Histadrut* to foster Arab-Jewish collaboration for the purpose of collective bargaining. In practice, however, these attempts were few and ineffective. Moreover, except for the single case of a common union of railroad workers (founded in 1923 and whose membership never exceeded 500), these efforts concentrated on the establishment of a "sister" Arab labor union to be federated with the *Histadrut*. Such a union – the Alliance of Palestine Workers – was indeed set up in 1932, and after all but disappearing in the turbulent years of the Arab revolt (1936–39), was reactivated during World War II, with a negligible membership of 2,500 (Horowitz and Lissak, 1978, chap. 2). In other words, by endoge-

---

[5] Employees include self-employed members of workers' cooperatives and of communal agricultural settlements – *kibbutzim* and *moshavim* (see Sussman, 1974, chap. 4).

nizing the ethno-national divide, while attempting to accommodate Arab workers, these moves could be viewed as an additional manifestation of the segregated coexistence of Arabs and Jews.

Another not unrelated aspect of the Arab-Jewish divide is revealed by the "economic destination" of the massive influx of Jewish immigrants and capital. The sizable supply of labor generated by waves of immigration over the entire period was absorbed, by and large, within the "economic boundaries" of the Jewish community. According to recently constructed estimates, about 96.5 percent of the 130,000-strong Jewish labor force in 1935 were either self-employed (including members of *kibbutzim*, *moshavim*, and workers' cooperatives), or were employed by Jewish institutions and private employers; 3 percent were government employees; and a negligible 0.5 percent were either employed by or provided professional labor services to Arabs (Metzer and Kaplan, 1990, chap. 5). The same is true of imported Jewish capital: investments financed by these imports were confined to the Jewish economic sphere; there is no evidence of Jewish investment in Arab enterprises (or of Arab investment in Jewish projects, for that matter), or of joint ventures of any significance.

Shifting to geography, it can clearly be inferred from table 1.1 that the regional and local clustering along ethno-national lines, driven largely by the tension between Arabs and Jews, constituted another segregating factor. The Jews, led by the regional availability of land for sale and utilizing the geopolitical advantages of geographic consolidation, were building up their rapidly growing community by settling primarily in spatially contiguous areas stretching north along the coastal plain and then east through the northern valleys to the Jordan valley and north again to the eastern Galilee and the Huleh valley. The only area of major Jewish settlement lying outside this stretch was Jerusalem. Over 90 percent of the Jews in Palestine resided in only two well-defined regions: the central and northern coastal plain and Jerusalem. The Arabs, on the other hand, were concentrated in the central hilly region, with a more dispersed presence along the entire coastal plain and in the Galilee (Bachi, 1977, chap. 5).

Equally significant was the ethnic segregation between (and within) localities. Rural areas were completely segregated, since none of the villages and rural settlements had a mixed (Arab-Jewish) population. In the urban areas the picture was more complex. The share of Arab town-dwellers living in "all-Arab" towns – about 58 percent in 1922 – stabilized around 50 percent in 1931, with the rest residing in the country's five "mixed" towns (Jerusalem, Jaffa, Haifa, Tiberias, and Safed). The proportion of the Jewish urban population living in "all-Jewish" towns had increased steeply from 22 percent in 1922 to 52 percent in 1946, along

Table 1.1. *Regional distribution of Palestine's population (%)*

	1931		1944	
	Arabs	Jews	Arabs	Jews
coastal plain				
central and north	23.8	58.6	25.3	75.2
south	10.1	0.4	11.2	0.5
central range				
Jerusalem sub-district	11.5	31.4	12.2	18.1
others	32.2	0.1	29.0	0.0
northern valleys	1.3	1.6	1.6	1.7
Galilee	11.5	3.5	11.4	2.2
Jordan valley	3.7	4.4	4.2	2.3
Negev	5.9	0.0	5.1	0.0
all regions	100.0	100.0	100.0	100.0

Sources: distribution calculations based on *Census of Palestine* (1933), vol. II, tables II, III; *Vital Statistics* (1947), tables A6, A7; Bachi (1977), tables 5.4, 5.5, and appendix 6

with a decline in the "mixed" towns' share from 77 percent to 48 percent (*Survey*, 1946, vol. I, p. 148; *Supplement to Survey of Palestine*, 1947, pp. 12–13). It should also be noted that even in so-called "mixed" towns Arabs and Jews usually resided in separate, ethnically distinct neighborhoods.

Another characteristic is the difference in the rural-urban mix (table 1.2). Notwithstanding the significance of its town-based commerce and the rise in urbanization since the 1880s, the Arab community remained primarily a rural society. Its rural population share, while declining from its peak of 79 percent in 1880, did not shrink below 64 percent in the Mandate period, and the socio-economic organization of the typical Arab village remained largely "traditional" throughout this period. It was dominated by hierarchical lineage-descent groups (*hamulot*), and was still partly (though decreasingly so) based on communally held and periodically redistributed land (*musha'a*) within the village (Kamen, 1991; and chapter 4). The Jewish rural population share, on the other hand, although it rose from a negligible 0.7 percent in 1881, never exceeded 27 percent. Thus, despite the Zionist back-to-the-land ethos, epitomized by promoting agriculture as the focal activity of the Jewish "nation building," the *yishuv* remained essentially an urban community.

This distinction is closely associated with the dissimilarities between the two communities in the composition of employment and production by industry. Of particular note are the differences in the labor and output

Table 1.2. *Percentage shares of rural population*

	Arabs	Jews
1880	78.6	0.7
1914	68.4	12.9
1922	70.9	18.1
1931	69.9	26.4
1946	63.9	26.4

Sources: Bachi (1977), tables 1.1, 1.2, A12, A13;
McCarthy (1990), table 2.18

shares of agriculture and manufacturing. Over 50 percent of all Arab employed persons were engaged in domestic agricultural production, and no less than 30 percent of Arab product originated in agriculture, while the share of manufacturing remained less than 10 percent on both counts. The Jewish industrial structure had entirely different proportions: agricultural workers (Jews and Arabs employed by Jewish farmers) constituted less than 30 percent of total employment, and agricultural output accounted for less than 13 percent of total product. Manufacturing, which utilized between 16 and 20 percent of total labor before World War II (during the war this proportion came to exceed 30 percent), was the largest industry, output-wise, and generated about 20 percent of Jewish domestic product as early as 1922 (see chapter 5).

These dissimilarities, whose broader implications for secular growth, cyclical patterns of economic activity, and inter-communal trade are discussed below, obviously strengthen the case for the "separate economies" approach. It would therefore severely circumscribe our documentation and analysis of the economic record of Mandatory Palestine, if – besides treating such topics as the monetary apparatus, the balance-of-payments and trade policy, and the tax structure on an aggregate, country-wide basis – we failed to examine the economic life of each community separately, bearing in mind the interrelation between them.

It should be emphasized, though, as Owen (1982) has rightly pointed out, that the case for two economies should by no means be based on the assertion that economic relations between Arabs and Jews were either nonexistent or negligible. Such relations, as demonstrated below and in chapter 5, were, in fact, quite substantial, at least until the outbreak of the Arab revolt of 1936–39, and to some extent again in the course of World War II (see also Abramowitz, 1945). Furthermore, precisely the same marked dissimilarities that distinguished the two economies from one another were largely responsible for their different comparative advantages, and were thus instrumental in facilitating bilateral trade (see below).

Granted the appropriateness of the "two units" approach, the question is whether the ethno-nationally divided economy of Mandatory Palestine could usefully be treated within a more generalized framework. Following Sussman (1973) and Horowitz and Lissak (1978), I have argued elsewhere (Metzer, 1982; Metzer and Kaplan, 1985) that the "dual economy" notion serves this purpose well. However, since various versions of "dualism" can be found in the literature,[6] and since some doubt has recently been cast on the appropriateness of the concept in the context of Mandatory Palestine (Kamen, 1991, chapter 4), a clarification regarding the meaning of "economic dualism" in our particular context is called for.

Let me start by way of elimination. In applying the dual-economy approach to Mandatory Palestine I do not allude to any of the variants of (social) dualism (stemming from the work of Boeke, 1953, and widely used in the sociological literature) that characterize a dual economy as consisting of a market-oriented, modern sector functioning alongside a traditional sector that is only marginally responsive, if at all, to market signals. The concept that I refer to is a rather generalized notion of "economic dualism": the coexistence, within some broader frame of economic reference (state, region), of two interacting economic sectors that differ from one another in level of economic development, *both* of which are "rationally" responsive, in the economic sense, to their respective environments and material opportunities and constraints.

More specifically, reference is here to economic units that differ from one another on the following Kuznetsian developmental counts: urbanization, the weight of agriculture (versus manufacturing industry) in employment and production, the institutional structure of farming and the nature of the financial markets, the extent of school enrollment, the skill composition of the labor force, and the level of income per capita (Kuznets, 1973; Chenery and Syrquin, 1975).

The less developed, or so-called (somewhat misleadingly) "traditional" sector is typified by substantial peasant-based husbandry and by other small "household" firms, all of which are often served by dated financial instruments of a personal nature. This sector is also typically distinguished by being relatively non-urbanized and under-industrialized, by poor school attendance, and by low levels of income per capita. The advanced sector (designated as "modern" in the development literature)

---

[6] See Meier (1989), chap. III, for a critical review of the literature.

is primarily urban, and is characterized by substantial, or at least fast-growing, manufacturing industry, by a comparatively well-educated and skilled labor force, by modern financial institutions and capital markets, and by relatively high income per capita.

While separate, the two sectors in a typical dual economy tend to interact. Lewis (1979), one of the founding fathers of the concept of dualistic development, has identified four such channels of inter-sectoral interaction, the first of which is the labor market. The fast-growing modern sector generates large demand for unskilled labor, especially in cash-crop agriculture and in manufacturing. The wages offered in the modern sector are higher than the alternative earnings in the traditional sector, thereby attracting labor from the latter to the former.

The second channel is the market for goods. The expansion of the modern sector raises overall demand for food, raw materials, and intermediate products. This demand can be partly met by increased production in the traditional sector, which in turn may "import" some manufactured goods and professional services from the modern sector.

The third area of interaction is in the public sector. The less-developed sector tends to benefit from the physical facilities of modern infrastructure (in transportation, communication, public utilities, and medical services), which are built to meet the needs of the advanced sector. On a broader scale, the incidence of taxation and public expenditures – which commonly direct more public services to the traditional sector than it pays for – provides a useful vehicle for the inter-sectoral diffusion of the benefits generated by the process of development and growth.

Finally, the relatively advanced technological and institutional level of the modern sector may inject – through demonstration and other effects – modernization of institutions and of modes of production and distribution into the entire economy, thus bringing about some inter-sectoral convergence over time.

The potential patterns of convergence notwithstanding, it is the structural stability, long since observed in the literature, that is the dominant feature of a dual economy. In a highly illuminating article Myint (1985) suggests that the persistence of multi-faceted dualism in developing countries can be best understood by resorting to a general framework of what he defines as "organizational" dualism. His viewpoint is that "dualism is pre-eminently a phenomenon of an under-developed organizational framework," which, when combined with various distortions, makes for "clogged up" inter-sectoral connections "creating the weak links between the sectors concerned and segmenting the economy" (Myint, 1985, pp. 25, 26).

Myint identifies weak inter-sectoral links in four dualistic manifestations, roughly analogous to Lewis' four channels of interaction: the market for goods, the labor market, the capital market, and the government's fiscal and administrative apparatus (see also chapters 4 and 6 below). The goods market, though likely to be the most integrated of the four, may still exhibit dualistic wholesale-retail price differentials for agricultural products, which could be caused by relatively high transport and marketing costs in the less-developed economies. In the labor market, institutionally caused distortions (such as those imposed by minimum-wage legislation and collective bargaining), combined with relatively low labor productivity in the traditional sector, would tend to preserve segmentation and wage differentials along sectoral lines.

As for dualism in the capital market, Myint blames transaction and information cost differentials for causing diverse structures of financial markets and wide interest-rate gaps between the two sectors. In the modern sector, the well-organized and cost-efficient capital market is operated by banking institutions capable of utilizing economies of scale in gathering information and minimizing risks. In the traditional sector, where such economies rarely exist, the capital market is operated mainly by individual moneylenders who serve a dispersed peasantry and household firms at relatively high cost.

In the workings of government, dualism is manifested primarily by the comparatively limited availability of publicly provided social services in the traditional sector and by their relatively low quality. These deficiencies are typically caused by the high cost of providing educational and health services in what are often remote, under-developed rural areas and by the low attractiveness of servicing them. The result is a persistent human capital gap between the populations of the two sectors.

With regard to the rural-urban mix and the industrial structure of employment and production, the persistent differences already noted between the Jewish and Arab communities in Palestine, coupled with the large disparities in the groups' income per capita (to be dealt with below), strongly suggest a dualistic posture along the lines portrayed here. This inference is reinforced by the following observations and findings: (a) a wide gap in school attendance; (b) persistent wage differentials and capital market segmentation along ethno-national lines; (c) "dualistic" inter-communal trade: unskilled labor services, agricultural produce, and raw building materials being sold by Arabs to Jews, in addition to land, in partial return for manufactured goods and professional services; (d) a net flow of resources transferred from Jews to Arabs via the government's fiscal system and activities; (e) various indications of improvements and productivity advance in Arab agriculture, partly facilitated by inter-sectoral demonstration effects and technological spillover. All these observations are elaborated on in the next section and in the following chapters of the book.

Taken in conjunction, these observations constitute a profile that is highly consistent with the structure, dynamics, and interactions that identify a "representative" dual economy in the economic development literature. In the case of Mandatory Palestine, however, the ethno-national divide distinguishes it from the typical "dual" economy. The self-imposed spatial and social segregation of the two peoples, and the operation of "community-specific" public institutions, partly complemented but largely substituted for the incompletely developed organizational systems, which in a typical dual economy tend to "clog" (to use Myint's terminology) the inter-sectoral connecting lines and sustain the dualistic structure.

All told, the demonstrated applicability of the dual economy approach to our subject of inquiry makes it a most appropriate organizing theme for the economic story of Mandatory Palestine. However, I should also point out that since in our case the two sectors are identified ethno-nationally, they are not as clearly socio-economically distinct from one another as in a "typical" dual economy (or, for that matter, in any other segmented structure, in which distinct groups or classes are characterized by "pure" socio-economic attributes). Thus, consideration should be given to the fact that neither the Arab nor the Jewish sector was completely homogeneous in terms of the dual economy dichotomy. Take, for example, the urban elite of highly skilled professional civil servants and merchants in the Arab economy, or various small household firms and other traditional segments in the otherwise advanced Jewish economy. With this clarification in mind, the next section begins the orderly exploration of Palestine's economic record with a broad comparative overview of aggregate economic performance and change in the two ethno-national communities.

Palestine's economic record: a comparative assessment

As far as the quantification of aggregate economic activity is concerned, 1922 marks the beginning of Palestine's "statistical age." In 1922 the newly confirmed Mandate government began systematically to record vital statistics, and on October 23 of that year it conducted the first population census (a second, more thorough census was taken in 1931). Together with additional government surveys of agricultural production in the early 1920s these data compilations provided a launching pad for contemporary and later estimates of demographic and economic statistics on an annual basis.[7]

Although there are no similar data for previous years, the late Ottoman era was not a complete statistical void. Using the available sources, students of the period were able to draw a picture of economic vitality and growth, with increasing external trade, in the six decades between the Crimean War and World War I (Gross, 1977; Owen, 1993, chaps. 6, 10). This period also saw the intensification of economic activity by European religious emissaries, most notably the 2,000-strong German Templar colony, whose members brought along some new crops and methods of cultivation (Carmel, 1975; Thalman, 1991).[8]

However, what emerged (in retrospect) as the most significant development of the period was the inception, in 1882, of the largely nationally driven Jewish immigration and the formation of the "new Jewish community" (*ha-yishuv he-hadash*) in Palestine.[9] According to Bachi's (1977, p. 79) estimates, at least 53,000 newcomers entered Palestine in the two immigration waves preceding World War I. Of those, about 40,000, or 5–6 percent of the Palestine population on the eve of the war, may have remained in the country permanently.[10] These growth patterns were cut short by the adverse economic and demographic effects of the war, but when hostilities ended in the fall of 1918, the British occupation authorities moved swiftly to consolidate the country's administration and took the measures needed for the resumption of orderly economic life. With stability restored in the early 1920s, the economy recovered, Jewish immigration resumed, and Palestine embarked on a long-run, albeit fluctuating, growth path that characterized the Mandate period.

In 1922 Palestine was a small and sparsely populated country. The census figures, slightly adjusted by Bachi (1977, appendix 6), report a total of 763,550 inhabitants (excluding members of the British armed forces and

---

[7] The 1922 census is referred to in the text as *Census*, 1922; and that of November 18, 1931 as *Census of Palestine*, 1933. The agricultural surveys are reported in Sawer (1923).

[8] The Templars, most of whom later became Nazis or Nazi sympathizers, were deported from Palestine by the British government at the outbreak of World War II.

[9] The new community should be distinguished from the traditional "old community" (*ha-yishuv ha-yashan*), which consisted primarily of orthodox Jews who trickled into Palestine in small numbers over the centuries for religious reasons.

[10] In deriving this net migration figure I adopt McCarthy's (1990, p. 23) assumption of a 25 percent re-migration rate. Estimates of Palestine's population in 1914 vary from the low official British figure of 689,300 (adopted by Bachi, 1977, p. 32), to a high of 798,400 (McCarthy, 1990, pp. 5–26, 37). The gap between assessments of the population's ethno-national composition on the eve of World War I is even larger. According to McCarthy (1990, pp. 13–26, 37), no more than 61,000 Jews resided in Palestine in 1914, whereas Bachi (1977, pp. 5, 32) estimates their number at 94,000.

their families) of whom 679,760 were non-Jews.[11] Since the personal status of the inhabitants was determined – as part of the Ottoman legacy carried over to the British Mandate – by their religious affiliation (Muslims, Jews, Christians, and others), the censuses and other official accounts classified the population by religion rather than by ethnicity. The number of Arabs in the population can therefore not be directly obtained from the population figures.

An attempt to partly rectify this informational deficiency was made in the census of 1931, when individuals were asked to state both their ethnicity (Arab, Jewish, or other) and their religion. The 1931 cross-classification by religion and ethnicity was officially published, in summary form, in 1937 (*Memoranda*, 1937); it reported a proportion of Arabs among non-Jews of 97.75 percent. Given this percentage, it seems quite reasonable to put the size of Mandatory Palestine's Arab population at the slightly larger number of people recorded in the official statistics and in later studies (e.g., Bachi, 1977) as belonging to non-Jewish religious communities. It follows that in 1922 Arabs made up 89 percent and Jews 11 percent of the country's population.

Production in the early 1920s was also dominated by the Arabs, whose economic activity accounted for 81 percent of Palestine's net domestic product (NDP) in 1922. But since the economic weight of the Jewish community was appreciably larger than its population share (19 percent versus 11 percent), its members' standard of living in 1922, crudely measured by the level of product per capita, was almost twice as high as that of the Arabs (table 1.3).

These orders of magnitude changed substantially in the course of time. From the 1922 census to the end of the Mandate, the total population of Palestine rose 2.6-fold (it doubled in the eighteen years between 1922 and 1940), reaching about 2 million by the end of 1947. Although the rapidly growing (primarily by natural increase) Arab population accounted for 55 percent of the total increase, it was the massive influx of Jewish immigrants that had the most telling impact on the ethnic composition of the population. Immigration raised the population share of the Jewish community from 11 percent in 1922 to about 17 percent by the 1931 census, and to 31 percent by the end of 1947 (Bachi, 1977, appendix 6; for further discussion of the demographic patterns see chapters 2 and 3).

---

[11] McCarthy (1990, pp. 28–29) suggests an upward adjustment of these figures to correct for underrecording of children in general and of prepubescent girls in particular. His "adjusted" numbers are 816,123 for the entire population and 722,763 for non-Jews. Since he applies his correction factor equally to all segments of the population, the percentage breakdown by religious groups remains unaltered.

Table 1.3. *Arab-Jewish comparative growth, 1922–47*

	annual growth rate 1922–47 (%)		Jewish/Arab ratio (Arab=1)	
	Arabs	Jews	1922	1947
population	2.8	8.5	0.12	0.46
NDP	6.5	13.2	0.26	1.19
product per capita	3.6	4.8	1.91	2.53

Sources: tables A.1, A.22

The changes in the economic sphere were even more dramatic. By 1931 the share of Arab production had shrunk to 56 percent of the country's output, and as early as 1933 it was surpassed by the Jews (43 percent versus 57 percent). From that year on, Arab economic weight remained relatively stable, fluctuating at about 42–45 percent of Palestine's total product.

The different rates at which the respective output and population shares changed were obviously reflected in the widening standard-of-living gap between the two communities. Jewish per capita income was already 2.6 times higher than that of the Arabs in 1929, and the differential remained fairly constant thereafter, except for a sharp increase (up to 4.8) in the first half of the 1930s (table A.22).

A small part of the income per capita differential could be attributed to differences in age structure between the two communities. Extremely high Arab fertility and the predominance of prime ages among Jewish immigrants (about 80 percent were in the fifteen-to-sixty-four age bracket) were principal causes of the Arab-Jewish discrepancies in the ordinarily measured dependency ratios (0.8–0.9 versus 0.5–0.6), which, for equal labor utilization and productivity, would have caused income per capita in the Jewish community to be 15 percent higher than in the Arab community in 1931, and 25 percent higher in 1944 (see chapters 2, 3, and 4). But this is, obviously, only a fraction of the observed income differential, which in the main resulted from substantial disparities in productive capacity.

The income per capita gap, however, should not be taken to portray an economically stagnant Arab community being bypassed by a vigorously expanding Jewish economy. The Arab record of economic growth, as the figures in table 1.3 clearly indicate, was very impressive indeed, even if it was overshadowed by the extraordinary economic performance of the Jews.

The remarkable achievement of the Jewish community is vividly illustrated by its capacity to accommodate a rapidly growing population (at 8.5 percent a year), within an even faster expanding economic base (at 13.2 percent annually). Arab output grew at half that speed (6.5 percent annually), but since the Arab population grew at a much slower pace (2.8 percent annually) than the Jewish population, the growth-rate differential of income (net national product) per capita between the two communities (4.8 percent and 3.6 percent for Jews and Arabs, respectively) was substantially smaller than that of total output.

Crude "growth accounting"[12] suggests that labor and capital accounted for about 75 percent of the growth of Jewish NDP between 1922 and 1947, leaving, at most, 25 percent of the rise in output to be explained by productivity advance (chapter 5). Comparatively, this extent of the growth-effect of productivity is rather on the low side. According to Maddison's (1987) calculations, the rise in productivity was "responsible" for no less than 50 percent of output growth in the developed countries between 1913 and 1973, and Chenery (1986) found that the average contribution of productivity to the increase in output in (twelve) developing countries reached about 31 percent in 1950–73.

However, the relatively large weight of inputs in the growth of Jewish output seems hardly surprising in view of the unusually high rates of growth of capital (11.6 percent annually) and labor (8.8 percent), facilitated by the massive influx of people and capital from abroad, which enabled the stock of reproducible capital per member of the Jewish labor force to rise at an annual rate of 2.8 percent (note that in the Arab economy, capital per member of the labor force grew at the much milder pace of 1 percent annually, thus raising the Jewish-Arab ratio of reproducible capital per labor from 1.4 in 1922 to 1.9 in 1945). Under these circumstances, the relatively moderate contribution of productivity to output growth should certainly not be taken to belittle the major economic achievement of the Jewish community, which managed to incorporate the vast inflow of inputs within the production process and foster a secular rise in the material well-being of a population that increased tenfold in twenty-five years (see also Syrquin, 1986).

In the Arab community, on the other hand, total factor productivity may have accounted for 50 percent (and possibly more) of output growth. This suggests that the mainly traditional Arab economy was able to gain from exogenous factors (such as the expanding world market for Palestine's citrus, the demand and demonstration effects of the fast-

---

[12] Growth accounting is a calculating procedure that decomposes the increase (decline) in output to: (i) a part attributable to a rise (decrease) in the quantity of inputs; and (ii) a part that is due to growing (diminishing) productivity (see chapter 5 for details).

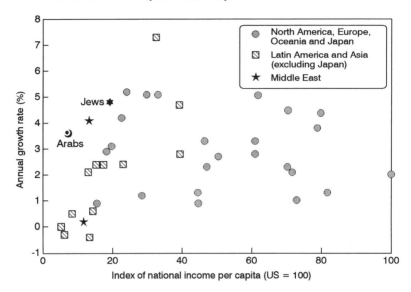

Figure 1.1 Income per capita: inter-war growth rates and levels
c. 1939
(source: table B.1)

growing modern Jewish economy, and government-provided economic services and infrastructure) and mobilize its resources – primarily land and labor – largely in response to these factors, so as to facilitate speedy economic growth.

Palestine's growth records become all the more impressive when put in a broader comparative context. This is done in figure 1.1, in which the level and growth rate of income per capita are plotted for the Arab and Jewish economies and for thirty-eight other countries (for which relevant data were available). The level of income per capita, about 1939, is reported for all forty economies in index numbers (with income per capita in the US = 100), and the growth records are presented for Arabs and Jews by their all-period (1922–47) annual growth rates, and for (most) other economies by the higher of the two inter-war decades (1919–29 and 1929–39). A distinction is drawn between Middle Eastern countries (Egypt and Turkey), Latin America, and Asia, on the one hand, and North America, Europe, Oceania, and Japan, on the other (for more details see the discussion in the appendix, and for the country data see table B.1).

With all the limitations of coverage and quality of data, the picture emerging from the comparison is quite unmistakable. It is seen that the Jewish growth rate of 4.8 percent annually in 1922–47 was among the fastest registered in the period under consideration. Only five economies

Table 1.4. *The expansion of foreign trade in the Middle East*

Percentage increase in the volume of trade (export and import) between 1928 and 1948

Palestine	515.8	Sudan	116.0
French Morocco	207.1	Turkey	85.9
Iraq	177.1	Egypt	72.6
Lebanon and Syria	136.9	Algeria	71.4
Iran	128.3	Tunisia	45.6

Source: Issawi (1982), table 2.2, pp. 26–27

(out of thirty-nine) experienced a more rapid growth of income per capita in the inter-war years than the Jews of Palestine (these were, in descending order, oil-producing Venezuela, France, Czechoslovakia, Finland, and Austria). Furthermore, of all the Latin American, Asian and Middle Eastern economies, it is shown that only those of Chile (with a growth rate of 4.7 percent) and the newly born modernizing state of Turkey (with a growth rate of 4.1 percent) exhibited growth of comparable intensity to that of the Jewish economy.

Not much less impressive was the growth performance of the Arab economy (3.6 percent per annum), which ranked thirteenth of the forty economies. Moreover, it is seen that Arab income per capita grew much faster than that of other economies of similar income levels. Note, in particular, the tiny growth rate of income per capita in Egypt (0.2 percent annually between 1913 and 1950); at this rate it would have taken Egypt at least eighteen years to achieve the same percentage increase of per capita income that the Arab economy of Palestine averaged in *one* year (3.6 percent).

Another piece of information regarding the economic performance of Middle Eastern countries is presented in table 1.4, which reports some comparative figures, calculated from Issawi's (1982) indexes, on the expansion of external trade between 1928 and 1948. The 516 percent growth in Palestine's trade over the period far exceeded that of any other country in the region. These numbers support the picture emerging from the comparison of output growth, and strongly suggest that Mandatory Palestine was by far the most vibrant Middle Eastern economy in the first half of the twentieth century.

But the impressive growth record of Mandatory Palestine should not be allowed to obscure the fact that it was a relatively low-income country. Palestine's Arab community was extremely poor; its level of income per capita was by the late 1930s the third lowest among the forty recorded economies (the poorest economy was China), and even in Egypt, ranking fifth from below, the level of income per capita was no less than 64 percent higher than that of the Arabs of Palestine. The Jewish community, on the other hand, obviously ranked much higher, with a third of the plotted economies (thirteen out of forty, including the Arabs) having lower per capita income than its own.

This wide – and persistent – disparity is another unmistakable manifestation of the "developmental gap" so characteristic of Palestine's dual economy. This gap remained essentially unbridged, implying that each of the two sectors went about its economic expansion, while not independent from one another, certainly within a different developmental regime.

Another implication of the structural divergence has to do with the significant differences in factor endowment and skill composition between the two economies (see chapters 3 and 4). These differences generated a diversity of comparative advantages forming the base for mutually gainful trade between Arabs and Jews, largely along the "dualistic" lines outlined above. Indeed, inter-communal trade seems to have been beneficial enough to surmount political obstacles raised by both sides prior to the outbreak of the Arab revolt of 1936–39 (Shapira, 1977; Porath, 1977). In the fifteen years that preceded these violent eruptions, inter-communal trade made an important contribution to output-inducing demand in the Arab economy, and was of no small importance in the Jewish economy as well.

The proportion of Arab sales to Jews (excluding land transactions) reached about 14 percent of Arab national product in 1935, and accounted for over half (56 percent) of total Arab export revenues (the sale of land, addressed in chapters 4 and 5, is excluded from the calculations because it constituted an exchange of assets, not a flow of output or resources). The corresponding output and export weights of Jewish sales to Arabs, while substantially smaller, made for no less than 7 percent of Jewish national product and 27 percent of total Jewish export in 1935 (chapter 5).

The expansion of inter-communal trade, especially the rise in Arab sales to Jews, was certainly a significant factor in inducing the observed increase in the utilization of land in Arab agriculture until the mid-1930s, and may also have fostered productivity-increasing resource reallocation in the economy as a whole. In performing these functions, inter-communal trade joined forces with other external factors (such as the growing export market for citrus fruit, or government-provided physical infrastructure) in contributing to long-run growth in the Arab as well as in the Jewish economy.

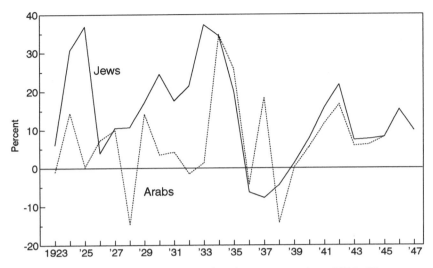

Figure 1.2 Net domestic product in constant prices, 1923–47
(annual percentage rate of change)
(source: table A.22)

Although secular economic growth in Mandatory Palestine was vigorous, it was far from smooth. As the annual rates of change of NDP demonstrate (figure 1.2), there were marked oscillations in both the Arab and the Jewish communities. It is also apparent that until the 1940s, at which time economic activity was largely determined by war-time conditions (Gross and Metzer, 1993), the two fluctuating patterns differed appreciably from one another. The Jewish inter-war growth profile was essentially dominated by two long swings, whereas Arab growth was characterized by much shorter cycles. This visual impression is confirmed by the statistically weak association between the two series; the correlation coefficient is just 0.333 for the entire period.[13]

A similar picture is revealed by the yearly rates of change of product per capita (figure 1.3), whose dispersion was even greater than that of total product. The coefficients of variation (the standard deviation divided by the mean) for the growth of total product and product per capita were 1.5 and 2.4 respectively in the Arab economy, and 0.9 and 2.1 in the Jewish economy. These numbers also imply that the yearly fluctuations of both growth aggregates were distinctly sharper in the Arab economy than in the Jewish economy (more on this point below).

[13] A correlation coefficient of $+1$ stands for perfect positive correlation, while -1 stands for perfect negative correlation; zero indicates no statistical association between the two series.

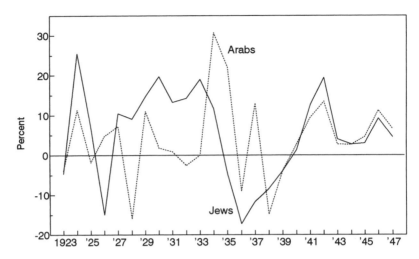

Figure 1.3 Product per capita in constant prices, 1923–47
(annual percentage rate of change)
(source: table A.22)

The swings in Jewish economic activity have long been recognized in the literature, and, for the inter-war years, have been linked primarily to the period's two major waves of the (highly correlated) inflows of immigration and capital.[14] The first wave began in 1920, with the establishment of the British civilian administration, peaked in 1925, and subsided in the second half of the decade. The second influx started in 1932, intensified after the Nazis' rise to power in Germany (1933), peaked in 1935, and then receded (for further discussion of the patterns and attributes of Jewish immigration see chapter 3).

The association between immigration, capital import, and the growth of NDP prior to World War II is illustrated in figure 1.4. This association has been systematically established in a recent econometric study (Beenstock, Metzer, and Ziv, 1995 [hereafter BMZ]), and found to have been generated by the stimulus provided by upswings in immigration and capital inflows to short-run upsurges in investment and productivity (figure 1.5). The former was mainly driven by the demand for housing and by the rising supply of investable funds (see chapter 4); the latter reflected, at least in part, the temporary increase in the utilization of

[14] For the periodization of the Mandatory Jewish economy based on the two long swings see Gross (1981). A partial list of references addressing the fluctuations in Jewish economic activity includes Grunwald (1932); Horowitz and Hinden (1938); Horowitz (1948); and Halevi (1983).

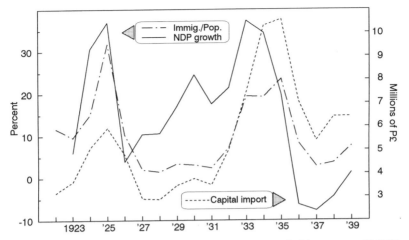

Figure 1.4 Ratio of immigrants to residents, capital import, and NDP growth (Jews), 1922–39
(sources: tables A.1, A.3 for immigrants–residents ratio; table A.24 for capital import; table A.22 for growth of NDP_J)

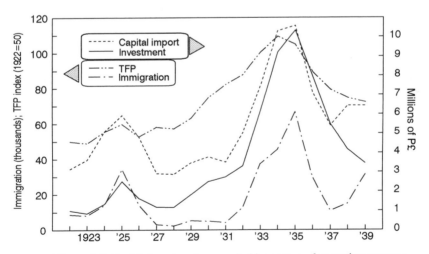

Figure 1.5 Jewish immigration, capital import, and gross investment (in 1936 prices), and TFP, 1923–39
(sources: table A.3 for immigration; table A.24 for capital import; table A.23 for gross investment; BMZ, table A6 for TFP)

resources and intensification of production in response to the immediate absorption requirements of newcomers and to the corresponding rise in aggregate demand.

Another – not unrelated – destabilizing factor was the periodic disruption of economic life associated with the violent eruptions of Arab resistance to the Jewish buildup in Palestine. Indeed, BMZ were able to show that, other things being equal, the disturbances of 1929 did adversely affect the level of output and that the Arab revolt of 1936–39 had a statistically independent role in inducing the economic downturn in the second half of the 1930s.

It is quite remarkable, though, that the cyclical profile of the Jewish economy shows very little resemblance to the fluctuations in the "world" economy in the inter-war period. The correlation coefficient between the 1923–39 annual rates of change of Jewish NDP and those of aggregate GDP for sixteen major developed economies[15] (denoted as "world") was -0.274. The two series are plotted together in figure 1.6. As can clearly be seen, the world depression years of the early 1930s were, for the Jewish economy, a period of relatively uninterrupted accelerated growth. It started with an internally induced recovery following the downturn of 1926, and continued with the above-mentioned economic impetus generated by the revival of immigration in the first half of the 1930s. By analogy, the declining phase of Jewish economic activity in the second half of the decade roughly coincided with renewed growth in the world economy.

This divergence was due mainly to the fact that neither the emigration of Jews nor their transfer of capital to Palestine in the 1930s seem to exhibit the "expected response pattern" to ordinary push factors operating in the world economy. Immigration and capital inflows remained quite limited from 1927 through the trough of the world depression in 1930–32; they intensified later, when overall economic recovery was already under way. Although the immigration pattern may, to some extent, have reflected a lagged response to changing conditions in the world economy, it was primarily shaped – within the confines of the Mandatory government's immigration policy – by the deteriorating conditions of European Jewry, and partly also by the economic and political state of affairs in Palestine.

As for the war years, the renewed expansion of the 1940s has long been recognized as having been driven by the demand of the allied forces in the region and by the substitution of domestic production for diminished

[15] Australia, Austria, Belgium, Canada, Denmark, Finland, France, Germany, Italy, Japan, the Netherlands, Norway, Sweden, Switzerland, the UK, and the USA (Maddison, 1991, chaps. 1, 4).

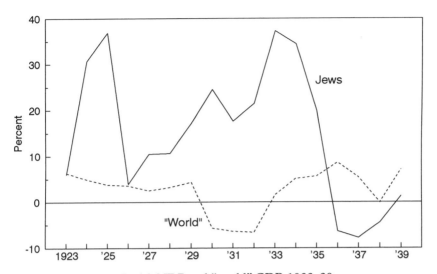

Figure 1.6 Jewish NDP and "world" GDP, 1923–39
(annual percentage rate of change)
(sources: table A.22 for NDP_J; Maddison (1991), table 4.7 for "world"
GDP)

civilian imports during the war. But the recent findings of BMZ imply
that a narrowly defined "non-war" counterfactual would have generated a
much stronger recovery than the one actually experienced in 1940–45.
This suggests that the war-related stimuli may not have been potent
enough to compensate fully for the otherwise disruptive economic effects
of the war.

The factors responsible for the path taken by Jewish growth may have
affected the Arab cyclical profile as well, particularly from the mid-1930s
on. But on the whole, the diverse pattern of aggregate economic activity
in the Arab sector, which, like that of the Jewish community, was also
unrelated to world-wide fluctuations (the coefficient of correlation
between the rates of change of Arab GDP and those of the sixteen developed countries was 0.242 for the inter-war years), seems to have been
independently determined by domestic mechanisms. This inference
follows from the correlation coefficients in table 1.5 which show the cor-
respondence, in each economy, between the annual growth rates of
aggregate product and those of the output of the material-producing
industries in 1922–39. In the Jewish economy, the highest correlation is
observed between the annual rates of change of total product and of
construction output. This finding is consistent with the "leading industry" role that construction played in the inter-war Jewish economy –

Table 1.5. *Coefficients of correlation between the growth rates of NDP and of the outputs of material-producing industries, 1922–39*

output of material-producing industries	NDP	
	Arabs	Jews
agriculture	0.958	0.350
manufacturing	0.699	0.795
construction	0.449	0.881

Sources: tables A.11, A.14, A.16, A.22

despite its modest product share (9.2 percent of Jewish NDP between 1922 and 1939, with a single-year maximum of 16.2 percent) – due to its high sensitivity to swings in immigration and in capital import (see also chapters 3 and 4). Second in descending order of association comes manufacturing, the largest material-producing industry in the Jewish economy (accounting for an average of 21 percent of Jewish NDP over the period). Agriculture, whose average product share (12.5 percent) was higher than that of the "front-running" construction industry, remained a distant third.

The ranking order in the Arab economy is a complete reversal of the ranking in the Jewish economy: the percentage changes in NDP are almost perfectly correlated with those of farm output. This observation is consistent with the high dependence of the largely rural Arab community on agricultural production, which comprised about 34.1 percent of its domestic product in 1922–39. It is thus apparent that crop cycles must have been instrumental in shaping the predominantly short swings in Arab agricultural and total output. Note, in particular, the sharp decline of Arab NDP in the extremely poor crop years of 1928 and 1938, and the acceleration of output growth in the bumper-crop years of 1934, 1935, and especially 1937 (figure 1.2).

Another illuminating observation is the high instability of the rates of change of Arab agricultural output, relative to those of Jewish farm production, revealed by the large discrepancy between their respective coefficients of variation (2.56 for Arab and 0.85 for Jewish agricultural output in 1922–39). This difference reflects the steeper fluctuating growth path of Arab total output, which could be ascribed to the renowned cycles in the annual yields of (predominantly Arab) olive groves and to the high dependence on climatic factors of the (mainly unirrigated) Arab extensive husbandry, compared with the largely irrigated intensive Jewish agriculture (see chapter 5).

In summary, the diverse cyclical patterns of economic activity are obviously consistent with and provide additional support to the contention that there were two separate economies in Mandatory Palestine. The evidence presented strongly suggests that the "Jewish-specific" attributes of immigration and capital inflow waves, on the one hand, and the "dualistic" traits distinguishing the two economic sectors from one another, on the other, were instrumental in shaping the different patterns and intensities of the short-run swings.

It is interesting to note, in this context, that as early as the mid-1930s Abramowitz (1935) used the differences in the time path of Jewish and Arab construction as the prime rationale for his conclusion that Palestine comprised two national economies. The inference drawn in the present chapter resembles the one drawn by Abramowitz, with one major difference: the leading economic role of the construction industry is shown to have been confined to the Jewish community; in the Arab community – as might have been expected – this role was assumed by agriculture.

2   The peoples of Palestine: a comparative account

In performing their dual economic role, as producers – who utilize their work power, skills, and initiative to produce and disseminate goods and services – and as final consumers – who are themselves the aim of production – people's behavior is closely linked to their demographic and socio-economic traits, and, as such, to their society's state of development. In Mandatory Palestine, the ethno-national divide and the socio-economic distinction between Arabs and Jews add to the picture an extra dimension, occupying, quite naturally, center stage in the account of the human factor in the country's economic life – the main concern of this chapter. What follows is a broad review, conducted within an internationally comparative framework, of the demographic, health, and educational attributes of Palestine's two peoples, and of their respective "human development" state during the Mandate period.

The pace and sources of population growth

Palestine's demography was dominated throughout the period by the extremely rapid (though fluctuating) growth of the Jewish community. The magnitudes and components of the country's population expansion are presented in table 2.1 in intervals that roughly correspond to the swings in Jewish immigration.[1] In percentage terms, the Jewish population grew faster than the relatively smoothly growing Arab community, not only over the entire period, but in each sub-period as well, including lulls in immigration (panel B, column 1).

---

[1] Bachi's continuous yearly estimates of the size of population, on which table 2.1 draws, starts on December 31, 1921 (Bachi, 1977, appendix 6, tables A12, A13). The figures for mid-1919, reported separately in panel A, are based on independent contemporary estimates of the settled population (quoted in *Statistical Abstract of Palestine 1929*, table 13) and on backwards-extrapolating Bachi's figures for the nomadic population in 1922, utilizing the average growth rate implied by his calculations (Bachi, 1977, appendix 6). The overall population figures in table 2.1, panel A are all inclusive. But since no data are available on the components of growth of the nomadic population, the rates pertaining to Arabs in panels B and C refer only to the settled population.

Table 2.1. *Growth of Palestine's population 1922–47*

A Absolute growth

	Arabs ('000)		Jews ('000)	Jewish share in total (%) (3)/[(2)+(3)]
	settled (1)	total (2)	(3)	(4)
population as of June 1, 1919	533.0	594.0	57.0	8.8
increase between June 1, 1919 and Dec. 31, 1921	71.0	72.1	17.7	19.7
population as of Dec. 31, 1921	604.0	666.1	74.7	10.1
increase in: 1922–26	93.2	95.4	74.9	44.0
1927–31	97.5	99.8	25.5	20.4
1932–35	95.3	98.5	180.0	64.6
1936–39	92.7	95.9	94.3	49.6
1940–45	193.8	199.0	114.4	36.5
1946–47	83.8	85.6	66.2	43.6
1922–47	656.3	674.2	555.3	45.2
population as of Dec. 31, 1947	1,260.3	1,340.3	630.0	32.0

B Components of population growth (average annual rate per 1,000 population)

		total growth (1)	natural increase (2)	"residual" (3)
Arabs (settled)	1922–26[a]	29.7	25.3	4.4
		(26.0)		(0.7)
	1927–31	26.5	24.9	1.6
	1932–35	28.7	24.2	4.5
	1936–39	25.1	24.6	0.5
	1940–45	30.5	28.3	2.2
	1922–45	27.5	25.7	1.8
Jews	1922–26	150.6	26.5	124.1
	1927–31	32.1	23.0	9.1
	1932–35	194.8	22.4	172.4
	1936–39	60.9	18.8	42.1
	1940–45	38.6	18.6	20.0
	1922–45	90.3	21.8	68.5

Table 2.1. (*cont.*)

C Growth of population accounted for by natural increase and by "residual" growth (%)

	Arabs (settled)			Jews		
	total growth (1)	natural increase (2)	"residual" [(1)-(2)] (3)	total growth (4)	natural increase (5)	"residual" [(4)-(5)] (6)
1922–26[a]	100.0	87.2	12.8	100.0	17.5	82.5
		(97.4)	(2.6)			
1927–31	100.0	93.7	6.3	100.0	70.8	29.2
1932–35	100.0	84.1	15.9	100.0	10.0	90.0
1936–39	100.0	98.1	1.9	100.0	30.7	69.3
1940–45	100.0	92.9	7.1	100.0	48.1	51.9
1922–45[a]	100.0	91.5	8.5	100.0	27.3	72.7
		(93.1)	(6.9)			

Note:
[a] Numbers in parentheses are net of the increase in the Arab population of Palestine (9,700 persons) in 1924 due to border changes; see Bachi, 1977, p. 393.
Sources: Statistical Abstract of Palestine 1929, table 13; tables A.1–A.3

Given the relatively small number of Jews living in Palestine at the beginning of the period, their substantial contribution to the growth of the country's population is all the more impressive. Between 1922 and 1947 the entire population grew by 1.2 million people (from 0.741 million to 1.970 million), of whom 555,300 (45.2 percent) were Jews (panel A, column 4). Jews accounted for 44 percent of the overall population growth as early as the first half of the 1920s, and while their weight shrank substantially (to 20.4 percent of the increase) during the immigration slowdown of the late 1920s, it more than recovered in the 1930s. Even during the relatively low immigration years of World War II, Jews accounted for about 36 percent of the country's entire population growth.

The years 1932–35 stand out most clearly. During these four years of intensive immigration the Jewish population grew by 180,000 people – almost double the Arab increase at the time (98,500). This highly visible growth disparity, and the resulting upsurge in the relative size of the Jewish community (the share of Jews in Palestine's population rose from 17 percent in 1931 to 27 percent in 1936) may have been crucial in determining the timing and intensity of the Arab revolt of 1936–39, which was directed against the British government and the Jewish buildup in Palestine.

Panels B and C of table 2.1 divide the growth of the population into two components: natural increase, and a "residual," calculated as the difference between total and natural growth. Measurement and estimation errors apart, the latter should obviously stand for net migration.[2] The proportion attributed to the "residual" in the Jewish community – 72.7 percent of the increase in 1922–45 – which is practically identical to the net immigration share as calculated from Sicron's (1957b) migration estimates (72.9 percent) – is enormous by any standard.[3] For example, in the United States and Argentina, the two main destinations of international migrants before World War I, the largest ten-year contributions of immigration to population increase recorded in the 1900s were about 33 percent and 50 percent respectively (Willcox, 1931, table 50; Maddison, 1970, appendix C; Haines, 1994, table 1). Even the mass immigration to the newly born state of Israel in the 1950s did not account for more than 65 percent of total population growth in 1948–61 (*Statistical Abstract of Israel*, 1992, table 2.2).

The data for the Arab community are substantially different and rather ambiguous. The shortcomings of the official vital statistics – particularly with respect to the predominantly rural Muslim population and Arab migration – have long been recognized in the literature (for example, Bachi, 1977; Gilbar, 1987; McCarthy, 1990). In his comprehensive study of the demography of Palestine and Israel, Bachi (1977) attempted to rectify some of these shortcomings. His revised official figures and original population estimates suggest that Arab net migration resulted in a net inflow of 40,000–42,000 people in 1922–45, excluding the 9,700 persons added to the country's Arab population in 1924 after the border adjustments of the early 1920s (Bachi, 1977, appendix 6). The percentages in panels B and C of table 2.1, while derived from Bachi's estimates, also include the population changes caused by these border adjustments (only the numbers in parentheses are net of them) and therefore imply a somewhat larger net immigration figure of about 49,000. This number (8.5 percent in total Arab growth; see panel C, column 3) may thus be interpreted as an upper bound estimate of net Arab migration, but even this does not alter the picture of a community whose growth was driven primarily by natural increase.[4]

---

[2] Although direct use could have been made of the independent migration estimates for the Jewish community (Sicron, 1957b and this vol., chapter 3), I preferred, for the sake of comparative consistency, to present the migratory growth component in terms of the "residual" for both communities.

[3] Due to various assumptions used by Sicron (1957b) and Bachi (1977) to estimate yearly figures of illegal immigration and Jewish emigration, the identity between the two measures does not hold in the intermediate time intervals.

[4] Gottheil (1973) suggested a much larger influx of Arab net migration, of up to 60,000 between 1922 and 1931. His numbers are based on the population totals reported in the

Note, though, that in 1932–35 Arab immigration took a sharp upswing from the average share of 8.5, reaching about 16 percent of Arab population growth. These were years of remarkable economic expansion in both the Jewish and the Arab communities (see chapter 1), which may have generated a strong pull factor for Arab in-migration. However, even the considerable proportion of 16 percent was a far cry from the relative weight of Jewish immigration that never fell below 29 percent of the total increase in the Jewish population, including the low immigration years 1927–31 (panel C, column 6).

Components of natural increase

Although the volume and intensity of immigration was the major factor demographically distinguishing Jews from Arabs, the two peoples differed substantially also in the components of their natural increase.[5] Problems of accuracy and coverage notwithstanding (see discussion in Bachi, 1977, appendix 6), the numbers clearly reveal a remarkably rapid rate of natural increase in the Arab community (25.7 per thousand population annually in 1922–45), generated by extremely high birth and death rates (49.5 and 23.8 per thousand respectively). Jewish natural increase over the same period, though slower, was also considerable (21.5 per thousand) owing to appreciably lower rates of birth (32.2 per thousand) and, more so, to substantially lower mortality rates (14.3 per thousand).[6]

A broader view, incorporating the dispersion of Palestine's vital changes and their developmental implications, can be obtained from examining them in a wider comparative context. This is done in figures

1922 and 1931 censuses without allowing for underreporting in the first census (see Gilbar, 1987). Bachi's (1977) convincing upward adjustment of the 1922 census figures for Muslim Arabs by 34,000 shows that Gottheil's estimates are exaggerated (see also McCarthy, 1990). Another claim, that unrecorded Arab immigration into Palestine from the late Ottoman period to the end of the British Mandate was substantially higher than suggested by the existing estimates, was made by Peters (1984). However, as Porath (1986) and McCarthy (1990) have unequivocally demonstrated, her numbers do not stand up to any scientific scrutiny and cannot be taken as a credible alternative for the range of estimates surveyed by Bachi (1977).

[5] There were marked demographic (and other socio-economic) differences between Muslim and Christian Arabs: the former had substantially higher birth and death rates. The vital rates of the Christians were closer to those of the Jews, who were themselves quite a heterogeneous community, particularly insofar as age of marriage and natality is concerned (see *Vital Statistics*, 1947; Bachi, 1977). Nonetheless, in order not to blur the basic comparative picture, and in view of the fact that 88 percent of the Arab population were Muslims, I chose to present and discuss in this chapter the demographic statistics and socio-economic parameters in aggregate form: all Arabs versus all Jews.

[6] The average crude birth and death rates for Arabs and Jews were derived from *Vital Statistics* (1947), tables A14 and A26, incorporating Bachi's corrections (1977, appendix 6).

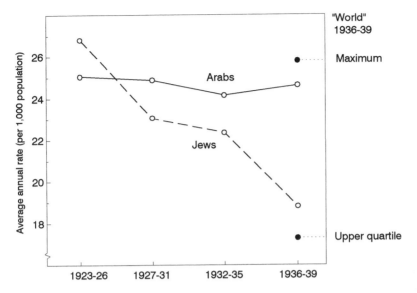

Figure 2.1 Natural increase: Palestine, 1923–39
(sources: tables A.1–A.3 for Palestine's natural increase;
Demographic Yearbook 1948, tables 14, 20 for "world")

2.1, 2.2, and 2.3, which show annual rates of natural increase, birth, and mortality for the Arab and Jewish populations.[7] These rates are combined with comparable "international data," derived from distributions of average yearly rates for 1936–39 in sixty-six countries for which such records are available (*Demographic Yearbook 1948*, tables 14, 20).[8]

As shown in figure 2.1, natural increase in Palestine was very rapid indeed. Throughout the inter-war period the Arab community maintained a stable and extremely high natural growth rate of 24.6 per thousand. In 1936–39, only three countries (Western Samoa, Paraguay, and Costa Rica) had faster growth rates. Jewish natural increase, although declining quite sharply from an initial rate higher than that of the Arabs to a much lower one (18.8 per thousand in 1936–39), nonetheless

[7] In view of the dubious reliability of the vital statistics figures for 1922 and (for the Arab population) in the war years (see Bachi, 1977, appendix 6), the rates presented in figures 2.1, 2.2, and 2.3 are confined to 1923–39.

[8] The international demographic data dealt with in this section, as well as the various countries' income figures and estimates of other socio-economic attributes discussed in the following sections, are obviously of uneven quality and reliability. Nonetheless, the profiles and the inter-parameter links they suggest are illuminating enough to justify their use as indicative devices within an internationally comparative framework.

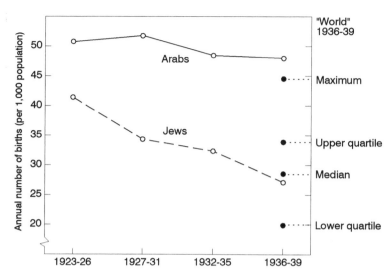

Figure 2.2 Birth rates: Palestine, 1923–39
(sources: tables A.1–A.3 for Palestine's birth rates;
Demographic Yearbook 1948, table 14 for "world")

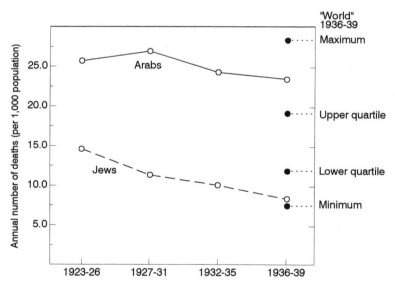

Figure 2.3 Death rates: Palestine, 1923–39
(sources: tables A.1–A.3 for Palestine's death rates;
Demographic Yearbook 1948, table 20 for "world")

remained in the upper world quartile of over 17.3 per thousand in the late 1930s.[9]

A comparison of birth- and death-rate patterns (figures 2.2 and 2.3) reveals a different picture. The international ranking of Arabs, with each component separate, remains as high as it was in terms of natural increase. In fact, their yearly inter-war birth rates (48.0 per thousand in 1936–39) were the *highest* on record, and their mortality rates (23.4 on average in 1936–39), though declining from the late 1920s on, were surpassed by only four countries – Mauritius (28.3), Egypt (27.0), Chile (23.6), and Mexico (23.5).

Note, however, that in a traditional society, deficiencies in official records of births and deaths may understate the true rates. For example, El-Badry (1965) revised the official Egyptian figures upward; his estimates for 1934–39 produce an average birth rate of 47.1 per thousand, and a death rate of 32.6, compared to the respective official rates of 42.7 and 27.1. While these revised figures do narrow the difference between birth rates in Egypt and the official figures for Arabs in Palestine, the latter still hold the record for the relevant years.

The secular decline in Jewish natality was appreciably faster than among Arabs (figure 2.2). The average Jewish birth rate for 1936–39 (27.1 per thousand) ranks three positions lower than the "world" median (28.6) – still very high, though, by Western standards. Of all the European and North American countries only one (Romania) had a higher average birth rate at the time.

But the truly outstanding feature of the Jewish vital record is its rapidly diminishing mortality rate (figure 2.3). The average death rate among Jews in the first half of the 1920s (14.6 per thousand) was roughly the same as the world median for 1936–39 (14.4), while the substantially lower rate in the late 1930s (8.3 per thousand) was second only to the world minimum in 1936–39 (7.4 per thousand among European settlers in South West Africa).

This comparative sketch of Palestine's vital statistics is related to the developmental differences between the two ethno-national communities. The Arab community is a clear case of a pre-modern society typified by excessively high birth and mortality rates. The decline in its death rates from the late 1920s onward, which was accompanied by a mild downturn

---

[9] The upper-quartile benchmark rate of 17.3 means that in ranking the sixty-six countries by rate of natural growth, in descending order, the seventeenth country (Cyprus) had an average rate of natural increase of 17.3 per thousand in 1936–39 (*Demographic Yearbook 1948*, tables 14, 20). With a growth rate of 18.8 per thousand, the Jewish community places just above the upper quartile benchmark, between the fifteenth and sixteenth countries.

in birth rates in the 1930s, does not change the general pattern. The decline may reveal some potential for a "demographic transition," but if so, it did not become manifest until the end of the Mandate period. In contrast, the "demographic performance" of the Jewish community, particularly with respect to mortality, besides the effect of its immigration-induced young age structure, points to a highly developed state, typical of the most advanced countries at the time.

This general characterization is derived from the crude birth and death rates. But a fuller appreciation of the vital movements and their socio-economic attributes requires going "behind the scenes" and examining the factors underlying birth and mortality.

Birth-rate determinants

Table 2.2 divides the crude birth rates of Arabs and Jews in three selected years into two components: (a) the relative population share of women of reproductive age (fifteen to forty-nine), as an approximation of the population's "fertility potential"; (b) the total number of live births per thousand women in the fifteen-to-forty-nine age bracket (general fertility), as an indication of the extent to which this potential was realized.[10]

It is hardly surprising to find that the Jewish immigrant community, with its "prime-age-tilted" age distribution (see below), had a clear advantage in potential fertility. But significant as this advantage may have been, it was completely overshadowed by the actual fertility gap.

A similar gap appears in the age-independent total fertility rates (table 2.3). These were, on average, over 2.5 times higher in the Arab community.[11] Moreover, while Jewish total fertility was within the upper-middle range of the European rates, Arab total fertility was the highest recorded rate in the world (Gurevich, Gertz, and Bachi, 1944 [henceforth GGB], p. 172; *Demographic Yearbook 1948*, table 31). Since confinements of unwed mothers were quite rare in Palestine (GGB, p. 111), this divergence hinges on differences between the two communities in (a) the portion of women's fertile years spent in wedlock (marriage intensity) and (b) disparities in marital fertility.

[10] Taking the fifteen-to-forty-nine age bracket as the relevant child-bearing period is supported by the available data on age-specific fertility in Palestine in 1938–44: *Survey* (1946), vol. III, p. 1166.
[11] Total fertility rates for a given year cite the number of children a woman would bear throughout her entire reproductive period, if she survived to the age of fifty, and provided her age-specific fertility rates were the ones calculated for that particular year. Since the official fertility rates from 1943 on were, by government admission, overstated (see *Survey*, 1946, section I, table 9), table 2.3 reports estimates of total fertility only up to 1942.

Table 2.2. *Birth-rate determinants in Palestine: 1931, 1936, 1940*

	1931	1936	1940
1. percent women aged 15–49 in the population			
Arabs	23.2	21.9	21.8
Jews	27.1	29.8	29.4
2. total number of births per 1,000 women aged 15–49			
Arabs	220.8	229.3	206.7
Jews	116.5	96.1	79.4
3. [=1.×2. / 100] birth rate per 1,000 of population			
Arabs	51.2	50.2	45.0
Jews	31.6	28.7	23.3

Sources: table A.1 for total population figures; *Vital Statistics* (1947), table A1 for population by sex figures, table A14, for number of births; Sicron and Gill (1955), table 1 for age by sex breakdown of the Jewish population; McCarthy (1990), table A4–5, for age by sex distribution of the Arab population

Table 2.3. *Total fertility rates (annual averages)*

	Arabs		Jews
	Muslims[a] (1)	total (2)	(3)
1926–27	6.37		3.86
1928–30	6.50		3.35
1931	6.72		3.10
1932–33	6.41	6.13	2.72
1934–36	7.14	6.75	2.67
1937–39	7.50	7.06	2.36
1940–42	7.83	7.31	2.36

Note:
[a] Muslims' fertility figures are used, since data for non-Muslim Arabs are available only from 1932 on.
Sources: (1) and (3) – *Survey* (1946), vol. III, section I, table 9. (2) – average of the fertility rates by religious groups, as reported in the *Survey* (1946, vol. III, section I, table 9), weighted by the respective shares of those groups in the non-Jewish population of women aged 15–49, which were, in turn, calculated from the *Census of Palestine* (1933), vol. II, table VIII

In his major study, Bachi (1977, p. 170) inferred from the 1931 census data that while Arab women spent 73.7 percent of their years aged fifteen to forty-nine in wedlock, the figure for Jewish women was only 66.3 percent. He also showed that the Arab marriage proportion was significantly higher than in North America, Oceania, and most of Europe in 1930 (as low as 50 percent in Scandinavia to as high as 65 percent in North America and Oceania; Bachi, 1977, p. 171), that it was comparable to the percentages found in Bulgaria, Turkey, and India (about 75 percent in the early to mid-1930s), but was lower than in Egypt (84 percent in 1927; GGB, p. 131). In other words, the proportion of married women among the Arabs of Palestine was well within the range observed in societies commonly characterized as traditional or pre-modern.

On average, Jewish women were married during a shorter span of their reproductive period, but nevertheless had a high marriage intensity in international terms. This was so in 1931 (66.3 percent – somewhat higher than the upper bound of the Western countries: 65 percent), and certainly in 1948, when marriage intensity reached 71 percent (Bachi, 1977, p. 170). This finding probably reflects both the influence of traditional-religious groups in the otherwise "modern" and secular Jewish community, and the strong family ethos prevailing in all walks of Jewish society.

The age-specific marriage rates in table 2.4 reveal that the major disparities between the proportions of married women in the two communities were concentrated, at least in 1931, in the younger age group. This strongly suggests a significantly younger age of first marriage among Arab women. Note, in particular, the extremely large proportion – about 32 percent – of married Arab women in the fifteen-to-nineteen age group, compared with only 11.5 percent among Jewish women. Another illuminating piece of information is that 34 percent of all Muslim brides in 1936–41 were under fifteen years of age, and 52 percent were under seventeen on their wedding day (Bachi, 1977, p. 179).

The higher Arab propensity to marry young was sufficient to make for a 1.17 Arab-Jewish ratio of marriage intensity over the entire reproductive period, but Arab-Jewish fertility ratios were substantially higher: 1.90 for general fertility in 1931 (table 2.2); 2.25 for total fertility in 1932–33 (table 2.3). Therefore, Arab marital fertility must, on the whole, have been more than twice as high as that of Jews.

In order to get some idea of the differences between marital fertility rates by age, table 2.4, panel B combines the ratios of births by mother's age in 1940 with those of marriage intensity in 1931, yielding Arab-Jewish marital fertility ratios broken down by age group. However, since the accuracy of the derivation depends on the implied (uncertain) stabil-

Table 2.4. *Percent married, births, and marital fertility by women's age*

A Percent married and number of births by community

	percent women who were married in 1931		no. of births per 1,000 women in 1940	
	Arabs	Jews	Arabs	Jews
age group	(1)	(2)	(3)	(4)
15–19	31.7	11.5	77.6	23.3
20–29	80.3	63.9	400.7	158.0
30–39	87.3	85.2	242.9	70.9
40–49	72.9	78.0	53.1	7.8

B Arab-Jewish ratios

age group	marriage intensity [(1)/(2)] (5)	number of births [(3)/(4)] (6)	marital fertility [(6)/(5)] (7)
15–19	2.8	3.3	1.2
20–29	1.3	2.5	2.0
30–39	1.0	3.4	3.3
40–49	0.9	6.8	7.3

Sources: Census of Palestine (1933), vol. II, table VIII, for the marriage figures by age; *Survey* (1946), vol. III, section I, table 3, for the number of births by age; Sicron and Gill (1955), table 1, for the age distribution of Jewish women; McCarthy (1990), table A4–5, for the age distribution of Arab women by religious group

ity of the marriage-(or births)-by-age distributions between the two years, they should be viewed as indicative only.

This exercise suggests that contrary to the Arab-Jewish differential in marriage intensity, which declined with age, that of marital fertility rose with age. In the thirty-to-thirty-nine age bracket, Arab married women gave birth to three times as many children as did their Jewish counterparts; in the forty-to-forty-nine age group, the differential factor widens to seven. These findings are compatible with Bachi's estimates of the time elapsed between a (surviving) woman's marriage and her last delivery (14.8 years for Muslims, 5.5 years for Jews in the late 1930s; GGB, pp. 202–203); they imply considerable differences in marital birth control between the two communities.

Alongside the disparities in the age at which women marry, the discrepancies in marital fertility reveal the differences between the traditional characteristics and norms of Arab family formation and reproduction patterns and those of modern Jewish fertility regulation. Following Easterlin (1978), and drawing on his conceptual formulation, it is useful to categorize this distinction in terms of supply of and demand for surviving children, and the cost of fertility control.

On the supply side, the two key parameters are an infant's probability of survival to adulthood and the "natural fertility" of households that do not practice birth control. Thus defined, "natural fertility" is determined by: (a) biological determinants of fecundity and of full-term pregnancy which, besides being affected by genetic and evolutionary factors, seem to be positively associated – as is the survival probability of children – with the level of nutrition, the quality of individual and public health, and the overall standard of living; (b) cultural and social norms such as sexual taboos and the attitude to breast-feeding, affecting marital coital frequency, the length of a mother's temporary sterility intervals, and the spacing of births. Insofar as the "marriageable" age is determined by social customs and by economic considerations that are not related to the desired number of children, it, too, may be regarded as an attribute of natural fertility.

Social and economic modernization generally involves an improvement in living conditions and a reduction in morbidity and mortality. It may also moderate various traditional fertility-restricting customs. These developments should raise the survival chances of children and the rate of natural fertility, thereby providing a positive link between modernization and the "supply" of children.

As for the demand for children, the modern literature in economic demography applies standard demand theory to the analysis of the desired number of children by utility-maximizing households. Children are perceived as utility-generating objects, similar to consumer goods (for which they may be substitutes), and their demand is, likewise, taken to be determined by tastes, income, and prices in a state of cost-free fertility control.

Households' "tastes" for children (versus goods) are formed by their social and cultural norms and by their own preferences regarding the desired family size. In order to "enjoy" the surviving children, a household needs to "produce" them, so that the extent of infant mortality is a crucial factor in determining the required number of live births per surviving child (into adulthood). Hence, changes in infant mortality may well affect the number of births required for any desired number of surviving children. Similarly, the formation of preferences for "higher quality" children (particularly insofar as educational attainment is concerned), which tends to accompany modern economic growth, may reduce the number of children desired by a household for any level of child-raising cost.

Income is assumed to affect the demand for children in the ordinary way – namely, a rise in family income, other things being equal, will increase its consumption possibilities and therefore raise the demand by now richer households for all (normal) goods and services, including children.

Prices are also expected to operate in the normal fashion: an increase (decline) in the price of child-raising will reduce (increase) the desired number of children. Properly considered, the price of children is a composite of a variety of cost items whose most obvious component is the direct costs of child raising which tend to rise with economic development. For example, consider the development-linked level of education required to maintain (let alone improve) one's relative income position. In addition, an increase in years of schooling can be viewed as part of the structural and institutional changes that, in modernizing societies, tend to erode the economic gains parents can expect to derive from their offspring, either as contributors to the family's income or as providers of support at old age. Moreover, the parental (largely the mother's) time involved in child raising imposes opportunity costs that are positively correlated with women's education and alternative earnings. These costs are quite low in traditional communities, which tend to impose effective social and cultural constraints on women's school enrollment and labor-force participation, but can become substantial in modern societies that are relatively free of such bounds. All that said, it seems reasonable to expect the full price of children to rise with modernization and economic growth.

Finally, consider the costs of fertility control – cultural/ethical, psychological, and/or informational. These costs tend to introduce an "excess supply" wedge between the number of children that parents actually have and the number they would have chosen to have, had birth control been costless. Unlike the costs of child raising, the costs of fertility regulation, and the resultant wedge between actual and realized fertility, can be expected to diminish with modernization.

Economic demographers examining past and present patterns of fertility have portrayed a stylized profile of fertility change associated with economic and social modernization. It is characterized by two phases: an early phase, in which fertility rises, and a later one, in which it secularly declines as part of the well-known "demographic transition." The increase in fertility in the early phases of modernization and economic growth could be generated by the development-related rise in the supply of children and/or by the possible income-induced growth in the demand for them. With further economic development, the increasing costs of child raising tend to lower the demand for children. But if the cost of fertility control remains too high, preventing the decline in demand from reducing the actual number of births, the number of surviving children will still rise. It is probably only later in the developmental process that the cost of fertility regulation starts to decline and birth control becomes socially acceptable so as to cause a secular downturn in actual fertility with continuing economic growth (Kirk, 1969; Easterlin and Crimmins, 1985, chaps. 1, 7).

The extremely high (and rising) fertility in the Mandatory Arab community (table 2.3) places it, quite naturally, in the early developmental phase, in which the number of surviving children per typical household is growing. In view of the growth in income per capita, the improvement in health conditions, and the decline in infant, child, and overall mortality (see the discussion below), it seems highly probable that the supply of surviving Arab children did increase in the Mandate period. Likewise, the very low labor-force participation rates and school attainment of women – as well as the small number of school years for men (see below) – should have kept the price of child raising low; this, combined with the demand-augmenting growth of family income, should have made for a high (possibly even rising) demand for children throughout the period.

Moreover, the relatively high natality observed in Muslim communities around the world, possibly linked to "Islam-specific" religious and cultural norms (see Kirk, 1966), and the extremely high fertility rates among Arabs in contemporary Israel and in the West Bank and Gaza (Metzer, 1988), suggest that, other things being equal, the Arabs of Palestine maintained a social and individual preference ("taste") for large families, and/or that the social and psychological costs of fertility control remained persistently high. These factors may have been instrumental in prolonging the period of rising fertility and postponing the reduced-birth-rates phase of "demographic transition" in the Arab community. As far as the Muslims of Palestine and Israel are concerned, this transformation did not come about until the early 1970s (Keysar et al., 1992).

The Jewish record of relatively low and declining fertility compared with that of the Arabs presents a different socio-economic state.[12] Concurrent with the shrinking share of the traditional-religious segment in the Jewish community, vigorous economic growth, improved living and health conditions, steeply declining infant mortality, and relatively high labor force participation and school attainment of women and men, the

[12] From 1943 on, Jewish fertility was on the rise, generating a baby boom similar to the one observed in the West after the war. In Jewish Palestine it may have reflected, among other things, a "catching up" mechanism commencing after the removal of the German threat from the Middle East, following the Allied victory in the Western Desert in 1942, that counter-balanced the postponed births of the late 1930s and early 1940s.

Jewish experience was a typical case of fertility decline generated by a decrease in the demand for children and the diminishing costs of fertility regulation. This pattern, largely a reflection of substituting individual for social control of fertility (Easterlin, 1978), is characteristic of modern societies in the nineteenth and twentieth centuries (for example, in the Jewish and general population in inter-war Europe; Bachi, 1977, p. 199) and of contemporary modernizing societies in advanced stages of demographic transition.

Mortality

Demographers have observed that developing (high mortality) countries are characterized by a U-shaped profile of death by age, with early childhood mortality as high, or even higher, than at old ages. In developed (low mortality) societies, the analogous profile has been found to be J-shaped, indicating that early childhood mortality is exceeded by death rates at advanced ages (*Demographic Yearbook 1948*, table 22; Hull and Jones, 1986). In view of the developmental and overall mortality differences between Arabs and Jews in Mandatory Palestine, one should not be surprised to find that their respective profiles of age-specific death rates do indeed fit this distinction (figure 2.4).[13]

The figure also shows that Arab mortality was appreciably higher than that of the Jews in all age brackets below sixty. These differentials can probably explain most (92.7 percent) of the discrepancy between the crude death rates in the two communities. The remaining 7.3 percent are accounted for by the Jewish age distribution, which – with relatively fewer children under the age of five and relatively more young and prime-age adults (see below) – was more conducive to low mortality.[14]

The patterns of age-specific death rates can be usefully translated into a composite parameter of life expectancy at birth. Being a capsule index, independent of the age structure, life expectancy at birth provides a standard measure for comparing mortality rates, and relating them to standards of living across and within societies at a given period and over time.

Estimates of life expectancy in inter-war Palestine are presented in table 2.5. While life expectancy at birth rose substantially among Arabs and Jews alike, the sixteen-to-seventeen-year gap between the two

---

[13] The yearly age-specific death rates were calculated by dividing the number of deaths during the year of people in a given age group by the number of people in that age group who were alive at the beginning of the year.

[14] When applying the Arab age distribution to the Jewish pattern of age-specific mortality, the death rate in the Jewish community rises from 8 to 9.1, thus reducing the total mortality gap between the two communities by a mere 7.3 percent, from $(23 - 8 =)$ 15 to $(23 - 9.1 =)$ 13.9.

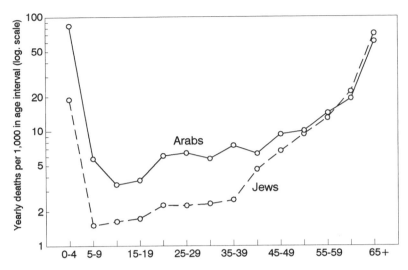

Figure 2.4 Death rates by age: Palestine, average 1932, 1937, and 1941
(sources: *Census of Palestine*, 1933, vol. II, table XVI; *Vital Statistics*,
1947, table A29)

communities barely changed during this period. However, in view of the
well-established cross-sectional association between income per capita
(as a proxy for a population's living standard) and life expectancy
(Preston, 1975, 1976, 1980; *Levels and Trends of Mortality Since 1950*,
1982), this persistent gap seems to be on a par with the stable income
differential between the two communities (see chapter 1).

The positive link between income and life expectancy is demonstrated
by figure 2.5, in which estimates of life expectancy at birth are plotted
against national income per capita (income per capita in the US=100) for
forty countries, and for Arabs and Jews, around 1939.[15] A distinction is
drawn between the Middle Eastern countries (Egypt and Turkey), countries in Latin America and Asia, and the group including North America,
all of Europe, Oceania, and Japan.

The Arab and Jewish positions are shown by their life expectancy as of
1939/41 (see table 2.5) and by their average annual income in 1935–39.[16]
The Jewish population is also drawn by the average amount of resources

[15] These are all the countries for which estimates of both income and life expectancy are
available (see table B.1). The positive association between these two parameters, as
shown in the figure, is also borne out by their high correlation coefficient (0.855).

[16] In the case of Palestine, annual averages for 1935–39 of income and resources per capita
were used in order to avoid the possible distortion caused by using Palestine's exceptionally low income (and resource) figures in the sharply depressed years of the late 1930s
(see chapter 1 and table A.22).

Table 2.5. *Life expectancy at birth (years of age)*

	Arabs		Jews
	Muslims[a] (1)	total (2)	(3)
1926/27	37.49		54.40
1933/35	42.01	43.27	60.62
1936/38	47.60		62.63
1939/41	46.44	47.77	63.39

Note:
[a] Estimates of life expectancy of non-Muslim Arabs are available only for 1933/35 and 1939/41.
Sources: Survey (1946), vol. III, section 1, table 6, for life expectancy by sex and religious community; Bachi (1977), table A.13, for population figures by religion; Sicron and Gill (1955), table 1, and *Vital Statistics* (1947), table A1, for the population's sex composition

per capita (which, in 1935–39, was about 44 percent larger than its average level of national income per capita; see tables A.22, A.24, B.1), reflecting the contribution of the massive volume of net capital imports to the material resources available, over and above the level of national income, and hence to the standard of living and economic growth in the Jewish community (see chapter 1).

Besides the overall positive association between income and longevity (note that countries in the Middle East, Latin America, and Asia are positioned in the "southwest" part of the scatter diagram and that all the other countries are in its "northeast" part), by the end of the inter-war period people in developed countries had a higher life expectancy than those in the less-developed ones at the same or similar income level. The mortality record of the Jewish community in Palestine was truly remarkable in that sense: it ranked twenty-seventh from the top among the forty-two national populations by income per capita, but had the tenth highest level of life expectancy. None of the poorer fifteen populations had a higher life expectancy, and in seventeen of the twenty-six richer ones (including, among others, the UK, Germany, France, Luxembourg, Belgium, Italy, Finland, Austria, Czechoslovakia, and Hungary) the expected age of death at birth was lower than among the Jews of Palestine. The closest richer population with longer life expectancy is Norway, whose income per capita was more than double that of Palestine Jews (table B.1). Moreover, it can easily be seen that even if we considered the level of resources per capita as a proxy for the Jewish standard of living (placing

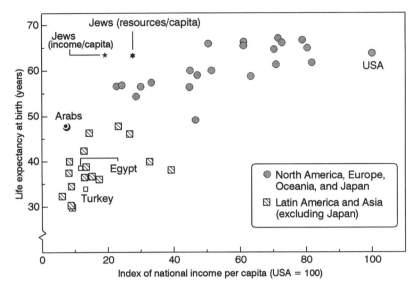

Figure 2.5 Life expectancy at birth by national income per capita
c. 1939
(source: table B.1)

them twenty-third instead of twenty-seventh in the international ranking order of income per capita), the observation regarding their outstandingly advanced state in terms of low mortality would remain unchanged.

Thanks to the declining mortality of the 1930s, life expectancy in the Arab community, although significantly lower than that of the Jews, is equally impressive considering its comparatively low income level. In 1939–41 the Arabs – whose income exceeded only that of India – could expect to live longer than the inhabitants of seventeen countries (sixteen of which had higher per capita income). It thus shared the less-developed world's lowest mortality rate with Taiwan. The life-expectancy advantage of Palestine's Arabs over Egypt and Turkey is especially revealing: these are the only two other Middle Eastern populations for whom age-specific mortality estimates are available for the period concerned (table B.1).

Of all the age-specific components of life expectancy, the extent of infant mortality (the number of deaths of infants under one year of age, per thousand live births in a given year), and under-age-five mortality, are closely associated with a society's socio-economic state. Consequently, patterns of decline in infant (or early-childhood) mortality have long served as an important indicator of socio-economic progress and

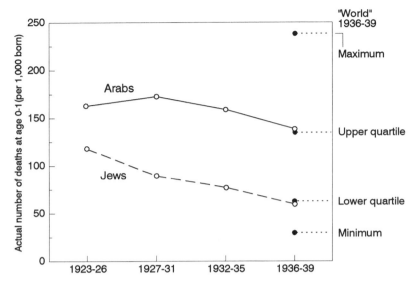

Figure 2.6 Infant mortality rates: Palestine, 1923–39
(sources: *Vital Statistics*, 1947, tables A31, A31a for Palestine;
Demographic Yearbook 1948, table 24 for "world")

modernization (see for example, *World Development Report*, various years,
and Aturupane, Glewwe, and Isenman, 1994).

The inter-war record of infant mortality in Palestine (figure 2.6) *vis-à-
vis* benchmark rates of the "world" infant mortality in 1936–39 (composed of eighty-two countries; see *Demographic Yearbook 1948*, table 24)
fits this notion well. Although declining moderately from the late 1920s
onward, early-age mortality in the Arab community remained within the
upper quartile of the world's distribution (only seventeen of the eighty-
two countries had higher infant mortality in 1936–39), while mortality
among Jewish infants fell sharply, from above the median for the late
1930s to within its lower quartile (nineteen countries had lower mortality
rates). The wide Arab-Jewish gap thus remained quite stable throughout
the period.

Health

Among the socio-economic attributes of society, the state of public and
individual health stands out as instrumental in accounting for the level of
and changes in mortality. It is in this context that some comparative statistics of health services, morbidity, and fatal disease in Palestine will be

Table 2.6. *Admission to hospitals and clinics, 1935 and 1944*

A Admissions per 1,000 population

| | 1935 | | 1944 | |
	Arabs	Jews	Arabs	Jews
hospitals	29.4	78.7	26.8	70.1
clinics	326.2	2,580.5	282.0	2,380.8

B Composition of admissions by ownership of facilities (%)

| | 1935 | | | 1944 | | |
	Arabs	Jews	% Jews in total	Arabs	Jews	% Jews in total
hospitals						
G&M[a]	37.1	7.9	14.7	53.5	8.7	15.5
Jewish	0.2	80.1	99.7	2.4	69.7	97.1
others	62.7	12.1	13.5	44.1	21.6	35.7
all	100.0	100.0	44.9	100.0	100.0	53.1
clinics						
G&M[a]	41.4	0.9	4.8	54.7	1.6	9.6
Jewish	7.6	95.3	96.8	5.2	97.0	98.6
others	51.0	3.8	15.3	40.1	1.4	11.3
all	100.0	100.0	70.6	100.0	100.0	78.5

Note:
[a] Government and municipal health facilities.
Sources: Memoranda (1937), p. 139; *Survey* (1946), vol. II, p. 634

discussed and further illuminate the diverse living conditions and developmental characteristics of the Arab and Jewish communities.

Summary figures of hospitalization and attendance at out-patient clinics are presented in table 2.6, which shows a wide and persistent disparity between Arabs and Jews in the utilization of health facilities. The discrepancy is extremely large in out-patient clinics: visits by Jews were about eight times more intensive (on a per-population basis) than by Arabs. But even the smaller differential in hospital admissions (by a factor of roughly 2.5) is very noticeable indeed.

The question that springs to mind is whether this disparity reflected an unequal supply of health services or differences in demand. A possible departure point for the examination of the supply side could be the distribution of hospital beds by ownership. A government health survey conducted in 1943 (*General Monthly Bulletin of Current Statistics* [*MBS*], September 1944) indicates that by the end of 1943, 912 (28.7 percent) of the 3,178 hospital beds serving the entire population were "governmental," 835 (26.3 percent) were run by church and private non-Jewish establishments, and 1,431 (45.0 percent) were in Jewish hospitals of all kinds.

Strict reference of non-Jews (i.e., Arabs) *only* to government and other non-Jewish hospitals, and Jews *only* to Jewish ones would imply the availability of 1.5 hospital beds per thousand Arabs compared with 2.8 beds per thousand Jews. For Arabs, the calculation based on this segregative assumption is actually quite close to reality: only 2.2 percent of all Arabs hospitalized in 1944 were treated in Jewish hospitals, and these constituted 3 percent of all the patients admitted to these hospitals.

Jews, however, made quite extensive use of non-Jewish hospitals: 8.7 percent of all Jewish patients in 1944 were admitted to government hospitals, and no less than 21.7 percent to other non-Jewish hospitals. These made for about 15 percent and 36 percent of all the admissions to hospitals in these two categories respectively (table 2.6). Thus, while the number cited (1.5 hospital beds per thousand population) is a reasonable approximation of the supply available to the Arab population, 2.8 beds per thousand is certainly a lower-bound estimate of the facilities available to the Jewish community in the mid-1940s.

A related parameter is the supply of medical personnel. By 1921, 44 percent of the physicians in Palestine were Jewish; their share rose to 60 percent in the late 1920s; owing to the large number of Jewish professionals entering the country in the 1930s (see chapter 3), this proportion climbed to about 90 percent by the end of the decade. Using the segregative assumption, Bachi (1977, pp. 238–39) has shown that the ratio of Jewish physicians to Jewish population was extremely high and rose rapidly, from twenty-four per ten thousand in the 1920s to more than forty in the 1930s and 1940s. This was far higher than the highest recorded ratio in 1940 (seventeen per ten thousand in Switzerland). As for the Arabs, the rather stable ratio of about 2.4 physicians per ten thousand fell within the Middle Eastern range: similar rates were found in Egypt (2.2), lower ones in Iraq (1.7), Trans-Jordan (0.9), Turkey (0.8), and Saudi Arabia (0.1).[17]

These supply considerations do not preclude the possibility that

[17] If one discards the segregative assumption and assumes that the people of Palestine could have used the services of all physicians, irrespective of ethnicity, the physicians-to-population ratio in Palestine (about 15.5 per ten thousand in the 1930s and 1940s) remains among the highest on record on the eve of World War II (in 1940 the USA had 14.2 physicians per ten thousand, and the UK 10.6; Bachi, 1977 p. 239).

differences in demand may also have played a role in the Arab-Jewish "utilization" discrepancy. One should bear in mind the internationally observed positive association between the propensity to use "conventional" medical services and such attributes as the level of education (see below), income per capita, and overall modernization (see, for example, *World Development Report*, 1993). This suggests that, other things being equal, the tendency of Arabs to avail themselves of modern health services may have been smaller than that of Jews. Some indication that this may indeed have been the case is provided, for example, by the extremely low percentage of hospitalized maternity cases per confinement in the Arab population – 3.3 percent in 1943, versus 86 percent among Jews (Bachi, 1977, p. 234; *Vital Statistics*, 1947, table A17). Another observation that may at least in part be explained by demand factors, given the country's relatively short travel distances, is the substantial divergence in the utilization of hospital services by the urban and rural segments of the two communities. The rate of hospitalization among urban Arabs was, by the end of 1943, 41.5 per thousand, and only 19.5 among the more traditional villagers. In the Jewish community, the respective shares were 56.4 per thousand in towns and 60.0 per thousand in rural settlements (*MBS*, September 1944).

So much for the "input" side of the health system; we now move on to its "outcomes" end and look into the causes-of-death statistics. The single most significant parameter here is the intensity of fatal infectious and parasitic diseases. As it reflects the state of public health, this parameter is widely accepted as an indication of a society's ability to prevent, contain, and treat diseases effectively. Before the advent of antibiotics in the early 1940s, and the post-World War II progress in immunization programs and coverage, the crucial factors in this respect (still of major importance in the developing world) were: sanitation, hygiene, quality and safety of water and fresh foodstuffs, and general awareness of the importance of health maintenance and disease control (see *The Determinants and Consequences of Population Trends*, 1973, and the references cited there; and *World Development Report*, 1991, chap. 3 and 1993, chap. 4). No wonder, therefore, that both life expectancy at birth and income per capita have been found to be negatively correlated with the death-causing proportion of infectious diseases.[18]

---

[18] On the basis of the life tables in Preston, Keyfitz, and Schoen (1972), the relative share of infectious, parasitic, and diarrheal diseases among the causes of death has been related to life expectancy at birth in 100 national populations between 1861 and 1950. The correlation coefficient between the two variables is –0.903. Similarly, the correlation coefficient between the same disease variable and the level of income per capita in a subset of fourteen national populations in the 1930s (see table B.1) is –0.863.

Table 2.7. *Distribution of natural deaths by disease (%)*

A Urban Palestine, all inhabitants, 1929–1945

	1929–31	1932–34	1935–37	1938–40	1944–45
infectious and parasitic diseases					
diarrhea and enteritis	23.9	23.2	20.0	20.6	18.2
pneumonia and bronchitis	26.5	25.0	23.5	22.1	19.2
others	10.0	11.1	10.7	9.3	9.4
all infectious and parasitic					
diseases	60.4	59.3	54.2	52.0	46.8
other causes of natural death	39.6	40.7	45.8	48.0	53.2
total	100.0	100.0	100.0	100.0	100.0

B Urban Palestine by community, 1944–45

	Arabs	Jews
infectious and parasitic diseases		
diarrhea and enteritis	26.6	2.9
pneumonia and bronchitis	23.4	11.4
others	9.9	8.6
all infectious and parasitic diseases	59.9	22.9
other causes of natural death	40.1	77.1
total	100.0	100.0

Sources: SAP (1936), table 27 and 1941, table 37

The major sources of data on the causes of death in Palestine are the detailed mortality records in urban localities, compiled by the Mandatory government and published on an annual basis starting in 1929. The percentage distributions of deaths by causes, calculated from these records, are presented in table 2.7, panel A, for 1929–45. The causes of death are grouped in two general clusters: (a) infectious and parasitic, including diarrheal diseases; and (b) all other death-causing ailments. The weight of infectious and parasitic diseases among the causes of death in urban Palestine is seen to have declined steadily: in 1929–31 about 60 percent of all the recorded deaths resulted from these diseases; by 1938–40 their proportion went down to 52 percent, with a further decline to about 47 percent in 1944–45. The decline in deaths attributed to enteritis and diarrhea, and pneumonia and bronchitis, is particularly significant, being facilitated, at least in part, by progress in improving the standard of public health and hygiene (see also Bachi, 1977, p. 252).

The official records of urban mortality by cause of death in 1944 and 1945 also allow for a distinction along ethno-national lines. The observed differences between Arabs and Jews (table 2.7, panel B) are extremely large and suggest that there must have been a considerable gap between the quality of public health and sanitation enjoyed by Arabs and Jews, not only in rural areas but in major towns, including adjacent ones. Note, for example, that in Jaffa, where Arabs constituted 70 percent of the population, infectious diseases caused 70 percent of all the recorded cases of natural death in 1940, whereas in the all-Jewish adjacent town of Tel Aviv the share was only 30 percent (*Statistical Abstract of Palestine* [*SAP*], 1941, table 38; see also Kamen, 1991, chap. 2). Moreover, existing records of infectious diseases that were reported by physicians to the department of health during 1938–45 point to an average death-disease ratio of 11 percent for Arabs and 6 percent for Jews in those years (*SAP*, 1944–45, table 23). These imply a Jewish advantage in treating infectious diseases, not just in preventing them.

Education

Educational attainment has long been associated in the growth and development literature with productivity advance and economic performance, and is known to have a strong effect on various characteristics of modernization. Among the latter, the literature emphasizes (usually in connection with education in general, especially with women's education) the increasing ability to utilize preventive and therapeutic medical care effectively, and the rising demand for such care; infant and overall mortality; increasing participation of women in the labor force; and the transition from high to low fertility regimes (see, for example, Schultz, 1981; Meier, 1989, chap. IX; *World Development Report*, 1991, chap. 3 and 1993, chaps. 2–3). With such wide-ranging (potential) developmental links and effects, education naturally becomes a major component of a society's socio-economic profile, perhaps *the* major one.

Not being compulsory, formal education in Mandatory Palestine was very unevenly distributed between Arabs and Jews. In the Jewish community, where education was regarded a top national, social, and cultural priority, Jewish-owned and autonomously run public and private schools were universally available and extremely well attended. In 1931, about 73 percent of the Jewish population aged five to nineteen were enrolled in schools, and enrollment continued to rise – to 76 percent in 1940 and 77 percent in 1944. In the Arab community, educational services, most of which were provided by the government (50–60 percent of the total) and by religious and other private schools, were rather limited and attendance

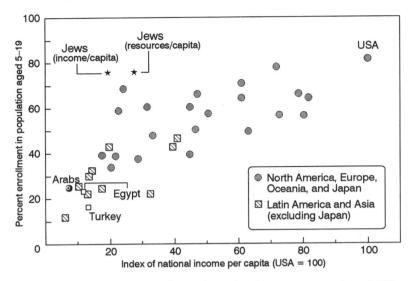

Figure 2.7 School enrollment by national income per capita *c.* 1939
(source: table B.1)

was low. No more than 19 percent of the Arab population aged five to
nineteen were enrolled in school in 1931; and even by the end of the
period, in 1940 and 1944, enrollment did not exceed 25 percent of this
age group.[19]

How do these rates fare comparatively? A partial answer to this question may be found in figure 2.7, which displays enrollment in the inter-
war period by income per capita around 1939 in thirty-four countries
(see table B.1). In view of the productive and developmental
ramifications of education, on the one hand, and the cost involved in providing educational services to the school-age population, on the other, the
positive association (correlation coefficient of 0.783) between enrollment
and income, as demonstrated by figure 2.7, is certainly expected.

Arab school enrollment in 1940, though low, was not "too low" for the
community's income level. Moreover, compared with other countries in
the same income range, including the two Middle East representatives
(Egypt and Turkey), the Arabs of Palestine did rather well. While Arab

---

[19] The school enrollment ratios for both communities were calculated from attendance data
in *SAP* (1941), table 165, and from the population by age composition, derived (a) for
Arabs, from: *Survey* (1946), vol. III, section 1, table 1; McCarthy (1990), table A4–5, and
Bachi (1977), table A13; and (b) for Jews, from Sicron and Gill (1955), table 1. Note that
the low Arab enrollment reflected the extremely poor school attendance of Muslims,
while that of Christians was much higher and similar to Jewish attendance.

school enrollment was largely compatible with income, Jewish enrollment in 1940 was a true outlier, substantially surpassed only by the USA, the richest of all the thirty-four countries in figure 2.7 (where income per capita was over five times larger than Jewish income, and resources per capita 3.6 times larger).

Enrollment figures point to the investment in education made at a certain time; but what we need in order to get an idea of a society's educational achievements, at that or at any other point in time, is "stock" measures such as literacy rates and the number of completed years of schooling. Some information on these parameters in 1931 can be obtained from Palestine's population census.[20]

Illiteracy rates (for ages fourteen and over) derived from the census show a very large disparity between Jews and Arabs. Among Arab males, 70.3 percent were illiterate in 1931, and among females 92.3 percent. This results in an extremely high overall illiteracy rate – 81.4 percent. The corresponding Jewish figures were 5.7 percent for males, 22.5 percent for females, and 14.1 percent for both sexes (Census of Palestine, 1933, vol. II, table IX(A); see also Bachi, 1977, table 15.7).

The substantial gender differences in literacy in the Jewish community probably reflected the social norm of discouraging women's education, common in some religious and other traditional strata. But the Arab gender gap, which, except for a tiny minority, left virtually all women in a state of illiteracy, was undoubtedly a manifestation of an overall pre-modern developmental state.

Figure 2.8 places the illiteracy rates of Palestine in a comparative framework, showing the negatively correlated illiteracy and income per capita figures for thirty-nine countries (with a coefficient of –0.775). The extraordinary extent of illiteracy among the Arabs of Palestine is quite clear; it was surpassed at the time by only two countries: India (86.5 percent) and Egypt (84.9 percent) (table B.1).

As for the educational attainment of literate adults (aged over twenty-one), the census reveals that in 1931 Arab men had completed 4 median years of schooling, and Arab women 4.7 years. The comparable Jewish figures were 7.7 years for men and 6.8 years for women. Thus, apart from the large discrepancy in the proportion of people with any education at

---

[20] Estimates of years of schooling and literacy in Palestine are available only for 1931, not for later years. Hence, they do not reflect the effects of the expanding government school system on Arab educational attainment, nor do they incorporate the contribution of human capital, "imported" by the well-educated immigrants of the 1930s, to the Jewish pre-statehood stock of schooling. Nonetheless, the large enrollment differences between the two communities, which persisted throughout the period, strongly suggest that the Arab-Jewish educational gap of 1931 would not have narrowed significantly, if at all, over time.

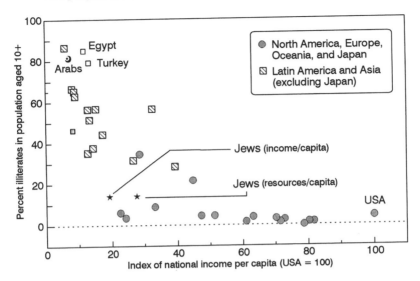

Figure 2.8 Illiteracy by national income per capita *c*. 1939
(source: table B.1)

all, the two communities differed substantially in the average schooling accumulated by their educated members.

When the calculation is made for the entire adult (over twenty-one years) population, literate and illiterate (assuming that illiterates never attended school), the figures for the Arab community naturally decline sharply: 0.7 median school years for men and 0.5 for women, implying that the average schooling of the adult Arab population was negligible in 1931. The high literacy rates in the Jewish community made for only a small change in the number of school years: 7.6 and 5.1 for *all* men and *all* women, respectively (*Census of Palestine*, 1933, vol. II, table IX).

Human development

The standard approach to economic development views "human improvement" in education and health primarily as investment in human capital, which, like physical capital, is expected to generate positive returns in the form of future income streams. Consequently, better education and improved health are regarded as inputs to society's output-generating activity, and therefore as a means to achieve the prime developmental goal of increasing people's overall access to goods and services (see, for example, Schultz, 1981; *World Development Report*, 1991, 1993).

In the past decade, however, an extended human development approach to economic development has emerged, inspired largely by the writings of Amartya Sen (1984, 1985a, b, 1987a, b). It emphasizes people's choices, and perceives their ability to lead long and healthy lives, and to acquire knowledge, as *independent* components of "well-being." These components are taken to be developmental ends in themselves, separate from – and regardless of their effect on – the access to material resources (Anand and Ravallion, 1993). These ideas were translated into a quantitative cross-country human development index (HDI) devised by the United Nations Development Programme (UNDP) and published since 1990 in its annual *Human Development Report*. For each country, this index combines parameters of longevity, educational attainment, and income-based standard of living into an average "measure" of human development.[21] The HDI has attracted wide attention and extensive debates. The final verdict on its interpretation and applicability has not yet been rendered, but it is already fairly evident that the HDI comes closer than an income-exclusive indicator to a comprehensive, comparative measure of a society's all-inclusive state of development.[22]

Applying the same procedure to the available estimates of life expectancy at birth, adult literacy, and income per capita in the inter-war period, table 2.8 presents a human development index and ranking for Arabs, Jews, and thirty-four other countries around 1939 (see table B.1). The numbers in parentheses give each country's ranking by income per capita only, which is highly correlated with that of the HDI (the rank correlation coefficient between the two is 0.93).

Table 2.8 shows that when development is broadly viewed as encompassing attributes of well-being such as longevity and educational attainment (in addition to income) both Jews and Arabs advance in the international ranking – a finding that largely supports the international comparisons made in the previous sections. Specific factors that may account for this outcome in the Jewish community may include extensive demand for social services, institutional emphasis on their provision, and a relative abundance of professional and skilled labor. As for the Arabs,

---

[21] Each of the three HDI components is calculated for any single country as a fraction whose numerator is the difference between its own and the world's lowest values of the parameter concerned; and the denominator – the difference between the world's highest and lowest values of that same parameter (i.e., each component stands for the country's position on the respective zero-to-one world scale). For more details on the parameters chosen and their adjustments see *Human Development Report* (1991), technical note 1, pp. 88–89 and 1993, technical note 1, pp. 100–01.

[22] For coverage of the debate on the HDI see *Human Development Report* (1993), pp. 104–24; Streeten (1994); Srinivasan (1994); Aturupane, Glewwe, and Isenman (1994); and the works cited in these articles.

Table 2.8. *Human Development Index c. 1939: an international comparison*

rank	rank by income per capita	country	HDI
1	(1)	USA	0.954
2	(4)	Sweden	0.921
3	(3)	Switzerland	0.905
4	(6)	New Zealand	0.893
5	(5)	Australia	0.886
6	(2)	UK	0.881
7	(7)	Canada	0.861
8	(9–10)	Denmark	0.850
9	(9–10)	Netherlands	0.842
10	(8)	France	0.780
11	(11)	Luxembourg	0.747
12	(13)	Ireland	0.735
13	(12)	Belgium	0.723
14	(16)	Finland	0.642
15	**(22)**	**PALESTINE'S JEWS**	**0.626**
16–17	(20)	Czechoslovakia	0.624
16–17	(14)	Italy	0.624
18	(21)	Hungary	0.607
19	(18)	Greece	0.499
20	(19)	Puerto Rico	0.428
21	(15)	Chile	0.413
22	(25)	Philippines	0.362
23	(29)	Panama	0.331
24	(17)	Venezuela	0.296
25	(23)	Colombia	0.255
26	(33)	Thailand	0.251
27	(26)	Mexico	0.238
28	(24)	Brazil	0.205
29	(28)	Peru	0.196
30	**(35)**	**PALESTINE'S ARABS**	**0.182**
31	(34)	Honduras	0.150
32	(31)	Nicaragua	0.138
33	(30)	Egypt	0.101
34	(32)	Guatemala	0.091
35	(27)	Turkey	0.086
36	(36)	India	0.017

Sources: table 2.5, figure 2.8, and table B.1

poor as their health and educational record may have been, they may have had a more equal income distribution and/or better access to social services than that dictated by their (even lower) income ranking. These general factors (see Streeten, 1994) may also have operated in the same direction in the Jewish community.

The rank improvement of the Jews – the largest among all fourteen countries whose HDI ranking was higher than their rank by income per capita, and matched only by Thailand – placed the Jews ahead of all the non-Western populations, and ahead of four European countries (Czechoslovakia, Italy, Hungary, and Greece).[23] The Arabs, although climbing from the penultimate (thirty-fifth) position in the income per capita ranking to the thirtieth HDI position, remained in the lowest quartile of the distribution, alongside the least-developed poor countries. Moreover, the Arab-Jewish HDI ranking discrepancy was somewhat larger than it was according to income per capita (fifteen versus thirteen places); this suggests that non-income (though not income-independent) differentials may have been even more important than the wide income gap in generating the socio-economic disparities between these two communities.

---

[23] Using resources per capita instead of income per capita in constructing the HDI for Jews (see the discussion in the previous sections) does not affect the direction of change: their income ranking rises from twenty-second to nineteenth place, and their HDI ranking from fifteenth to fourteenth place.

3   Patterns and characteristics of Palestine's (Jewish) immigration

It has already been noted that immigration was a major, if not the major, force making for the ethno-national mix of the country's population in the Mandate period, and certainly for the demographic and socio-economic profile of the Jewish community, let alone for its economic performance. But while it has, so far, lingered backstage, this chapter moves Palestine's (Jewish) immigration into the limelight. The discussion is divided into three parts: the first deals with Jewish international migration in a comparative framework; the second takes up Palestine's changing weight in Jewish migratory movement over time; and the third part considers the demographic and socio-economic attributes of the immigrants.

Jewish international migration

During the three decades of British rule (1919–48), about 550,000 people immigrated to Palestine; 483,000 (88 percent of the total) were Jews, and the rest (12 percent) mainly Arabs. While most Arab immigrants crossed into Palestine from neighboring countries (for example, 80 percent of the 4,000 registered immigrant Arabs in 1938–45 were recorded as originating in Jordan, Syria, and Lebanon; *SAP*, 1944/45, chap. 4, table 14), the vast majority (88 percent) of the incoming Jews set sail from Europe.[1]

The major European source of migrants destined for Palestine lay in the east: about 59 percent of all the European Jewish immigrants originated in Eastern Europe, and of these, over three-quarters were from Poland. Departures for Palestine from Central Europe, which intensified considerably following the rise of Nazism, contributed 23 percent of the overall European influx, the Balkans added another 16 percent, and all the other (West and North) European countries accounted for the

---

[1] The remaining 12 percent of Jewish immigrants were distributed as follows: 9 percent originated in Asian countries, 2 percent in America and Oceania, and 1 percent in Africa (see Sicron, 1957b, table A9).

remaining 2 percent (Sicron, 1957b, table A8, A9; Bachi, 1977, chaps. 8, 9).[2]

The timing, dimensions, and origins of Palestine's Jewish immigration identify it as an integral component of the international Jewish migratory movement that has been a major feature of European and world Jewry since the early 1880s. About 3.3 million Jews are thought to have left Europe between 1881 and 1939 (some 38 percent of the entire Jewish European population at the turn of the century). The largest group, nearly 2.6 million, left for the USA, and the second largest, 420,000, for Palestine (GGB, p. 13; Lestschinsky, 1965, table 8; Bachi, 1977, table 8.1).

This extraordinary flow transformed the geographical make-up of world Jewry. The weight of Europe sank from 88.3 percent of the global Jewish population in 1880 to 56.8 percent in 1939 (with a further drop – resulting from the Holocaust – to 31.5 percent by 1945); the share of America leaped from 2.6 percent to 33.4 percent, and that of Palestine rose no less impressively, from a negligible 0.3 percent to 2.8 percent (Bachi, 1977, table 7.1).

The Jewish exodus was apparently part (although, as we shall see below, quite a distinct one) of the massive European outflow in which about 50 million people left the continent for the New World (primarily to the USA) between 1846 and 1930. Some sought security and freedom from persecution, but most made the move in expectation of material betterment in the relatively labor-scarce countries of destination.

The temporal pattern of all-European inter-continental migration (figure 3.1) shows an extremely rapid rise from the 1880s until the outbreak of World War I, with Southern and Eastern Europe becoming the prime "sending" areas toward the turn of the century. This upturn was mainly a response to intensified driving forces pushing emigrés away from the "old world," and is evidence of the stress and dislocations prevailing in the newly industrializing and modernizing European periphery on its rapidly growing population. These were reinforced both by reductions in information and transport costs associated with advances in shipping and communications technology, and with the growth and development of the international economy (Kuznets, 1975; Baines, 1991).

Other factors contributing to enhanced migration were, on the one hand, informational, material, and social support provided by friends and relatives who had already settled in the countries of destination and, on

---

[2] In order to maintain consistency with the common international classification, Eastern Europe here consists of: the Soviet Union, Estonia, Latvia, Lithuania, and Poland; Central Europe – Austria, Czechoslovakia, Germany, and Hungary; and the Balkans – Bulgaria, Greece, Romania, and Yugoslavia.

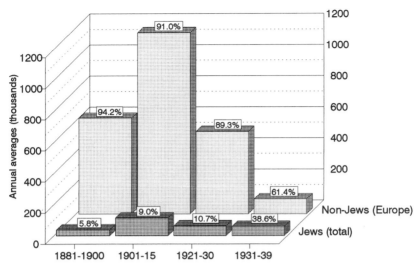

Figure 3.1 International migration, 1881–1939
(sources: GGB, p. 13; *The Determinants and Consequences of Population Trends*, 1953, chap. VI, table 16; Sicron, 1957b, table A1; Lestschinsky, 1965, table 8; Bachi, 1977, table 8.1)

the other hand, the growth of income in the countries of origin that enabled an increasing number of potential emigrants to bear the cost of migration (see Hatton and Williamson, 1994).

World War I interrupted this rising trend, and the post-war revival of inter-continental migration was both modest and brief. The 1920s witnessed a diminishing propensity to emigrate from the "old emigration" countries of Northern and Western Europe (due, in part, to the negative effect of falling birth rates and war casualties on the supply of prospective emigrants; see Hatton and Williamson, 1994). But the major migration-reducing factor of the decade was the effective constraint on the "new" (inter-continental) emigration from Southern and Eastern Europe.

In its Quota Act of 1921 the United States – the major destination for European out-migration – limited the annual number of (non-western hemisphere) immigrants of each nationality to 3 percent of its foreign-born American residents in 1910. These limitations were replaced by the Immigration Act of 1924, with even stricter quotas, which set the annual national limit to 2 percent of the foreign-born nationals as recorded in the census of 1890.

The quotas set in 1924 admitted about 24,000 immigrants annually from all the "new" emigration countries (compared with 158,000 under the Quota Act of 1921), and 126,000 from "old" emigration countries. These constituted 5 percent(!) and 91 percent of the actual number of Americans who had emigrated from those countries, respectively in 1921 (521,000 and 139,000; Kirk, 1946, p. 85; Gemery, 1994, p. 182). It follows that the American quotas, aimed mainly at reducing the influx of migrants from Southern and Eastern Europe, were highly effective. At that time, other countries of destination provided only a partial substitute for the lost American option (Hatton and Williamson, 1994).

Curtailment of emigration by some European governments, notably the Soviet Union, was an additional factor contributing to the overall decline in inter-continental migration. A further reduction in the depression decade of the 1930s (during which the American quotas, interestingly enough, did not effectively constrain immigration from either the "old" or the "new" emigration countries) brought the flow of international migration down to a trickle.

Jewish migration, however, enters the scene, as shown in figure 3.1, with a continuously rising weight. Its share in total European emigration grew from 5.8 percent in 1881–1900 to 9 percent in the peak (all-European) years 1901–15, and to 38.6 percent in 1931–39. This progression reflected the comparatively rapid growth of world Jewish migration prior to World War I, and its relative stability (in yearly averages per decade) in the face of shrinking international migration thereafter.

Underlying these patterns were the extremely high Jewish emigration rates, which exceeded the all-European rates throughout the entire period. The rate at which Jews left Europe in 1881–1914 (7.2 per thousand annually of the Jewish population of Europe at the turn of the century) was about three times higher than the figure for the European population as a whole (2.3 per thousand). The difference between the two flows widened further after World War I, to 4.9 times in 1921–30 and 17.5 times in 1931–39 (the annual emigration rates in the two inter-war decades, based on various population estimates for 1920–30, were: 5.4 and 7 per thousand for Jews, and 1.1 and 0.4 per thousand for all of Europe, respectively).The Jewish European emigration rates were also among the highest of the single-country rates, exceeded only by the exit from Ireland (10.0 per thousand) and Italy (7.8 per thousand) before World War I, and from Spain and Ireland again (6.3 and 5.9 per thousand) in the 1920s (Baines, 1991, table 3). But even these rates were lower than the record rate of Jewish out-migration from Tsarist Russia in 1881–1914 (12.0 per thousand annually; see Kuznets, 1975, table V), constituting about two-thirds of all the Jewish European emigration at the time.[3]

Furthermore, Jewish international migration was characterized by remarkably low return rates. Between 1908 and 1941 the proportion of foreign-born Jews who left the USA fluctuated between 1.1 percent and 7.1 percent of those who arrived, while the overall rate of departure from the USA ranged between 25.6 percent and 78.6 percent of all entrants (GGB, p. 15). The lowest return rate among all the non-Jewish peoples who emigrated to the USA in the peak immigration years of 1908–24 – the Irish (10.1 percent) – was double the Jewish rate (5.2 percent) in those years (Willcox, 1931, table 203). Assuming that these ratios were representative of overall net international migration in the period concerned (1908–24), they demonstrate that Jewish emigration was far more permanent in nature than that of European non-Jews.

Since the material "pull" factors in the countries of destination were not unusually favorable to Jews, their relatively high rates of emigration and low rates of return migration point to the force of "push" factors operating in the countries of origin. In view of the discrimination and frequent persecution of Jews in Eastern Europe since the early 1880s, in Central Europe in the 1930s, and the horrors of World War II, it is hardly surprising to observe that once the cost of moving went down, Jews were more likely than other European ethnic groups to emigrate, and to do so permanently.

This brings us to the question of selectivity. When individuals voluntarily consider migrating, they expect to gain at least as much from the move – materially, psychologically, socially, politically, and/or ideologically – as the pecuniary and non-pecuniary costs of leaving a familiar environment and adjusting to a new one. Other things being equal, the anticipated benefits of migration should be larger, and their costs smaller, the longer the potential migrant expects to live in the country of destination and the shorter the time he spent in the country of origin. It has been observed that young adults (mid-teens to the mid-forties) were heavily represented

---

[3] The emigration rates reported in this paragraph were calculated as follows: European Jewish emigration (assuming that it accounted for 85 percent of all Jewish world migration) was estimated from the global Jewish migration figures quoted in GGB, p. 13; Lestschinsky (1965), table 8; and Bachi (1977), table 8.1. Jewish population estimates for 1900 and 1939 were taken from the entry "Population" in *Encyclopedia Judaica*, 1971, vol. XIII, and from Bachi (1977), table 7.1. The population figure for 1930 was derived from the calculated annual growth rate between 1900 and 1939. The estimates for all European inter-continental migration are those reported in *The Determinants and Consequences of Population Trends* (1953), chap. VI, table 16. The sources for European population figures are Ferenczi and Willcox (1929), vol. I, pp. 200–201; and Mitchell (1992), table B1.

(60 percent–80 percent) in inter-continental migration during the period under review, whereas these age groups never comprised more than 50 percent of the population in their European "sending" societies (Ferenczi and Willcox, 1929, pp. 210–14; *Demographic Yearbook 1948*, table 4; *Sex and Age of International Migrants*, 1953; *The Aging of Populations*, 1956, table III; Easterlin, 1982).

Another distinct attribute of international migration in the late nineteenth and early twentieth centuries was the large proportion (around 70 percent) of males. In association with the high return rates and with typical patterns of "stage migration," the observed young-male-biased sex-by-age structure points to the individual and temporary nature of migration. This profile was particularly prominent in the new emigration from Southern and Eastern Europe, while the old emigration from Western and Northern Europe retained some of the permanent and family characteristics so typical of international migration in the first half of the nineteenth century (Baines, 1991).[4]

Only in the 1920s did the proportion of males and the share of young adults among international migrants decline (to around 55 percent), accounted for by family reunions after World War I. These were reinforced in the United States by the humanitarian clauses included in the newly introduced restrictions on immigration (Easterlin, 1982). The percentage of men continued to decline in the 1930s (in fact, in the USA and Canada men were outnumbered by female immigrants), reflecting the intensification of the refugee component of international migration throughout the decade (*Sex and Age of International Migrants*, 1953).

Jewish migrants usually occupied an intermediate position in terms of age and sex. On the one hand, they were less biased toward young adults than non-Jews – in 1899–1914 the fourteen-to-forty-four age bracket accounted for 70 percent of all Jewish immigrants to the USA, versus 84 percent for non-Jews; in 1920–41 the comparable figures for the sixteen-to-forty-four age group were 58 percent and 72 percent respectively (see GGB, p. 76; and Kuznets, 1975, table X). On the other hand, Jewish migrants were unquestionably age selective with regard to the Jewish communities from which they were drawn, where the relative size of the fourteen-to-forty-four age bracket ranged between 40 and 50 percent (Bachi, 1977, table 8.11).

---

[4] Note, for example, that of the 1.2 million immigrants who entered the USA in 1907, 72 percent originated in Southern and Eastern Europe, and three-quarters were males. Males were also overrepresented among the newcomers from Northern and Western Europe, who constituted 25 percent of the total flow of immigrants to the USA in that year, but their share was substantially lower – only 62 percent (Willcox, 1931, vol. II, p. 112).

A similar picture is revealed by the pre-World War I sex distribution of migration. The proportion of males among Jewish immigrants to the USA in 1899–1914 was 56 percent, and among non-Jews 70 percent. However, shortly after the war the sex ratio of Jewish immigrants was reversed (the Jewish American immigration of 1920–24 was 45.6 percent male and the immigration of non-Jews 58 percent male), suggesting an extremely strong family-reunion effect in the countries of destination (see Kuznets, 1975, table X).

It therefore appears that discrimination – above and beyond the general factors pushing both Jews and non-Jews out of Europe before World War II – may have accounted for the extraordinary stability of Jewish migration and for its more family-oriented structure. Nonetheless, at least until the mid-1930s, these elements were not pervasive enough to turn Jewish migration into a non-selective, involuntary flow of refugees and it retained the selectivity characteristics of voluntary migratory movements (Kuznets, 1975; Baines, 1991).

Palestine in Jewish migration

The early 1880s, during which large-scale Jewish international migration commenced, also marked the beginning of (largely nationally oriented) modern immigration to Palestine. At first, no more than an increment to the continuing stream of traditional migrants, driven primarily by religious feelings toward the Land of Israel, this flow soon overshadowed the immigration of the old type.

The modern immigration before World War I was instrumental in laying the foundations for the "new" Jewish community – as distinct from the traditional, "old" religious community – which took form as a well-functioning ethno-national entity during the Mandate period. Indeed, the standard immigration-related periodization of the history of the modern Jewish community in Palestine identifies the immigration waves of 1882–1914 as the First (1882–1902), and the Second (1903–14) Aliya.[5] However, important as immigration during the late Ottoman period may have been for future developments in the country's Jewish community, its size in relation to the world's overall Jewish migration was extremely modest, barely reaching 3 percent before World War I (Lestschinsky, 1965, table 8). Only in the inter-war period did Palestine's

---

[5] The literal meaning of the Hebrew word *aliya* is "ascent." In Jewish religion the term was originally used to denote walking up to Jerusalem, both literally and figuratively; it was later transformed in Jewish religious and national terminology to apply to the immigration of Jews to the Land of Israel (Palestine), and has come to mean exactly that in modern Hebrew as well.

Table 3.1. *Jewish world migration by destination, 1920–39*

	Palestine	USA	others	total	total
		(%)			('000)
1920	27.8	48.3	24.0	100.0	29.6
1921	5.9	84.3	9.8	100.0	141.2
1922	10.1	62.4	27.5	100.0	85.8
1923	9.8	59.6	30.6	100.0	83.4
1924	16.4	59.0	24.6	100.0	84.7
1925	52.1	15.6	32.3	100.0	66.0
1926	28.5	21.1	50.3	100.0	48.6
1927	7.7	29.2	63.1	100.0	39.4
1928	5.5	29.3	65.2	100.0	39.7
1929	11.4	27.2	61.3	100.0	45.9
1930	11.5	26.9	61.6	100.0	42.9
1931	15.6	21.8	62.5	100.0	26.1
1932	53.0	11.6	35.4	100.0	23.7
1933	47.8	3.0	49.2	100.0	78.1
1934	70.4	6.4	23.2	100.0	64.3
1935	80.4	5.9	13.7	100.0	82.6
1936	53.6	11.3	35.0	100.0	55.2
1937	30.2	32.2	37.6	100.0	35.2
1938	26.0	35.0	38.9	100.0	56.3
1939	31.4	43.7	24.9	100.0	99.4

Sources: non-Palestine immigration – GGB, p. 13; Lestschinsky (1965), table 8. Palestine – table A3

share climb sharply, and in the 1930s it became the largest destination country for Jewish international migrants, absorbing 46.8 percent of the total flow in that decade (table 3.1).

In view of the changing migration destination patterns, the question that comes to mind is what role did Palestine play in the considerations of prospective migrants as to whether, when, and where to go. Since in 1940–47 the Holocaust and its aftermath had turned Jewish migration largely into a matter of resolving the plight of refugees, this question is mainly relevant to the inter-war period.

However, we should bear in mind that the British government (and its Ottoman predecessor) did not pursue an unrestricted free-entry policy. Until the outbreak of the Arab revolt in 1936 the government criteria for granting immigrant visas were overtly non-political, being based primarily on the perceived "absorptive capacity" of Palestine. Although the implementation of the absorptive-capacity criterion and its translation into immigration certificates was often a matter of dispute between the government and the Jewish national institutions (GGB; Friedlander and Goldscheider, 1979; Halevi, 1979, 1983), it seems reasonable to assume, as a first approximation, that until the mid-1930s the Mandatory immigration policy did not constitute a binding constraint on the number of immigrants.

In the late nineteenth and early twentieth centuries just a tiny fraction of all Jewish migrants – those driven by religious and/or national fervor – sought to reach the poorly developed and politically unstable Palestine. The revealed preference of the vast majority in solving the choice-of-destination problem was to take advantage of the unrestricted American option. Hence, and given the intensifying "push" factors operating in the countries of origin, Palestine seems to have been prior to World War I the clear choice of only a highly self-selected segment of Jewish international migrants.

A similar conclusion can apparently be reached for the early phase (the Third Aliya, 1919–23) of the first major inter-war migratory influx of 1920–26. Between 1920 and 1923 the number of Jews immigrating to Palestine remained stable at about 8,000 per annum, while world Jewish migration fluctuated widely, rising from about 30,000 in 1920 to its inter-war peak of 141,000 in 1921, and then declining sharply, following the imposition of the American immigration quotas, to about 85,000 annually in 1922–24. A particularly revealing fact is Jewish immigration to "other" countries, which grew from 14,000 in 1921 to around 25,000 annually in 1922–23, indicating the availability of alternative destinations substituting for the restricted access to the USA.

The relatively high proportion of men (63.2 percent) and low percentage of children (20.8 percent under the age of sixteen) among immigrants to Palestine in 1919–23 (table 3.3), compared, for example, to Jews immigrating to the USA in 1920–24 (45.6 percent and 29.7 percent respectively; Kuznets, 1975, table X), suggests a clear selectivity element in the former group. Indeed, besides being driven by general factors pushing Jews (and non-Jews) to emigrate from Eastern Europe, such as hardship following World War I, the Bolshevik revolution, the Russian civil war (1918–20), and the war between Russia and Poland (1919–20), a good number of newcomers to Palestine in those years were young, idealistic pioneers, motivated by high expectations for the fulfillment of national and socialist Zionist ideologies under the new Mandatory regime. Note, however, that the Zionist Organization's policy at the time, of discouraging mass Jewish immigration to Palestine before adequate absorption was assured, seems to have added an involuntary institutional element to the self-selective nature of immigration in the early 1920s (Giladi, 1982).

The picture changed markedly toward the middle of the decade, when two independent developments coincided: one was the high inflation and stabilization policies in Poland, including state control over a wide range of economic activities and taxation on trade; these intensified Poland's "emigration push" factors, affecting mainly urban, middle-class Jews. The other development was the tightening of American immigration policy in 1924, which had a particularly adverse effect on immigration from Southern and Eastern Europe. These two developments seem to have been the major factors underlying the surge in Palestine's immigration in 1924 and particularly in 1925 – the early years of the Fourth Aliya (1924–31) – while overall Jewish international migration declined by about 22 percent between these two years (table 3.1).

As seen in table 3.1, the unprecedented increase in the influx of immigrants – over half of all Jewish migrants turned to Palestine in 1925 – stands out not only *vis-à-vis* the sharply shrinking American Jewish immigration (by about 80 percent from 1924 to 1925), but also with respect to the more moderate change in the inflow to other destinations. This observation leads to the conjecture that Palestine may have been the alternative of choice for prospective Jewish emigrants who were barred from entering the United States in the mid-1920s. By the same token, since the 1924 acceleration of immigration began before the upswing of Jewish economic activity in Palestine (see Halevi, 1979, 1983, and the income per capita figures in table A.22), it could be ventured that the Zionist "pull" effect played a non-trivial role in attracting Jewish immigrants to Palestine at the time.

The second half of the 1920s presents a different story. Palestine's immigration surge receded in 1926, with the further deterioration in the wealth of the Polish middle class, the erosion of its sterling value (following the sharp decline in the zloty exchange rate), new restrictions on cash transfers from Poland, and the slowdown of economic activity in the "receiving" Jewish community (see chapter 1). The violent upheavals of 1929 and the ensuing political unrest in Palestine may have added another (short-term) immigration-deterrent effect.

Consequently, gross immigration in 1927–31 shrank to about 4,000 annually, an all-period low for Mandatory Palestine. And since Jewish migration to the USA and to other destinations remained fairly stable, the volume of international Jewish migration in 1926–30 was, on average, less than half the 1921–25 flow. This suggests that besides some possible weakening in the propensity to emigrate from Eastern Europe in the second half of the decade, the recession in Palestine may have lessened its attractiveness as an alternative to the sharply diminished American option, leading many would-be Jewish migrants to reconsider emigrating.

As shown in table 3.1, the early 1930s witnessed a revival of immigration to Palestine (the Fifth Aliya, 1932–39), marked by the exodus of Jews from the depression-stricken and politically troubled Eastern and Central Europe and from Nazi Germany. Interestingly enough, this acceleration, in which Palestine was the destination of choice for 65 percent of the fast-growing flow of Jewish international migrants in 1932–35, took place while the stream of Jews entering the United States was minuscule (a mere 5.7 percent of total Jewish migration), although American immigration quotas were not met at the time. Moreover, except for 1933, when a relatively large number of Jews may have left Germany for other European countries as an immediate reaction to the Nazi accession to power, immigration to "other" destinations did not change appreciably (GGB, p. 13).

This pattern suggests that Palestine may have regained its position as preferred destination by Jewish emigrants in those years, reflecting the fact that unlike the depressed American and world economy, Palestine enjoyed an economic upturn between the late 1920s and the mid-1930s. This upturn was fueled largely by the renewed inflow of people and capital (see BMZ).

In the last four inter-war years, however, circumstances altered drastically. Palestine suffered a severe economic downturn (chapter 1), while the USA and world economies had already passed the trough of the depression. In addition, in 1937, and following the outbreak of the Arab revolt, the Mandatory government introduced non-economic restrictions on Jewish immigration, which culminated in the extremely restrictive "White Paper Policy" of 1939.

These developments, which reduced both the relative attractiveness of and access to Palestine as a destination for migrating Jews, drove increasing numbers of Jews to the United States, whose share in overall Jewish migration (33 percent) matched that of Palestine (35 percent) in 1936–39. It should be stressed, though, that while none of the broadly defined categories of American immigrant quotas was filled as late as the end of 1939 (Gemery, 1994), many Jews tried but failed to flee Europe before the war broke out.

To sum up, although a systematic examination of "whether and where to migrate" decisions requires several counterfactual exercises precluded by the paucity of data, our impressionistic review of inter-war Jewish migration by destination does allow the following generalizations. For a self-selected minority among the immigrants, Zionist-national ideologies provided both a trigger for emigration and a clear choice of destination. For the majority, however, the decision process was more complicated; national attitudes may have added extra flavor to Palestine's attractiveness, but they were certainly not sufficient to prompt mass Jewish emigration. Indeed, the above quantitative record suggests that the patterns of immigration were largely affected by discriminatory factors, policy constraints, and/or material considerations. These were perceived by the typical prospective Jewish migrant as major determinants of Palestine's comparative advantage *vis-à-vis* the option of staying in one's country of residence or emigrating to other destinations.

The country's migratory movements can be further illuminated by examining the patterns of emigration and net migration. Table 3.2 presents estimates of emigration and emigration-to-immigration ratios in Palestine's Jewish community, showing that the latter fluctuated widely, in inverse relation to the waves of in-migration. In the peak immigration years (the mid-1920s), and more so in the first half of the 1930s, outflows were rather small; when in-migration was slack, they intensified substantially. During the 1940s, emigration was no doubt closely linked to wartime and post-war conditions; but the inter-war record of out-migration is apparently compatible with and provides additional support for the links, suggested above, between the variations in Palestine's comparative status (economic and otherwise) and the fluctuating volume of immigration.

Viewing the entire inter-war period, Palestine's ratio of out- to in-migrating Jews (13.6 percent), although higher than the figure for American Jewish immigrants (4.6 percent in 1908–41, with a peak of 7.1 percent in 1908–14: see GGB, p. 15), was clearly at the low end of the range observed for overall migration in the major countries of destination (30–70 percent in the USA, Argentina, Australia, and Canada between 1880 and 1939: see *The Determinants and Consequences of Population Trends*, 1953; Kuznets, 1975, table X). This very modest extent of emigration, coupled with the extremely large influx of immigrants, made Palestine's net migratory inflow, relative to the resident population, among the highest on record.

The average yearly rate of net immigration (Jewish and Arab combined) of 1.5 percent per annum of all Palestine's residents in 1923–39 (table 3.2) was unmatched in the inter-war period. Only in the heyday of international migration, prior to World War I, were similar rates observed in some of the principal "receiving" countries (notably Argentina, Australia, and Canada: Taylor, 1994, pp. 95, 114).

Moreover, when Jewish net immigration is compared to the size of Palestine's Jewish community, which was largely responsible for the economic and social absorption of the in-migrating Jews, the scope of net immigration becomes even more impressive. As seen in table 3.2, the average annual rates of net Jewish immigration reached unprecedented heights in the peak years of the two inter-war influxes (21.3 percent of

Table 3.2. *Immigration, emigration, and net migration, Palestine 1919–47 (yearly averages)*

A Jewish immigration and emigration: numbers and rates

	immigrants	emigrants	emigrants as % of immigrants
1919–23	7,037	1,494	21.2
1924–25	24,139	2,094	8.7
1926–27	8,444	6,218	73.6
1928–31	4,111	1,565	38.1
1932–35	40,407	555	1.4
1936–39	21,523	4,218	19.6
1940–45	10,052	462	4.6
1946–47	20,429	3,124	15.3
1919–39	17,358	2,355	13.6
1940–47	12,647	1,127	8.9
1919–47	16,058	2,016	12.6

B Net immigration rates

	Jewish net immigration as % of Jewish resident population	all net immigration (Jews and Arabs) as % of all resident population
1919–23[a]	7.9	0.7
1924–25	21.3	2.8
1926–27	1.7	0.4
1928–31	1.6	0.3
1932–35	17.1	3.7
1936–39	4.5	1.4
1940–45	1.9	0.7
1946–47	3.0	1.0
1919–39[a]	8.5	1.5
1940–47	2.2	0.8
1919–47[a]	6.8	1.3

Note:
[a] The "all-Palestine" net immigration rates refer to 1923 only.
Sources: table A.3; *Statistical Abstract of Palestine 1929*, pp. 33, 40; GGB, pp. 24, 6* (sic), 7* (sic); *Statistical Handbook* (1947), pp. 112–13; Sicron (1957b), table A2; Bachi (1977), chapter 9 and appendix 6, sections 6.5, 6.6

Palestine's Jewish population in 1924–35 and 17.1 percent in 1932–35). Furthermore, even in the late 1920s, when the flow of immigrants dwindled, the average rate of net Jewish immigration never sank below 1.5 percent per annum. Consequently, the extremely high all-period average net immigration rate (8.5 percent of the Jewish population of Palestine annually in 1919–39, and 6.8 percent in 1919–47, surpassed only by the 16.9 percent net annual migration rate to Israel in 1948–51) clearly set the Jewish community of Mandatory Palestine apart from all the countries of destination in the history of modern migration.

The immigrants' demographic and socio-economic profile

Table 3.3 summarizes the available information on the sex composition of Jewish immigrants, their age, and family status upon arrival in Palestine. Though incomplete, the data provide a crude demographic profile of the immigrants, and allow further reference to the selectivity element in distinct immigration waves (*Aliyot*).

Unfortunately, detailed age distributions are available only from 1928; information on earlier inflows is limited to a dichotomized distinction between "under sixteen" and "sixteen plus" age groups. But when compared with the age structure of Jewish communities in major countries of origin (Bachi, 1977, table 8.11) and in Palestine (table 4.3), the percentages of panel A in table 3.3 leave little doubt that the working ages were overrepresented in all Palestine's immigration waves (including the 1930s, when the weight of refuge-seeking immigrants grew steadily), and were thus instrumental in facilitating the low dependency ratios of the country's Jewish population (see chapter 4).[6]

Some differences in the immigrants' age structure by sub-period can nonetheless be clearly distinguished. Assuming that the proportion of the over-sixty-five group changed relatively little, the numbers in table 3.3 imply that the proportion of working-age immigrants was higher in 1919–23 and (even more so) 1927–31 than in 1924–26 and 1932–39. This observation reaffirms the relatively selective nature of the Third Aliya when compared with the large influxes early on in the Fourth Aliya (1924–26) and the Fifth Aliya (1932–39).

Interestingly enough, the large proportion of working-age immigrants in the latter years of the Fourth Aliya (1927–31) suggests that the meager

---

[6] As for Arab immigrants, besides for the very small numbers involved, the limited information available suggests that their overall age structure (in 1935–45) was similar to that of Palestine's Arab population (*SAP*, 1944/45, chap. 4, table 16), so they could hardly affect the population's dependency ratio.

Table 3.3. *Jewish immigration to Palestine by age, sex, and family status, 1919–45 (%)*

A Age distribution of immigrants

	under 16	0–14	15–44	45–64	65+
1919–23	20.8				
1924–26	25.2				
1927–31	15.8				
1932–39	23.0				
1940–45	30.1				
1928–31		13.2	73.5	9.4	3.9
1932–38		18.9	63.7	13.7	3.7
1939–45		16.0	70.4	11.5	2.1

B Adult immigrants (age 16+) by sex and family status

	sex (% of all adult men/women/total)	family status (% of all adult men/women/total)		single
		married		
		migrating with family	migrating alone	
men				
1919–23	65.7	21.3	11.3	67.4
1924–26	54.6	36.7	10.5	52.8
1927–31	51.7	33.1	8.0	58.9
1932–39	48.1	56.6	8.6	34.8
1940–45	54.8	41.8	8.9	49.3
women				
1919–23	34.3	47.6	9.2	43.2
1924–26	45.4	52.2	6.5	41.3
1927–31	48.3	42.5	12.8	44.7
1932–39	51.9	57.4	16.8	25.8
1940–45	45.2	55.4	13.9	30.7
all				
1919–23	100.0	30.3	10.6	59.1
1924–26	100.0	43.7	8.7	47.6
1927–31	100.0	37.6	10.3	52.0
1932–39	100.0	57.0	12.9	30.1
1940–45	100.0	47.9	11.2	40.9

Sources: Statistical Handbook (1947), pp. 98–99; GGB, pp. 14* (sic), 15* (sic); Sicron (1957b), table A17

inflow during these years consisted primarily of highly motivated, self-selected immigrants (such as in the early 1920s), who made the move in spite of the weakening push-and-pull effects prevailing at the time. Similarly, the high concentration of working-age immigrants during World War II and its aftermath seems to reflect, besides the age structure of European Jews who escaped or survived the Holocaust, the self-selection of those who were prepared to face the challenge of illegal immigration, as did about 35 percent of all the Jews who immigrated to Palestine in those years (Sicron, 1957a, chap. 5; 1957b, table A1; Bachi, 1977, chap. 8).

The diminishing selectivity of the immigrants' age structure over the inter-war period is reinforced by the steadily declining share of men prior to World War II, from about 66 percent to 48 percent of all immigrating adults (aged over sixteen), and by the changes in the immigrants' family status. Two major patterns are revealed in panel B of table 3.3. First, the shrinking weight of unmarried adult immigrants, from almost 60 percent of the entire inflow in the early 1920s to 30 percent in the 1930s, most notably of single men (who accounted for 75 percent of all the single immigrants in 1919–23, and 55 percent in 1932–39). The second pattern is the rising component of family immigration. In the Third Aliya only 30 percent of the adult newcomers were married persons arriving with their spouses and/or children, a share that rose to no less than 57 percent in 1932–39.

Note, however, that whereas the percentage of married men who had left families behind was relatively low and declining (pointing to the possibility that "stage migration" of families, widely observed in international migration, might have been of some importance in the early 1920s, but became less significant later on), the opposite is observed for women. The share of married women immigrating on their own (about 9 percent of all immigrating women in 1919–23) first declined, started rising again in the late 1920s, and continued to rise until the outbreak of World War II.

A full explanation of these fluctuations is difficult to come by, but it may be conjectured that the large proportion of unaccompanied married women in the early years of the Mandate reflected, in part, "lagged" family reunions following World War I and what little stage migration there was. The resurgence can probably be attributed to fictitious marriages between immigrating women and male residents of Palestine, a device often resorted to as means of obtaining immigrant entry visas (Sicron, 1957a, chap. 6; Bachi, 1977, p. 98).

As mentioned above, "absorptive capacity" was the Mandatory government's guideline in controlling the flow of people into Palestine between

1922 and the eve of World War II. To implement this policy, immigration certificates were issued in four basic, loosely defined and periodically modified socio-economic categories into which prospective immigrants were classified (GGB, part I).

The first category was "labor." People were granted entry certificates according to their employment prospects in Palestine. It was the obligation of the Jewish Agency to demonstrate to the government that the (Jewish) economy was capable of gainfully absorbing the newcomers for whom it requested "labor" immigration permits (usually twice a year). This procedure provided an arena in which considerable bargaining took place between the Jewish Agency and the government over the extent of the country's absorptive capacity and the derived number of persons who were allowed to immigrate under this provision (Friedlander and Goldscheider, 1979; Halevi, 1979, 1983).

It should be pointed out, however, that the Jewish Agency did not opt to support unregulated entry of immigrants in the "labor" category. Perceiving the immigration of able-bodied Jews as a major element in fulfilling the Zionist nation-building task, it promoted the idea of preselecting candidates for "labor certificates," primarily through a process of ideological preparation and occupational training in their countries of origin organized by Zionist youth movements and other institutional organs (such as the *He-Halutz* [The Pioneer] organization).

The second category, often somewhat misleadingly called "capitalists" (see, for example, *Statistical Handbook*, 1947, p. 106), referred to individuals (or families) possessing a certain amount of wealth, varying between a minimum of P£500 and P£1,000 (P£250 for skilled artisans) and/or assured a secured income stream of P£60 annually. The admission of this group into the country was not restricted before 1939.

Newcomers demonstrably supportable by relatives already residing in Palestine (who had to submit a request for entry certificates) composed the third category of "dependents." In 1926 a fourth category was added: "pupils" – young people with assured maintenance who immigrated by themselves in order to study in Palestine.

Using the available data we can classify about 88 percent of the interwar Jewish immigrants according to these categories (table 3.4, panel A), and provide some clues as to their socio-economic features. "Labor" was clearly the largest group (47.3 percent of all the classified immigrants over the entire period), with the so-called "capitalists" accounting for slightly above a quarter (26.2 percent). The "dependents" were a little more than a fifth (21.9 percent), and the rest (4.6 percent) were "pupils." This breakdown comes as close as one can get to a size distribution of wealth. Assuming that the average amount of physical capital and financial means

Table 3.4. *Jewish immigrants to Palestine, their age structure and occupation abroad by "entry category" (percentage distribution)*

	labor	capitalists	dependents	pupils	total	total categorized as % of all immigrants
A Immigrants by category						
1922–23	50.3	15.5	34.2		100.0	90.5
1924–26	51.2	31.7	16.9	0.2	100.0	96.1
1927–31	59.8	16.2	22.4	1.6	100.0	96.2
1932–39	44.9	26.4	22.3	6.4	100.0	84.7
1922–39	47.3	26.2	21.9	4.6	100.0	87.7
B Immigrants of 1928–42 by category and age						
0–16	18.4	25.8	23.6	33.6		
17–25	41.6	11.2	13.7	61.1		
26–35	30.9	18.4	9.4	5.0		
36–50	7.9	27.2	10.5	0.3		
51–60	0.7	10.6	21.3			
61+	0.5	6.8	21.5			
total	100.0	100.0	100.0	100.0		73.0

C "Labor" and "capitalist" immigrants of 1928–42: earners by occupation abroad

	labor	capitalists
farming: work and training	17.7	3.3
non-farming material production & transport	68.4	16.7
commerce	2.7	46.4
liberal professions	7.8	19.5
religious services	0.2	8.8
clerks	3.2	5.3
earners:		
total	100.0	100.0
95% of all immigrants in category	39.8	33.5

Sources: GGB, pp. 72, 24* (sic); *Statistical Handbook* (1947), pp. 103, 106

possessed by "labor" immigrants was negligible (and certainly did not reach the "capitalist" threshold per household), most of the voluminous non-institutional capital, which was transferred by Jews to Palestine (about 75 percent of all Jewish capital imports over the period; see chapter 4 below) and not invested there by Jews living abroad, was probably concentrated in the hands of no more than a quarter of the immigrating population.

The proportion of "capitalists," however, fluctuated widely. While accounting for 15.5 percent of the immigrants in 1922–23, their share more than doubled (to 31.7 percent) in 1924–26. It is this difference, coupled with other factors (already mentioned) underlying the nature of "mass" immigration in the middle of the decade, that led contemporary members of the self-proclaimed Zionist-socialist *avant-garde* to disapprovingly characterize the Fourth Aliya as being dominated by "landlords" and "profit-seeking" bourgeoisie, in contrast to the ideologically motivated "worker pioneers" of the Third Aliya (Giladi, 1973, pp. 40–44).

The numbers reveal, however, that the average weight of "labor" remained stable, and even grew, between the two intervals (50.3 percent in 1922–23 and 51.2 percent in 1924–26), and that the rising share of "capitalists" was compensated for by an equivalent reduction in the proportion of "dependents."[7] Nonetheless, it appears that "capitalist"-type immigrants may indeed have given the Fourth Aliya its urban characterization. By using their material resources to promote small businesses and stimulate the growth of Tel Aviv into the major city of the Jewish community (its weight in the Jewish urban population grew from 22 percent in 1922 to about 35 percent in 1931; *Statistical Handbook*, 1947, pp. 38, 48), the contribution of wealth-owning immigrants to the evolving modern urban economy was quite noticeable in the mid-1920s.

This observation is also supported by the statistical record of Tel Aviv. In 1925, no less than 44 percent of the residents of Tel Aviv (34,200) were newcomers who had immigrated to Palestine that year or the year before (*Tel Aviv*, 1926, p. 73). Furthermore, the *Census of Jewish Workers* (1926) implies that at least 65 percent of the breadwinners among newcomer Tel-Avivians were either self-employed or had independent sources of income; only 35 percent were wage earners and members of producer cooperatives.

As might be expected, the proportion of "capitalists" shrank during the immigration and economic lull of 1927–31 (down to 16.2 percent of the inflow), but bounced back (to an average of 26.4 percent) in 1932–39. The growth of the 1930s was partly facilitated by the "transfer" (*ha'avarah*) arrangement, according to which the German (Nazi) government allowed emigrating Jews to transfer their private wealth to Palestine in the form of German export goods via a well-defined commercial mechanism (see Fraenkel, 1994; Niederland, 1996, and the references cited

---

[7] The relatively high percentage of "dependents" in the early 1920s (34.2 percent in 1922–23), and the later downturn, may point to intensified family reunions after World War I, and to a closing phase of "stage immigration," which, as already indicated, may have had some impact in the early years of the renewed post-war immigration.

there). Likewise, the Zionist Organization did its best to provide a safe haven in Palestine for Jewish children and young people from Nazi Germany (and in 1938–39, from Austria and Czechoslovakia as well) by utilizing the allowance for pupils and students, thereby quadrupling the proportion of pupils from 1.6 percent in 1927–31 to 6.4 percent in 1932–39. The relative share of labor naturally fluctuated in opposite directions, rising to 59.8 percent in the late 1920s and declining to 44.9 percent in the 1930s.

The immigration-intensive 1930s also revitalized the trend toward urban concentration, which had begun in the mid-1920s, largely by attracting immigrants of the Fifth Aliya to larger towns, notably Tel Aviv and Haifa. The (Jewish) population of Tel Aviv just about tripled (from about 46,000 to 132,000) between 1931 and 1939, and the total population (Arabs and Jews) of Haifa more than doubled (from 50,000 to 106,000), with the influx of about 50,000 Jews accounting for most of the increase (*SAP*, 1940, table 10; *Statistical Handbook*, 1947, p. 48).

Besides the gross classification of immigrants by entry category, the available statistics also provide some within-category characterization. Panels B and C of table 3.4 report the age composition of registered immigrants in each category, and the occupational structure abroad of "worker" and "capitalist" immigrants who were gainfully occupied (or trained) in their countries of origin. Unfortunately, the data cover only 207,000 people who registered with the Jewish Agency between 1928 and 1942 (they constituted 73 percent of all the immigrants in those years), and lump them together without further division into sub-periods. Nevertheless, the reported age and occupational variations seem quite revealing.

An examination of the two economically active categories shows that most (72.5 percent) of the immigrants who were granted "labor" entry certificates were young (seventeen to thirty-five). About 40 percent of them had been gainfully employed abroad, including those being trained in "useful" occupations – primarily farming – in preparation for the move to Palestine.[8]

This setup largely explains the high proportion (17.7 percent) of the "labor" immigrants in 1928–42 who were occupationally classified as farm workers and trainees abroad. By way of comparison, the share of farmers in the gainfully employed Jews of Poland in 1931 and Germany

---

[8] Such training was usually provided in various farms in Europe to groups of prospective immigrants organized by Zionist-socialist bodies and youth movements (primarily under the auspices and supervision of the *He-Halutz* organization) in preparation for "productive" absorption, preferably – but not exclusively – in communal settlements (*kibbutzim*) in Palestine.

in 1933 was 4 percent and 1 percent respectively (GGB, p. 73). Moreover, among the highly motivated immigrants of the Third Aliya (1919–23), no less than 30 percent of the wage earners (in all entry categories combined) listed their pre-immigration occupation as agriculture (Sicron, 1957b, table A26). Adding to agriculture the percentages of manufacturing, construction, transportation, and unskilled manual occupations, one finds that 86 percent of the "labor" immigrants in 1928–42 had been engaged or trained in blue-collar occupations prior to their arrival in Palestine. On the other hand, the "capitalists," at least those aged up to fifty, were more evenly age distributed. While their relative share in the seventeen-to-thirty-five age bracket (29.6 percent) was less than half the size of the "labor" segment, their proportion in the younger and older age groups was substantially larger. Note that 17.4 percent of the "capitalists" were over fifty years old upon arrival, whereas only 1.2 percent of the "labor" migrants were as old as that.

The occupational structure of the "capitalists" also differed substantially from that of "labor." With 46.4 percent of the economically active having registered their pre-immigration occupation as commerce, and 19.5 percent belonging to the liberal professions (versus 2.7 percent and 7.8 percent respectively among the "labor" immigrants), the dominance of skilled white-collar occupations in the middle-class "capitalist" group is quite prominent.

Earners, however, accounted for 33.5 percent of all the "capitalist" immigrants, compared with 40 percent for "labor." This difference mirrors the higher percentage of children (aged below sixteen) and the larger component of family migration in the former group; only 18.8 percent of the "capitalists" immigrated other than as part of an immigrating family in 1928–42, in contrast to 32.5 percent of the "labor" group (GGB, p. 16*).

As for "pupils," these were obviously concentrated in the young age groups (95 percent were twenty-five years old or younger). But "dependents" had a different, U-shaped, age distribution. This is what one would expect in view of the function of the "dependent" category, namely, to facilitate family reunions (even by forming pro-tem and often fictitious family links) and providing entry opportunities for immigrants who were either ineligible for "capitalist" status or were too old to qualify for "labor" immigration certificates (90 percent of these certificates had, by government order, to be allocated to persons aged eighteen to thirty-five: see GGB, p. 27). In general, this took some pressure off the often tight supply of "labor" certificates, regardless of age.

Overall, the reviewed age structures are compatible with the commonly observed economic attributes of migration. The age composition of "labor" immigrants seems to reflect the decline in the expected net material gains from migration with the age of moving (reinforced by the age constraints imposed by the government). The age distribution of the "capitalists" appears to have been affected both by the relatively age-independent (even age-augmented) prospects of earnings from wealth, liberal professions, and other wealth-related occupations (such as commerce), and by the lack of administrative age-specific constraints on their entry to Palestine.

These observations support the notion that Jewish immigration retained some of the characteristics of voluntary migratory movements even during the turbulent 1930s. This claim seems eminently plausible, especially as 78 percent of the immigrants in 1928–42 arrived between 1932 and 1935, at which time the refuge-seeking incentive to emigrate from Europe may not have been as forceful as it became in later years.

What remains to be examined is the immigrants' "self-imported" educational capital, obviously a key element in evaluating their socio-economic contribution to the Jewish community in Palestine. Unfortunately, neither the government nor the Jewish Agency regularly collected data on the newcomers' schooling experience, so that no direct figures on their educational attainment are available. Some inferences can nonetheless be drawn from various sources and fragments of direct and indirect information.

It has already been indicated that in 1931 the male Jewish population of Palestine (aged over twenty-one) had 7.6 median years of schooling (5.1 for females). It can be conservatively assumed that at least half of these adults were foreign born, and had completed their formal education abroad.[9] Some of the formal or informal education acquired abroad by immigrants in the 1920s (and probably by those arriving in the 1930s as well) was Palestine specific. For example, of the 30,000 foreign-born adults surveyed in the *Census of Jewish Workers* (1926), about 47 percent reported that they had been able to read, write, and speak Hebrew prior to immigration; since about a quarter of those surveyed did not respond to the language question at all, this percentage should actually be viewed as a lower bound estimate of the extent of the worker immigrants' comprehension of Hebrew upon arrival in Palestine.

Another source of relevant information is Israel's 1961 population census. As reported by Bachi (1977, p. 296), the median school attain-

---

[9] This conjecture is based on the age distribution of Palestine's Jews in 1931 (see table 4.3), indicating that 104,000 were over twenty-one years old, and on the scattered information regarding the age structure of immigrants, as reported above, suggesting that of the immigrants of 1919–31 (whose average age was probably between twenty-five and twenty-nine), about 60,000 may have been over twenty-one years old.

ment of foreign-born Jews who immigrated to Palestine before 1948 aged over twenty, and who were still alive and residing in Israel in 1961, was about ten years for men and nine for women. These numbers are visibly higher than the figures for the entire Jewish population in 1931.

Furthermore, given the age at immigration, we can safely assume (following Bachi) that the reported educational level of these foreign-born immigrants was mostly, if not entirely, acquired abroad, implying that simply by "importing" their stock of educational capital, other things being equal, they would have raised the average level of education among Palestine's Jews. It thus seems plausible that the declining extent of illiteracy, from 14.1 percent of the adult (over fourteen) Jewish population in 1931 to 6.3 percent in 1948 (Bachi, 1977, p. 295) was also due, at least in part, to the pre-statehood influx of well-educated immigrants.

Additional evidence on the level of schooling of immigrants and of Palestine-born Jews is presented in table 3.5. The figures in this table were derived from a sample of 6,000 records containing detailed personal demographic and socio-economic information drawn from files of local Jewish recruiting committees. In the first half of the 1940s these committees registered those Jewish men of Palestine aged seventeen to forty-five who answered the call of the Jewish national institutions for a general (voluntary) mobilization aimed at participating in the Allied war effort and/or joining the Jewish defense organization in Palestine (see Gelber, 1979, chap. 4 and 1981, chap. 1).

The sample is admittedly very small, rather arbitrary, and hardly representative. Moreover, since most of the surviving records in these files relate to requests for exemption, the sample may also suffer from selectivity biases, possibly linking the length of stay in Palestine and/or the level of education to the desire to obtain such an exemption. Nonetheless, being a unique source of information on schooling by age and by period of immigration, this body of data should be used – with all due caution – if only illustratively, to illuminate the issues at hand.

Two major features are forcefully demonstrated by the distributions in table 3.5. The first is the educational advantage of *all* the sample's foreign-born adult males (2,419 aged over twenty-five at the time of registration) over their Palestine-born counterparts (271 registered), regardless of the timing of immigration and the country in which schooling was acquired. The same holds true with respect to the subset of the foreign born who had completed their schooling abroad (i.e., 923 adults who immigrated to Palestine at the age of over twenty-five). This suggests that the relatively high propensity to acquire secondary and higher education, typical of the immigrating population in the countries of origin, may have been carried over into Palestine.

Table 3.5. *Educational attainment of adult Jewish males registered with Jewish "recruitment committees" in 1940–44 (percentage distribution)*

	primary	secondary	post-secondary	all schooling levels	absolute figures
adult males, aged 25+ at time of registration					
born in Palestine	59.4	32.8	7.8	100.0	271
foreign born, immigrated in:					
1918–32	45.3	40.7	14.0	100.0	563
1933–39	31.3	43.1	25.6	100.0	1,610
1940–44	40.6	35.8	23.6	100.0	246
1918–44	35.5	41.8	22.7	100.0	2,419
foreign born, aged 25+ at time of immigration					
1918–32	35.9	50.0	14.1	100.0	64
1933–39	34.2	43.1	22.7	100.0	657
1940–44	39.1	36.6	24.3	100.0	202
1918–44	35.4	42.2	22.4	100.0	923

Sources: CZA, files in section S-37, and text

Secondly, the immigration of 1933–39 (and largely also that of 1940–44) had an educational edge over the influx of 1918–32, particularly in the acquisition of higher education. This observation is compatible with the aggregate profiles of the immigrants' occupations; it is known that over 14 percent of the earners in the 1932–38 and 1939–45 immigration waves had held liberal professions in their countries of origin, compared to only 8 percent among the immigrants of the 1920s and 11 percent of all the economically active Jews in Palestine in 1931 (*Census of Palestine*, 1933, table XVI; Sicron, 1957b, table A26). A similar picture is revealed by numerous impressionistic accounts pointing to the high skill and profession intensity of the Fifth Aliya, attributed mainly to the rising weight of immigrants from Germany in that decade (see Gelber, 1990; Niederland, 1996, and the references cited there).

These pieces of evidence reinforce the suggestion that, apart from endowing the Jewish community of Palestine with "free" human capital, the continuous flow of immigrants raised the per capita amount of schooling and skill content of the country's Jewish population. In the long run this accumulation of educational stock certainly contributed to economic growth and prosperity; in the short run, however, problems of excess supply and imbalances in the labor market, which called for occupational adjustments and flexibility, were widespread. But this part of the story belongs to the next chapter.

4   Production resources in a divided economy: land, capital, and labor

The demographic and socio-economic features, discussed at length in the previous chapters, provide a clear developmental distinction between Arabs and Jews. But the prime cause of the emergence of Mandatory Palestine as a divided economy must be sought in the markets for primary factors of production – land, reproducible capital, and labor. The exchange, ownership, and allocation of land, capital, and labor services have therefore played a major role in the extensive literature dealing with the history of the Arab and Jewish communities in Palestine and with the dynamics and policy implications of their ethno-national conflict.

Historians and social scientists have long dwelt upon both general and "Palestine-specific" features underlying the segmentation of the factor markets and their inner structure, making extremely important contributions to our knowledge and appreciation of the subject. As might be expected, research in the field has not converged to a consensus description, let alone interpretation, of the complex issues involved.[1] This chapter will neither systematically survey the literature nor offer an alternative comprehensive treatment of the subject. Rather, it will concentrate, while reflecting on relevant scholarly contributions, on the economic features that were instrumental in shaping the structure and modus operandi of the factor markets in Mandatory Palestine and in determining their allocative and distributional implications. In so doing, several unresolved questions will obviously be raised, and some tentative answers provided. Naturally enough, the discussion is divided into three sections: the first deals with land, the second with reproducible capital, and the third with labor.

---

[1] See, for example, Abramowitz and Guelfat (1944); Asfour (1945); Granott (1952); Hadawi (1957); Sussman (1973, 1974); Shapira (1977); Taqqu (1977, 1980); Metzer (1977, 1978, 1979); Horowitz and Lissak (1978); Reichman (1979); Flapan (1979); S. Greenberg (1980); Kimmerling (1983a, b); Gross (1984a); Stein (1984); Gorny (1985); Shafir (1989); Firestone (1990); Grinberg (1991); Kamen (1991); Shalev (1992); Smith (1993). This list, though far from exhaustive, provides some idea of the variety of approaches and methodologies used in dealing with the questions at hand.

Land

In considering the economics of land in the Mandate period, two inter-related issues stand out. One concerns the volume, prices, and consequences of transactions in land; the other is the land-tenure regime and the size distribution of holdings within the Arab and Jewish communities.

Land transactions

Palestine's land regime, which was inherited from the late Ottoman era and improved upon by the Mandatory government, allowed for effective (if not nominal) private property rights in most of the country's land. By the end of the Mandate roughly 84 percent of Palestine's "non-desert" land area of about 15 million dunams were non-public. Public land was divided almost equally between state domain, on the one hand, and land held by religious institutions, municipalities, and other public bodies combined, on the other. A thriving land market developed, in which transactions involving a total of more than 3 million dunams were officially registered between 1921 and 1946, implying that if each piece of land had been exchanged only once, 11 percent of the country's entire land area (26.3 million dunams), or approximately 20 percent of the "non-desert" area, changed hands during the Mandate period.[2] But the actual land turnover was certainly larger, as a good number of land transfers were not officially registered for national-political reasons, tax considerations, or obscure property rights (Granott, 1952; Reichman, 1979; Stein, 1984). For example, according to the estimates of the Jewish Agency, Jewish land possessions grew by 1.2 million dunams, from 418,000 dunams at the end of World War I to 1.6 million dunams by the end of 1947 (Reichman, 1979, p. 79). But according to the above compilations of registered transactions, net Jewish acquisitions during the Mandate period were no more than 944,000 dunams. Adding only these "missing" transfers (of about 260,000 dunams) to the registered transactions, without taking into account the probable underregistration of intra-Arab land exchanges, would raise the recorded land turnover (of 3 million dunams) by no less than 8.5 percent.

The registered transactions were composed almost entirely of land transfers within and between the Arab and the Jewish communities (in 1929–46, for example, only 1.9 percent of the sales and 2.6 percent of the purchases were done by the government, municipalities, and by foreign-

---

[2] See the following sources: Granovsky (1938) and Granott [Granovsky] (1952); *SAP* (1942, 1944/45); *Village Statistics 1945*; *MBS*, March 1947.

ers combined). As land transfers from Jews to Arabs were negligible (in 1943–46 they constituted only 0.3 percent of the entire turnover), about 30 percent of the recorded turnover in 1921–46 was probably land sold by Arabs to Jews, and 70 percent consisted of intra-communal transfers (*SAP*, 1936–44/45, *MBS*, 1945–47).

However, when considering only land sold by Arabs, one observes that Jews bought 40 percent of all the registered sales between 1929 and 1946 (no similar breakdown is available for the 1920s), the share declining from 54 percent of all Arab land sold in 1929–39 to 22 percent in 1940–46. While the downturn of the 1940s may have resulted from the imposition of governmental restrictions in 1940 (see below), the proportion of unregistered (and thus unrecorded) transactions most probably increased at the same time in an attempt to circumvent those restrictions. This conjecture is indirectly supported by the rising gap between the officially registered net Jewish land purchases and the Jewish Agency's estimated addition to total Jewish land possessions (the former constituted 84.3 percent of the latter in 1920–37, but only 64.6 percent in 1938–47 (Gurevich and Gertz, 1938; Reichman, 1979, p. 79).

All told, Jewish land holdings (1.621 million dunams owned outright and 181,000 dunams of leased state land; Reichman, 1979, p. 79) amounted by the end of the Mandate to 11.4 percent of the non-desert area. However, 66 percent of Jewish land was located in the fertile and accessible coastal plain and the northern valleys: in 1945 Jews owned 23 percent and 30 percent of the area in the coastal plain and in northern valleys respectively, compared with 4 percent of the hill country (Gertz, 1945, p. 38). Therefore, a quality-based assessment would certainly raise the weight of Jewish land holdings. Consequently, the discrepancy between the (quality corrected) end-of-period proportion of land held by Jews and their much higher shares in other country-wide aggregates, such as population (31.3 percent) and output (58 percent), is narrower than the raw figures suggest.

However, modest as the accumulation of land by Jews may have been, its political and economic significance far exceeded its volume. Zionist ideology and politics of "nation building" made the acquisition of land – preferably contiguous – and its retention in Jewish hands a major (if not *the* major) vehicle for securing a territorial base for the nascent Jewish body politic. These considerations operated as an "extra-economic" component of demand in the land market, increasing the selling opportunities of non-Jewish landowners. But since the national directive of land retention was widely followed both by land-purchasing organs of the Zionist Organization such as the Jewish National Fund (JNF), which owned 52.2 percent of all Jewish land by the end of 1947 (Reichman,

1979, p. 79) and by private landowners, Jewish-acquired land was practically taken out of the intercommunal market. This unilaterally imposed segregation, besides its territorial-political connotations in the Arab-Jewish conflict, also implied a reduction in the overall land-buying options of non-Jews.

The non-economic components of Zionist demand probably raised the price that Jews were willing to pay for land, over and above the value of its added contribution to output (agricultural or otherwise). Moreover, whenever Arab sellers of large indivisible tracts could utilize monopoly power and capture at least part of the "buyers' surplus," the implicit demand price for land was pushed up even further. On the other hand, the major Jewish purchasing agencies (primarily the JNF and the Palestine Land Development Company [PLDC] of the Zionist Organization), although failing to coordinate all the land-buying activities, may have had some success in utilizing countervailing (monopsonistic) market power so as to restrain the price rise in the intercommunal market (Gurevich and Gertz, 1938, and the discussion below).

The question that naturally comes to mind is what effect, if any, did the political repercussions of Jewish land acquisition and retention have on the supply of Arab land in the intercommunal market. The historical literature tends to view the continuous transfers of land from Arabs to Jews as an indication that Arab landowners, drawn by the newly created opportunity to sell all or part of their possessions at attractive prices, were not deterred either by the strong opposition voiced by the Arab national movements or by government regulations aimed at rectifying the widely perceived deleterious effects on Arab landlessness (Porath, 1974, 1977; Reichman, 1979; Stein, 1984). Furthermore, evidence that some Arab offers were declined by the Zionist institutions for lack of funds has led scholars such as Stein to conclude that the "*only* [italics in the original] factor limiting the pace and scope of Jewish land purchase prior to and after the institution of the Mandate was insufficient funding" (Stein, 1984, p. 37, see also pp. 69, 120; Porath, 1974, 1977).

This characterization may accurately describe the silent features of the market, but it does not rule out the possibility that the price at which Jewish demand did not exhaust the entire supply of Arab land was higher than the minimum supply price at which land would have been offered for sale in a politically neutral market. In other words, it is not implausible that Arab political objection to, and the government's various restrictions on, intercommunal land sales induced Arab landowners to raise the threshold price at which they were ready to sell their property to Jews, thus reducing the actual volume of land transferred compared to what it would have been in a land market unaffected by political constraints. The

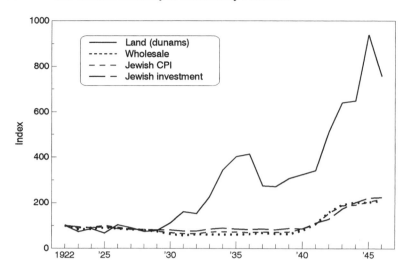

Figure 4.1 Price indices (1922=100)
(sources: for land values: Granovsky, 1938, p. 39; *SAP*, 1940, table 180, 1945, pp. 274–77; *MBS*, March 1945, table 10, April 1946, table 14, March 1947, table 13; for the other price indices: table A.21)

net "volume effect" of the political considerations, acted on and responded to by actual and potential sellers and buyers in the inter-communal land market, is therefore unclear. It is, however, highly proba-ble that these considerations contributed to the substantial increase in the prices at which land transactions were concluded (Reichman, 1979; Stein, 1984; Kamen, 1991).

The official data on the volume (in dunams) and total value (including improvements) of land turnover (*SAP*, 1936–45 and *MBS*, 1945–47) allow the derivation of an annual series of the average (per dunam) value of exchanged land, which is the closest one can get to aggregate land prices. Assuming that the pattern of this series closely resembles the price path of unimproved land, which is what we are actually after, this series is used as a proxy for the land price index presented in figure 4.1 together with all the available price indices of "non-land" aggregates for 1922–46.

The figure tells a clear story of rapidly rising overall land prices, by far outstripping all other price indices. Except for the depression in the second half of the 1930s the rising trend, which began in 1930, continued almost without interruption until the end of World War II, reflecting the demand-sensitive price determination of an asset whose overall supply is highly inelastic in the long run. The early phase of the rise in land prices (1930–36) seems to be related to the rapid growth in construction and economic activity generally (mainly in the Jewish sector), whereas the second phase (1941–45) may have been largely induced by the fast rise in demand for land as a hedge against inflation during the war, and also by expectations for renewed civilian construction toward its end.

Returning to the intercommunal land transactions, available data on Jewish land acquisition and possession (Gurevich and Gertz, 1938; Reichman, 1979) were used in conjunction with prices of unimproved rural land bought by Jews from non-Jews to arrive at a figure of P£13.4 million in current prices (or P£14.1 million in constant 1936 prices) for total payments Jews made for the (unimproved) land they purchased from non-Jewish landowners between 1921 and 1947.[3]

Whenever these payments were funded by donations from world Jewry to the JNF and by privately imported capital, as most of them were, the newly acquired land made for a net addition to the stock of productive resources in the domestic Jewish economy. As for the Arab economy, the intercommunal exchange should, in principle, be viewed as a mere substitution of one productive asset (land) for another (hard currency), changing the composition but not the size of the combined Arab domestic stock of land and capital. In fact, however, Jews, particularly up to the early 1930s, bought a large portion of their land from Arab owners who did not reside in Palestine. An examination of previous ownership of about 55 percent of Jewish-purchased land in 1878–1936 (Gurevich and Gertz, 1938, table 27, p. *39) and data on absentee Arab land ownership in 1932 (Stein, 1984, p. 179) suggest that no less than 74 percent of the acquisitions in 1920–32, and 19 percent of those in 1933–47, were of land bought from Arab landowners residing outside Palestine. The sharp decline of this proportion in the second half of the period reflects the rela-

---

[3] Gurevich and Gertz (1938) estimated some composite prices of rural land that Jews bought from non-Jews from 1878 to 1936 (rural land accounted for 95 percent of all the land acquired by Jews). Their prices cover 70 percent of all Jewish purchases over the entire period and during the inter-war years as a whole, but unfortunately only 35.6 percent of the transfers in 1933–36. Moreover, in discussing their procedures, Gurevich and Gertz concede that, unlike the earlier years, for which their figures may be regarded as a good approximation of the prices of all intercommunally transferred land, their estimated price for 1933–36 (P£4.91 per dunam) is extremely downward biased. To correct this deficiency I adjusted the average price quoted by Gurevich and Gertz upwards (to P£14.63 per dunam), assuming, on the basis of their impressionistic evidence, that the price of unaccounted-for intercommunally exchanged land (64.4 percent of the total) was P£20 per dunam. The adjusted series of Gurevich and Gertz's prices was extended to 1947 by applying the rates of change of the value of the officially recorded total land turnover between 1936 and 1947. The figure of P£13.4 million exceeds the accumulated value of the registered intercommunal land turnover (P£13.2 million; Metzer and Kaplan, 1990, table N-2), implying that the downward bias of the land turnover figures due to underregistration more than offset any possible upward bias caused by the fact that the official data record the value of improved land whenever such land was exchanged.

tively rapid exhaustion of the supply of large estates owned by Arabs residing abroad (in 1919 they possessed about half of all the Arab estates larger than 5,000 dunams), which was enhanced by the preference of Jewish (particularly institutional) buyers for singly owned chunks of land (Stein, 1984).

Assuming that these payments to absentee landowners were not reinvested or otherwise spent in Palestine, it is suggested that about 73 percent of the total sum (in current prices) that Jews paid for Arab land in 1920–47 (P£9.8 million) may have been retained in the domestic Arab economy. This implies that 27 percent of the value (or 46 percent in constant prices) of all the land sold to the Jews during the Mandate period could be viewed as an "effective loss" to the domestic Arab economy.[4]

As for the landowners, by exchanging land for cash at the going price they revealed their preference for selling over the alternative of holding on to their possessions: by doing so they obviously expected to improve their economic lot. This inference holds for poor peasants (*fellaheen*) who may have sold their land in order to pay off or at least reduce their debts (some even turning into tenants, cultivating their previously owned land), as well as for owners of large estates who used the proceeds from their land sales to finance ventures of sufficiently high expected profitability, in agriculture or elsewhere. Reference in this respect is to investments in capital-intensive citriculture; it has been estimated (Metzer and Kaplan, 1990, chap. 1) that total investments in planting and cultivating new citrus groves in the Arab economy in the inter-war years stood at about P£5 million in 1936 prices, accounting for between one-fifth and one-quarter of total Arab capital formation in those years (see below). Interestingly, this sum is only slightly lower than the estimated share of the revenue from land sold to Jews that was retained in Palestine during the same period (P£5.2 million in 1936 prices). The similarity in orders of magnitudes lends credence to the suggestion that the large and growing Arab demand for investment in citrus groves was a major inducement for Arab landowners to sell off part of their holdings (see for example, Porath, 1974, 1977).

However, unlike landowners, poor or rich, who elected to sell their property, displaced Arab tenants who might have been evicted by the incumbent or prospective landlords had practically no free choice,

---

[4] The extreme assumption regarding the outflow of payments received by absentee landlords may downward bias the estimated proportion of domestically retained payments. On the other hand, since information on most transactions involving purchases of large estates from owners living abroad was presumably recorded, adopting the percentage of absentee ownership based only on 55 percent of the area transferred intercommunally in 1920–36 may bias the estimates upwards. It is thus unclear whether (and if so, in what direction) the estimate of retained payments is biased, and it is therefore assumed that whatever the bias, it was probably small.

regardless of the cause of their displacement. Given the large land turn-over and the political connotations of its intercommunal component, it is only natural that the question of tenants' dispossession caused by the exchange of land became a major issue for the parties involved (see Stein, 1984; Kamen, 1991, and the references cited there).

The government sought to shield the Arab community from extreme socio-economic imbalances that would impose an extra burden on the public coffers and undermine the delicate equilibrium so crucial to its dual Mandatory role: promoting the Jewish National Home while main-taining the well-being and rights of the Arab population (see chapters 1 and 6). The government was troubled from the outset by the link between the intercommunal land transfers and growing Arab landlessness. This concern had been expressed as early as 1920 in the Land Transfer Ordinance. It intensified after the riots of 1929 and the official inquiries that ensued, gained impetus with the cultivators' protection and compen-satory regulations of the early 1930s, and culminated in the aftermath of the Arab revolt of 1936–39 with the restrictions on intercommunal land sales as per the Land Transfer Regulations of 1940 (*Survey,* 1946, vol. I; Stein, 1984; Kamen, 1991).

The government's definition of Arab landlessness employed for the purpose of resettlement and compensation was largely tailored to solve problems arising from the intercommunal conflict. It excluded cultivators displaced in consequence of land transfers within the Arab community (in view of the substantial volume of intra-Arab land transfers, there must have been numerous such cases). Moreover, people who owned land besides the tracts they had cultivated as tenants, who became tenants elsewhere, or who found stable employment after their displacement were also not deemed landless (hence deserving compensation) Arabs (*Survey,* 1946, vol. I, p. 296).

The political and academic debates over cultivators' displacement by intercommunal land sales, although partly framed in terms of the refer-ences set by the government, included such issues as the displacement effects on the socio-economic fabric of the Arab community in general and the "proletarization" of its peasantry. A related issue, raised in the lit-erature, was tenant displacement as a way in which immigrant Jewish set-tlers gained at the expense of Arabs in the zero-sum game dictated by the country's fixed natural resources and hence limited absorptive capacity (Kimmerling, 1983a, b; Shafir, 1989; Kamen, 1991, and its cited refer-ences; Shalev, 1992). Some of these issues will be dealt with as we proceed, but before doing so we should conceptually define those who became worse off by intercommunal land sales, and attempt to get some idea of the numbers involved.

From a purely economic point of view, all the evicted tenants suffered material loss simply by being unwillingly evicted – with or without compensation. Some were not offered any compensation; for others, the compensation (resettlement or cash) would not have sufficed to induce them to leave the land of their own volition.[5] Since the loss in well-being was caused by the tenants having to accept what they considered *ex ante* to be an inferior alternative, their welfare loss had nothing to do with the outcome of the move, which *ex post* could even be materially favorable.

Viewed thus, the number of displaced tenant households that suffered economic loss was certainly larger than the number of filed claims for inclusion in the government's Register of Landless Arabs (3,737), let alone the number of approved applications (899) (Stein, 1984, pp. 156–63; Kamen, 1991, p. 155). This is so partly because some eligible candidates for whom the compensatory schemes were unsatisfactory may not have applied at all, but mostly due to definitional differences. For example, some displaced tenants who were not considered eligible for landless status because they were not totally stripped of land possession, or because they found other gainful alternatives, should obviously have been included among those who, economically speaking, were adversely affected by intercommunal land sales. Furthermore, tenants whose tenancy was terminated by their Arab landowners in anticipation of selling the land to Jewish buyers were, in principle, also left worse off by the land-transfer process, even when the landowners' expectations that triggered the displacement did not materialize.

Unfortunately, data constraints do not allow us to move easily from conceptualization to estimation; the best we can do is to provide an upper-bound estimate of the number of Arab tenants who may have been forced off the land they cultivated during the Mandate period. Assuming that the land owned by peasants (*fellaheen*) was self-cultivated, and that the areas owned by non-cultivating landowners were *all* arable and had in fact been cultivated by tenants before their transfer to Jewish buyers – obviously a gross exaggeration of actual land utilization – the basis for estimating the number of displaced tenants should be the total area that Jews purchased from non-peasant Arab landlords.

. On the basis of the ownership distribution compiled by Gurevich and Gertz (1938) and Granott's assessment that 27 percent of all the land purchased by Jews in 1878–1947 had been owned by *fellaheen* (Granott, 1952, chap. 11), Jews acquired an estimated 800,000 dunams from non-

---

[5] In principle, these considerations should be extended to agricultural wage earners who were forced to seek employment elsewhere. However, since they had no legal claim to the land they worked, their exclusion from the picture, due to lack of data, would probably be inconsequential.

cultivating Arab landowners between 1921 and 1947 (these constituted 89 percent of all the acquisitions in 1920–36, 23 percent of the purchases thereafter, and 68 percent of the land acquired over the entire period). If the average holding size of a tenant household was assumed to be (a conservative) 100 dunams (Kamen, 1991, pp. 144–45, 186), no more than 8,000 tenant households *could* have been displaced by intercommunal land transfers.[6] Even this upper-bound estimate, which certainly overstates the "true" number, accounted for only a modest fraction of the Arab labor force. If a typical tenant household was composed of two working adult males, it follows that the possibly displaced 16,000 tenant-workers constituted 9 percent of the 184,200 males aged twenty and above who belonged to the Arab labor force according to the 1931 census. Moreover, since, as suggested below, the 1931 population census probably understated the size of the Arab male labor force, even this rather moderate percentage may be too high to serve as the lowest conceivable upper bound for the share of displaced cultivators in the Arab labor force.

Following the upper-bound estimate of the number of Arab members of the labor force who may have had to abandon the land they held in tenancy because of its sale to Jews, one might also suggest a plausible upper bound for their "contribution" to the change in the industrial structure of Arab employment. To do that, let us assume, unrealistically, that all the up-to-16,000 displaced working male adults moved out of agriculture. If so, they would still have constituted less than half (49 percent) the (counterfactual) required number (32,600) that should be added to the *actual* number of employed persons in Arab agriculture in 1945 (186,000) in order for the rate of growth of agricultural employment to equal that of total Arab employment between 1921 and 1945 (table A.5). Put differently, under rather strong upward biasing assumptions, the displacement of tenants caused by intercommunal land transfers could at most have accounted for half the relative decline of employment in Arab agriculture between 1921 and 1945 (see also chapter 5), the rest being employment shifts of former peasant owner-cultivators (*fellaheen*) who had sold their land to Jews, and of others: peasants, tenants, and wage earners who moved from domestic agriculture to different industries (including employment by Jewish farmers).

This appraisal supports the contention that the exit from the land, involuntary by tenants and voluntary by owner-cultivators, caused by

---

[6] Kamen (1991, pp. 155–57), using a different approach, arrived at a similar upper-bound estimate of 8,200 households. However, the (conceptually erroneous) inclusion in his figure of owner-cultivators who had sold their land in addition to dispossessed tenants makes it actually a lower estimate than mine.

intercommunal land transfers, was part – albeit a significant one – of larger structural changes generated by the pressure of the fast-growing Arab population on the land, coupled with increasing peasant indebtedness. These changes induced rural emigration to the (mainly coastal) towns, or at least partial reliance on earning opportunities outside domestic agriculture, and were closely linked to changes and adjustments in the structure of rural land tenure and ownership within the Arab community (Taqqu, 1977; Issawi, 1982; Gilbar, 1990; Kamen, 1991).

Land tenure and distribution

The Mandatory regime of property rights in land, largely inherited from the late Ottoman period, was originally shaped in the land legislation of 1858 as part of the *Tanzimat* reforms. The legal structure and classification of land tenure are well documented (see *Survey*, 1946, vol. I; Granott, 1952; and Stein, 1984, for summary descriptions) and need not be spelled out here, but some remarks on their economic aspects are certainly called for.

From an economic point of view the regime's most prominent feature was the embodiment of the principle of transferable property rights enjoyed by all landowners, either by title deed or by usufruct on state land. Moreover, property rights in land were individually specified; this was true not only of urban property and rural land permanently designated to individual households (*mafruz*), but also of co-owned land in *musha'a* villages – traditionally typified by periodic redistribution of peasants' scattered tracts to equalize their holdings.[7]

In the nineteenth century *musha'a* was the predominant mode of land tenure in the villages of Palestine and, in fact, in all of the rural Levant (Firestone, 1990). According to Firestone's (1981) well-known argument, it was the pre-*Tanzimat* rural tax system in the Ottoman Levant, mainly based on the village as a unit of assessment and imposition, that may have induced the equalization of the tax burden across village households, by periodically redistributing their holdings. But, as Firestone (1990) persuasively claims, regardless of its origins, the equalizing redistributive mechanism of *musha'a* land was rendered largely obsolete as the following developments unfolded: (a) the institutionalization of well-defined land ownership and tenancy rights underlying the individualization of rural taxes in the latter part of the nineteenth century, and the

---

[7] A distinction should be drawn between *musha'a*-type co-ownership, where individuals have claims to parts of, or relative shares in, common property, and communal ownership, in which property rights are bestowed on a communal body and not on its constituent parts (see Firestone, 1990).

attempts (although of limited success) to bring about land registration pursued by the late Ottoman regime and its Mandatory successor; (b) the evolving commercial land market in the Levant, prompted by the monetization of the rural economy, which became increasingly exposed to the world market, and by the growing demand for land by investors (and in Palestine, to a large extent by Jews), partly motivated by expectations for continually rising land scarcity and rental values due to the pressure of the rapidly growing rural population.

One outcome of these developments was the permanent partition of *musha'a* holdings and their conversion into specified, individually held, *mafruz* tracts. The literature assessing the changes in the proportion of *musha'a* land in Palestine (summarized by Kamen, 1991) suggests, indeed, a continuous decline from almost 100 percent of Palestine's rural land, on the eve of the 1858 land legislation, to 70 percent in 1917 and to 25–50 percent by the end of the Mandate. The discrepancy between the two "end of period" estimates may reflect the difference between the amount of land officially registered as *musha'a* and the much smaller proportion remaining effectively un-partitioned throughout the period.

This brings us to another kind of response to the exogenous developments, namely a gradual adjustment of the system without changing the status of the land as registered *musha'a*. Firestone, in his seminal work (1990), forcefully demonstrates how *musha'a* landholders in rural Palestine could adjust the system to the evolving market economy. Quantitatively, specifying the *musha'a* shares, thereby making them tradable, was a major step in this direction. It enabled the retention (or sale) of holdings by landowners leaving the village and facilitated consolidation of *musha'a* shares and/or their acquisition by outsiders without interfering with actual production, which could be conducted independently of property rights and considerations of distributive equity.

Given these circumstances, and in view of the fact that only land under field crops (and not fruit plantations) was subject to equalization to begin with, one can hardly blame – according to Firestone – the redistribution of land for the lack of medium- and long-term investment in traditional Arab agriculture. In any case, redistribution discontinued in many villages, so that the allocation of holdings was stabilized, further reducing that particular obstacle to economic development and change.

In a good number of these communities, however, co-ownership was officially retained instead of turning the stabilized *musha'a* into *mafruz* land. Maintaining the legal *musha'a* status may well have served the interests of the village community, or at least those of its more powerful members. It avoided disputes over partition and enabled enterprising villagers or outside notables to utilize holdings of others with minimum interference. It also prevented counter-productive fragmentation that would be the inevitable result of the dispersion of holdings and the pro-liferation of shares over time.

These adjustments vividly demonstrate the capacity of Arab rural com-munities to seize opportunities as they arose and to re-make their institu-tional framework, which might otherwise have hindered those beneficial adjustments from being realized. Viewed thus, the endogenous changes in the *musha'a* system support two well-known lines of thought found in the writings of development economists, economic historians, and "new" institutional economists. One line is based on the claim that peasants in traditional societies are material maximizers who, like any other eco-nomic agent, react rationally to the opportunities they face: their often-observed backward state probably reflects lack of opportunities rather than non-rational behavior (see also the discussion in chapter 1). The other line views institutions as endogenously determined rules of social, political, and/or economic behavior; it interprets their formation, modification, and possible demise as considered adjustments made by society to changing external conditions and prospects affecting the expected costs and benefits of the institutions in question (see, for example, T. W. Schultz, 1964, 1971; North, 1981; Stiglitz, 1988; Timmer, 1988).

In addition to economics, political considerations related to inter-communal land transfers may also have played a role in retaining the un-partitioned *musha'a*. Although *musha'a* shares were tradable, and there are even recorded cases of Jews buying them, it is quite obvious that Jewish potential buyers were generally more interested in purchasing clearly identified tracts, preferably of *mafruz* land. For exactly the same reasons, Arab national interests lay in preserving the *musha'a* system. In the short run, however, not partitioning *musha'a* land may have been a tactically sound practice for both Arab sellers and Jewish buyers of *musha'a* shares, since as long as the land remained un-partitioned, such transactions did not have to be revealed.

The dynamics that led to rural emigration and to the adjustments in the regimes of land tenure in Palestine (and in the entire Middle East) from the late nineteenth century onward should also have affected the size distribution of land ownership. Some of the underlying developments accompanying the evolving property rights in land, such as monetization and increasing exposure of the rural economy to external markets, concentration of power and wealth, and the rising indebtedness of the rapidly growing peasant population, should have enhanced consolidation of landed property via sales of smallholdings that were becoming even smaller and less manageable over time. On the other hand, the fragmentation of holdings should itself have reduced the mean size of holdings, and in the Arab community of rural Palestine, the sale of land to Jews who preferred to purchase large tracts from single owners should have also had a similar effect (Issawi, 1982; Gilbar, 1990; Kamen, 1991). Note, however, that the distribution of land holdings – although the single most important indicator of the dispersion of wealth in the Arab rural sector – had little (if any) bearing on the nature of husbandry. Agricultural production continued to be carried out – regardless of the changes in the size of holdings – primarily in small, household-size units, which were farmed either by peasant landowners or by tenants (under sharecropping or pecuniary rent arrangements).

On the whole, the evolving structure of land ownership in the Middle East was rather asymmetric, characterized by substantial, though varied, proportions of very large holdings, and extremely large numbers of small ones (Issawi, 1982, and the references he cites). A partial picture of Palestine is provided by the widely cited governmental survey of 322 Arab villages in 1936, which recorded 71,785 holdings by size in a total area of 3.25 million dunams – covering 50–60 percent of all Arab arable land north of Beersheba at the time. The main findings of the survey are reported in table 4.1; although it enumerates holdings, not owners (there were certainly many individuals who owned more than one holding), the numbers in the table are convincing enough insofar as the asymmetry of the size distribution of Arab rural land is concerned. Overall, the average holding in the surveyed villages was rather small (45 dunams), but the dispersion by size is extremely large, with a coefficient of variation of 14.472. Note, in particular, that properties smaller than 10 dunams (totaling 33,711) accounted for 47 percent of the number of holdings, but for a mere 3.4 percent of the total area. On the other hand, the 150 estates of 1,000 dunams and more constituted just two-tenths of a percent of all the holdings, but no less than 27.5 percent of the total area.

The data in table 4.1 let us depict the inequality of the distribution of Arab rural land holdings using a standard Lorenz curve,[8] drawn in figure 4.2 together with a similar curve for rural Egypt in 1940 (Warriner, 1948, p. 35). The two distributions are quite similar and both are highly unequal (the Gini coefficients for Palestine and Egypt are 0.778 and

---

[8] Each point on the Lorenz curve shows the share of total land by the corresponding fraction of the smallest holdings. The larger the area bounded by the curve and the diagonal – which stands for perfect equality – the less equal the distribution represented by the Lorenz curve. Based on this characterization, a widely used inequality index (the Gini coefficient) between zero and one is defined as the ratio of the area bounded by the diagonal and the Lorenz curve to the area of the triangle bounded by the diagonal and the horizontal and vertical axes. A Gini coefficient of zero stands for perfect equality; the closer it is to one, the less equal the distribution.

Table 4.1. *Size distribution of land holdings in 1936: 322 Arab villages*

size of holding (dunams)	number of holdings	area of holdings (dunams)	percent of	
			holdings	area
1–9	33,711	109,766	46.96	3.37
10–99	32,222	1,084,783	44.88	33.35
100–999	5,706	1,163,062	7.95	35.76
1,000–4,999	137	270,689	0.19	8.32
5,000+	13	624,435	0.02	19.20
all	**71,789**	**3,252,735**	**100.00**	**100.00**

Source: MBS, January–March 1946, table 76

0.752 respectively). The paucity of data does not allow for an extension of the comparison to other Middle Eastern countries, but the common patterns of change in the region, and scattered data on the size distribution of holdings in other countries, suggest that Palestine and Egypt were fairly representative (Issawi, 1982).

However, in order to address the question whether the increasing fragmentation of holdings and the large volume of land sales had a net effect on the distribution of ownership in the Arab sector, and in what direction, one needs information on the changes in the composition of landed wealth over time. Such information is scanty. The only available data on the number and size of private non-Jewish holdings at the beginning of the Mandate period are two lists of Arab large holdings, compiled by the Zionist institutions in Palestine. One list pertains to holdings larger than 2,000 Turkish dunams (TD) (1 TD=0.919 metric dunam), and the other to holdings larger than 5,000 TD each (CZA, Z4/1260/I; Stein, 1984, appendix I).

The accuracy and coverage of these lists are questionable, which makes any inference based on them highly tentative; moreover, since no breakdown of the data is available for holdings smaller than 2,000 dunams and these accounted for about 75 percent of all the privately owned rural Arab land north of Beersheba in 1919, any useful comparison with the structure of land ownership in 1936, with all the reservations regarding the quality of the data, is possible only for estates larger than 2,000 dunams. Comparison of the Gini coefficients of the distribution for 1919 (0.242) with that of holdings larger than 2,000 dunams in 1936 (0.615) reveals that inequality of ownership of large estates rose substantially between these two years. This finding suggests that whatever the effect of large tracts being purchased by Jews on reducing the size of the remaining Arab

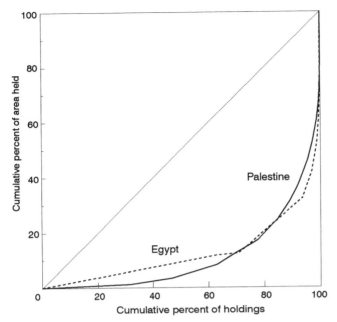

Figure 4.2 Arab rural land holdings, Palestine (1936) and Egypt (1940)
(sources: *MBS*, January–March 1946, table 76 for Palestine; Warriner, 1948, p. 35 for Egypt)

holdings, as far as the changes in the size distribution of Arab land is concerned, concentration of ownership within the Arab sector seems to have dominated the scene, alongside the continued fragmentation of smallholdings over the years.

Unlike the rural Arab community, with its extremely wide and skewed spread of private holdings by size, land-ownership schemes in the Jewish community were more diverse, the range of holdings by size much narrower and less dispersed, and their distribution appreciably more even. Note, too, that in the Jewish sector a single holding of rural land was virtually identical to the area of a typical unit of production: either a collective farm of commune-type settlements (*kibbutzim*), a single citrus grove, or a family farm (in completely private settlements – *moshavot* – as well as in those featuring various cooperative mechanisms in the purchase of inputs, marketing, and the provision of credit – *moshavim*).

As to property rights in land, the most prominent feature of the Jewish land regime was undoubtedly the continuously rising proportion of public ownership, resulting from the increase in volume and in relative weight of JNF possessions, which grew from 16,400 dunams (4 percent of all Jewish land) at the beginning of the British Mandate to 856,000 dunams (47.5 percent of the total) toward its end (Reichman, 1979, p. 79). The JNF was, of course, the institutional organ set up by the World Zionist Organization to acquire land in Palestine and retain it in perpetuity as a collectively owned "national" asset. The land legally owned by the JNF and not designated for public use (such as forestation) was typically leased to Jewish farmers and other lessees for specific predetermined uses such as husbandry, manufacturing, educational facilities, or residential dwellings.

In the first half of the 1940s the JNF had leased 65–70 percent of all the land it owned, 98 percent of which was farm land, and the rest land for urban and other non-agricultural uses. The rural lessees were either *kibbutzim*, which held about 66 percent of all the rural land leased by the JNF in 1942, or single-family farms, most of them in *moshavim* and some in *moshavot* (Granott, 1952, chaps. 11, 12; Gurevich and Gertz, 1947, for the agricultural census of 1941/42). All lessees were given long-term (forty-nine-year) renewable leases that provided for periodic revaluation of the leased tracts and, accordingly, adjustment of the annual rent payments. Individual leases were transferable and inheritable, which made them tradable assets and granted lessees of JNF land a holding claim of practically unlimited duration that was barely distinguished from outright ownership (for an extensive discussion of the JNF's leasing practices see Granott, 1952).

Nonetheless, the JNF proprietary rights were not merely nominal, and in implementing Zionist policies, it exercised them in a number of areas (a major one, to be dealt with below, was the contractual clauses preventing lessees from hiring non-Jewish farm labor). For the purpose of the current discussion, the relevant Zionist guidelines, translated by the JNF into land leasing practices, were the following:

a. Determining the size of leased units by what the settling institutions perceived to be the required area for an economically viable family farm in any region – given the nature of the terrain, available water resources and technology, and the derived type of husbandry, ranging from extensive dry to intensive irrigated farming.

b. Dividing the land within settlements into family farms defined by size, and providing clauses to enable the lessor to adjust the size of the single farm over time. Size adjustments (typically downward) of already established and newly leased farm units were called for by technological advances in production methods, investments in agricultural machinery, and drilling wells that raised the productivity of land by intensifying agricultural production, and thereby increasing the settlements' capacity to absorb additional (immigrant) farm households economically. Indeed, the average size of a single farm on JNF land – excluding *kibbutzim* – declined from 92 dunams in 1927 to 45 dunams in 1942 (see *Statistical Abstract of Palestine 1929* (1930), p. 109; Gurevich and Gertz, 1947, tables 1 and 2a).

c. Overseeing the transfer of leased holdings (by subleasing or by bequest) so as to prevent the agglomeration or fragmentation of farm holdings. Note that according to the Jewish agricultural census of 1942, the size of the smallest individual holding on JNF land was 8 dunams, and the largest no more than 206 dunams (Gurevich and Gertz, 1947, table 1).

The second largest single proprietor of Jewish land in the late Mandatory period was PICA – the Palestine Jewish Colonization Association – which owned about 22 percent of all rural Jewish land in 1942. The company was established in 1924 by Baron Edmund de Rothschild to manage his philanthropic colonizing endeavors. Upon registration in Palestine and obtaining title to Rothschild's land, PICA became in the mid-1920s the largest Jewish landowner, holding about 55 percent of all Jewish land (468,000 dunams). PICA also leased its land to Jewish farmers under long-term contracts, employing similar considerations to those of the JNF except for two major differences: it did not impose contractual constraints on non-Jewish farm labor, and it did not intend to retain possession of its land indefinitely. Rather, PICA gradually liquidated its possessions by selling already leased property to the farmer lessees, so that by the end of the Mandate, PICA's entire land holdings shrank to about 140,000 dunams. The size of holdings of PICA land, while also declining with agricultural intensification and spread of irrigation (from an average of 244 dunams in 1927 to 170 dunams in 1942), remained substantially larger than that of family farms on JNF land, since most of the "historically" extensive family grain-producing farms of 250 to 300 dunams each were concentrated in PICA-sponsored *moshavot* (Granott, 1952, chap. 11).

The rest of the Jewish rural land (200,000 dunams, or 26 percent of the entire rural area occupied by Jews in 1942) was held by privately owned single family farms, usually in multi-farm settlements. The size dispersion of holdings in this category was, not surprisingly, substantially larger than that of holdings on JNF and PICA land.[9]

In summary, taking all the Jewish rural land (excluding *kibbutzim*)

[9] The coefficients of variation of the JNF, PICA, and private size-of-holdings distributions in 1942 were: 1.074; 0.758; and 7.84, respectively.

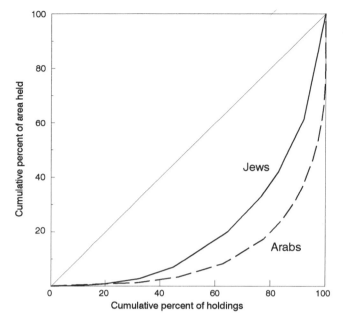

Figure 4.3 Farm land holdings, Arabs (1936) and Jews* (1927)
(sources: *MBS*, January–March 1946, table 76 for Arabs; *Statistical Abstract of Palestine*, 1929, table 52 for Jews)
* excluding *kibbutzim*

together, it is observed that the average size of holding declined by more than one half, from 120 dunams in 1927 to 55 dunams in 1941/42, reflecting the rising productivity of farm land. The size range of Jewish holdings, between 1 and 1,000 dunams, was about *fifty times* narrower than the range in the Arab sector (1 to 48,000 dunams in 1936, see table 4.1), and the dispersion of the distribution of Jewish landed possessions was substantially smaller.[10] These differences led to a considerably more equal distribution of rural land holdings in the Jewish community, as shown by the Lorenz curves in figure 4.3 and by the corresponding Gini coefficients: 0.778 for the Arab distribution of 1936 versus 0.597 for the Jewish distribution of 1927.

Much of the narrower range of dispersion and lower inequality of Jewish land holdings is explained by the land-allocation guidelines followed by the JNF and other settling institutions. As already indicated,

---

[10] The coefficients of variation of holdings by size in the Jewish rural sector were 1.302 in 1927 and 1.191 in 1942, and in the Arab sector 14.472 in 1936.

although the JNF leases turned into tradable assets whose prices were largely market determined, they were protected from both agglomeration and fragmentation. It follows that the size distribution of the holdings of JNF-owned land was determined primarily by the initial allocation and further institutional adjustments. Not so, however, in the case of privately owned, or even PICA-leased land, which could change hands quite freely.

Supplementary explanations for the relatively low concentration of Jewish landed wealth can probably be found in: (a) the more versatile options for capital buildup in the modern Jewish rural and general economy, relative to the largely traditional Arab rural sector, where the accumulation of wealth was largely confined to land; and (b) the more developed Jewish capital market and quasi-public credit facilities that served the Jewish farm economy, whereas Arab agriculture depended, at least in part, on personal providers of credit, making for concentration of land ownership throughout the Mandate period.

Capital

Moving from land to reproducible capital, the discussion in this section revolves around two themes. One addresses the patterns, orders of magnitude, and economic determinants and implications of investment, and the other deals with the nature of capital and financial markets in Palestine's divided economy.

Capital formation

The existing information on investment and distribution of capital goods, partial and impressionistic as it may be, suggests that fixed assets (structures and equipment) were accumulated and retained largely within the separate "economic confines" of the Arab and Jewish communities, with the government adding another component to the buildup of the country's stock of tangible capital by virtue of its infrastructure investments.

The quality and scope of the data on capital and investments are highly uneven, ranging from well-documented governmental outlays and quite detailed estimates of capital stock and formation in the Jewish sector to very scanty and extremely speculative figures on accumulation in the Arab sector. Nonetheless, and bearing these severe limitations in mind, a tentative picture is attempted in table 4.2, suggesting plausible orders of magnitude for the country's stock of fixed reproducible capital and its changes over the period.

Table 4.2 shows that capital formation in Mandatory Palestine was dominated by Jewish investment, which accounted for 60 percent of the addition to Palestine's overall net fixed capital during the period, and raised the share of the Jewish sector from 17 percent of the country's capital in 1922 to 52 percent in 1947. The intensity of Jewish fixed capital formation stands out not only *vis-à-vis* the much slower pace of Arab accumulation (in the Jewish economy the "end of period" stock of fixed capital was more than fifteen times larger than that of 1922, while the analogous growth in the Arab economy was probably only 2.5-fold), but in an international comparative context, as well.

The ratio of gross investment to gross national product (GNP) in the Jewish community, averaging 31.3 percent annually in 1922–47 (with the inter-war rate reaching 39.3 percent per annum) was extremely high. It exceeds by far the highest rates of investment (24 percent of GDP) cited by Chenery and Syrquin (1975) in their comprehensive study of the world's development patterns, which links the intensity of capital formation (among other developmental features) to levels of income per capita in 1950–70. Furthermore, none of the seventy-three economies surveyed by Sato (1971) had produced higher investment-to-product ratios in the post-war years of rapid growth (1950–64), and this includes the world record holder, Norway (29.1 percent), and the runner-up: Israel (28.9).

Moreover, if we consider an all-inclusive concept of fixed capital accumulation, it should include the estimated utilization of government capital by Jews and their newly acquired land. These two items accounted on average for roughly 4 percent and 10 percent, respectively, of overall Jewish capital formation during the Mandate period; the remaining 86 percent are Jewish own-investment in reproducible capital. Inclusion of these components raises the investment-GNP ratio even further, to 36.5 percent over the entire period and to 46.1 percent in 1922–39. When looked at as a fraction of the entire flow of resources available for domestic uses (GNP plus import surplus), the all-inclusive Jewish domestic investment naturally shrinks, to about 28 percent on average in the inter-war period and 24 percent in 1922–47. These, though, are still respectable investment rates by any standards.

As for the Arab community, the intensity of investment in reproducible capital (11.4 percent of GNP annually in 1922–47, and 12.2 percent in 1922–39) was quite low; and the same holds true for the essentially identical rates (11.2 percent of GNP in 1922–47 and 12.3 percent in 1922–39) generated by the increments to the all-inclusive stock of fixed capital. Note, however, that for the Arabs, the derivation of an all-inclusive capital-formation estimate requires, besides the incorporation of their share in government investments, *subtraction* of the value of land sold to Jews from total accumulation.

Table 4.2. *Capital and investment in 1936 prices*

	Jews	Arabs	gov't	total
A Total fixed reproducible capital, beginning of year		('000 P£)		
1922	5,056	22,246	2,000	29,302
1947	77,985	57,057	15,429	150,471
		(%)		
1922	17.3	75.9	6.8	100.0
1947	51.8	37.9	10.3	100.0
B Accumulated capital: total investment 1922–47[a]				
'000 P£	72,929	34,811	13,449	121,189
%	60.2	28.7	11.1	100.0

	Jews		Arabs
	in GNP	in resources	(in GNP)
C Rates of investment (%)			
own investment in fixed reproducible capital			
1922–39	39.3		12.2
1922–47	31.3		11.4
all-inclusive investment[b]			
1922–39	46.1	27.8	12.3
1922–47	36.5	23.7	11.2

Notes:
[a] Total investment is derived by subtracting the capital stock of 1922 from that of 1947.
[b] Including, in addition to own investment in fixed reproducible capital, investment in unimproved land (positive for Jews, negative for Arabs) and utilization of government investments.
Sources: tables A.24–A.26; Gurevich and Gertz (1938) and the discussion on land, above; BMZ, tables A3, A4, A5

The estimated Arab investment rates exceeded only those of ten economies, out of the seventy-three on the 1950–64 world scale (Sato, 1971), but they come pretty close to the investment GNP ratio (12.9 percent) predicted by applying the actual level of Arab income per capita and size of population to the econometric formulation of Chenery and Syrquin (1975). Moreover, the Arab rates of investment allowed for an increase in the stock of fixed reproducible capital per member of the labor force at a respectable annual rate of 2.1 percent in the inter-war years, and of 1.4 percent over the period as a whole.

It follows that while the allocation of resources for building the stock of reproducible capital in the very poor Arab community seems to have been compatible with income-linked international standards, the intensity of investment in the Jewish economy was a true upward outlier at any level of income per capita. What made this massive buildup of capital possible? The evidence clearly points to the external supply of resources made available to the Jewish community by a remarkably large, albeit fluctuating, flow of capital imports. This flow accounted, in 1932–46, for at least 85 percent of the influx of long-term capital to Mandatory Palestine from all sources combined (Halperin, 1954, chap. X); and, though secularly declining as a proportion of the extremely fast-growing output (see chapter 1), the annual inflow of capital to the Jewish community averaged about 64 percent of the size of its NNP in 1922–47, and no less than 87 percent in the inter-war period.

Most of these imported resources were private (75 percent of all Jewish capital imports in the inter-war period, and about half of them in 1940–47; *Statistical Handbook*, 1947, p. 375), consisting largely of immigrants' unilateral transfers and of private investments made in Palestine by Jews living abroad, and the rest being public resources, unilaterally transferred by the World Zionist Organization and its affiliated bodies and by other non-profit public institutions (see chapter 6). This influx of capital, which was closely associated with that of immigration (chapter 3), enabled the Jewish community to undertake massive investments before World War II without having to resort to foreign borrowing or to domestic savings.

In general, the demand of immigrants for housing, consumer durables, infrastructure, and public utilities, on the one hand, and their labor-force effect on raising the productivity of and returns to capital, on the other, should (other things being equal) increase demand for investment in immigrant-absorbing economies, and induce capital to chase after (in-migrating) labor. Since in Palestine the bulk of inflowing capital belonged to the immigrants themselves, the Jewish economy was characterized not so much by capital anticipating or chasing immigration as by capital accompanying (or rather being embodied in) immigration. Hence the influx of immigrants-cum-capital import generated both the demand for investment and the supply of resources to meet it, enabling the amount of reproducible fixed capital not only to catch up with the extremely fast growth of labor (at 8.8 percent per annum in 1922–47, see chapter 1), but to rise per member of the labor force at 2.6 percent annually and almost double between 1922 and 1947 (tables A.4 and A.24).

Indeed, as figure 4.4 demonstrates, Jewish domestic investment usually followed the combined pattern of immigration and capital imports rather closely, with the amplitude of the inflow of resources being shaped pri-

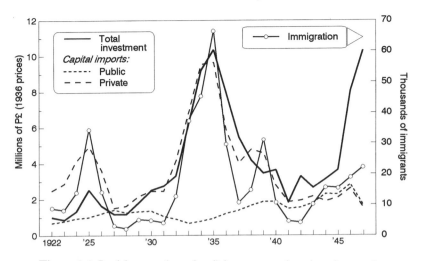

Figure 4.4 Jewish gross (non-land) investment, immigration, and
capital (public and private) imports, 1922–47
(sources: table A.23 for investment; table A.24 for capital imports; table
A.3 for immigrants)

marily by their private component. This association is also reflected by
the large proportion (53.2 percent on average, over the entire period) of
structures, most of them probably residential, in Jewish capital formation,
and by its fluctuations coinciding, prior to World War II, with the waves of
immigration (table A.3 and BMZ, table A3).

These rather impressionistic observations are supported by a recent
econometric analysis, in which Jewish investment is shown to be positively affected by the accelerator effect of changes in the growth rates of
output, by Jewish capital imports, and by the size of the government's
(infrastructure) capital stock. Interestingly enough, the latter finding
indicates that the two types of capital (government and Jewish) were
complementary, augmenting one another in the production of Jewish
output (BMZ).

In view of the large inflow of Jewish capital, one might ask whether any
part of it crossed the ethno-national "economic lines" to the Arab sector.
Unfortunately, data from which well-informed inferences on the matter
could be drawn are not available. Absence of evidence of the existence of
quantitatively significant joint Arab-Jewish business undertakings, on the
one hand, and the vast investment activity within the Jewish sector, on the
other, lead to the conjecture that intercommunal net capital movements
in the form of direct investments or long-term credit extended by Jews to

Arabs were probably quite small. This, of course, does not rule out the possibility that some transactions of this nature may have taken place in the course of Arab-Jewish trade in land and in goods and services (chapter 5). Taking the basic separation between the two economic sectors as given, one may even wonder whether the returns to capital in the Arab economy were not on the whole higher than in the immigration-absorbing Jewish economy, calling – other things being equal – for a returns-equalizing movement of capital from the Jewish to the Arab economy.

Some resources, though, were unilaterally (and involuntarily) transferred from Jews to Arabs indirectly, via the Mandatory fiscal mechanism, as shown in the study of government tax and expenditure incidence (Metzer, 1982; and chapter 6). These were rather minor transfers, constituting no more than 2–3 percent of Jewish capital imports on an annual basis (Metzer, 1982). In terms of Arab economic activity, however, these transfers had considerable weight. For example, the resources fiscally transferred from the Jewish to the Arab community in 1935 were estimated at P£330,000 (Metzer, 1982), or about 10 percent of Arab net domestic investment in that year.

In accumulating fixed capital, the Arabs may also have benefited from the rising prices of their land relative to the prices of reproducible assets for which some of this land was exchanged. Yet the orders of magnitude involved could not have been very large, as total receipts from inter-communal land sales constituted no more than one-fifth of Arab gross investment over the entire period, and those received by Arabs residing in Palestine only 12 percent.

All in all, the Arabs, unlike the Jews, had to resort to their own savings for a relatively large proportion of the resources demanded for domestic investment (possibly 31.3 percent of all Arab net investments in 1935). And although their saving rates were not insignificant (in 1935 they may have reached 5 percent of national income), their low income level certainly imposed an effective constraint on the amount of savings they could generate, and given the comparatively small inflow of capital (about 10 percent of Arab GNP, in 1935), on the extent of their capital accumulation and all their domestic uses as well.

The markets for investable funds

The process of capital formation, however, involves more than merely the supply of and demand for investable funds; it requires institutional mechanisms for collecting them from savers (domestic or foreign) and making them available to investors, who turn them into new capital. These mechanisms can generally be classified into two types: "organized" financial markets consisting of commercial and credit banks, security exchanges, and other impersonal financial intermediaries; and "unorganized" markets, encompassing a variety of institutions from friends and relatives, through specialized and occasional moneylenders, to credit cooperatives and government-sponsored agricultural banks and other credit-providing facilities (Tun Wai, 1956–57, 1957–58, 1977; Bell, 1988; Fry, 1988). These two institutional mechanisms coexist in any economy; but naturally, the more developed an economy, the more prominent the role of its organized financial markets. The same holds true for the monetized, market-oriented urban and (cash-crop-based) agricultural sectors in less-developed economies. But the traditional peasantry and (mainly rural) artisans in less-developed countries tend to rely heavily on moneylenders and other "unorganized" devices for meeting the demand for capital, particularly when such demand is seasonal and the required capital is circulating in nature, thus making for a typically dual structure of capital markets in developing economies.

These structural differences are functionally reflected in wide interest-rate gaps, which are part and parcel of the organizational dualism in developing economies as discussed in chapter 1. Due to both demand and supply factors, interest rates in an unorganized market are typically much higher and more widely dispersed than in organized ones. On the demand side, the low levels of income in traditional rural sectors limit their ability to save and self-finance, raising their relative demand for credit to facilitate ongoing productive activity (Tun Wai, 1957–58, 1977). On the supply side, the high cost involved in extending a large number of small loans to peasants and evaluating their creditworthiness tends to deter banks from extending their operations into the relatively riskier traditional sectors which are therefore left to be serviced primarily by local moneylenders largely out of their own resources. The opportunity costs of funds lent by moneylenders (and by other non-institutional credit providers) are commonly higher than those of organized banking institutions, which are not constrained by their own resources in generating loanable funds. This, however, may be partly compensated for by the advantage that the former have in obtaining inside knowledge on their rural clientele and in operating with lower overhead and administrative costs (Tun Wai, 1957–58, 1977; Myint, 1985; Bell, 1988).

The net effect of all these factors is a regime of relatively high and variable nominal interest rates to borrowers in the unorganized capital market; although, when considering the various non-interest costs attached to borrowing, it turns out that the nominal interest-rate gap considerably overstates the "true" cost differentials between unorganized and organized markets. Moreover, the accessibility of local moneylenders and indigenous bankers, and the flexibility of their lending procedures, may partly compensate for the high cost of borrowing in an unorganized market (Bell, 1988; Fry, 1988).

As for saving opportunities, the high cost of banking in a traditional economy lowers the interest rates offered by financial institutions to small, rural savers, inducing them to consider hoarding as a preferred alternative to channeling their savings through the organized capital market (Ali, 1957–58; Tun Wai, 1957–58; Myint, 1985). Hoarding obviously hinders the mobilization of funds from savers to investors, which may further raise the cost of borrowing.

However, divided as the capital markets in developing economies may be, their organized and unorganized segments are nonetheless linked. Large rural landlords and owners of cash-crop estates may be borrowers in the organized market and lenders in the unorganized market. In addition, institutions providing credit to the rural sector via the unorganized market, such as credit cooperatives and agricultural banks, may raise some of their working capital in the organized market. These links fulfill a supply-raising, risk-dispersing, and efficiency-increasing function, and reduce the cost differential between the two financial markets. Being aware of this role, we find that governments in both colonial and independent developing countries tend to encourage and sponsor institutional involvement in the unorganized financial markets serving their traditional (rural and otherwise) sectors.

The picture outlined in these general remarks describes the segmentation of the financial markets in Palestine's Arab community rather well. The available sources, though scanty, strongly suggest that non-institutional instruments dominated the provision of credit in the large sector of peasant agriculture in the inter-war period (Johnson and Crosbie, 1930; Himadeh, 1938; *Survey*, 1946, vol. I). And the government used limited economic resources and, from the early 1930s onward, its regulatory capacity, in a continuous but only partly successful attempt to institutionalize the provision of rural credit. For example, the government encouraged the setting up of credit cooperatives in the Arab sector, mainly on a temporary, seasonal basis, so as to broaden the range of financial options faced by Arab peasants, thereby reducing their dependence on private moneylenders, which was rather substantial prior to World War II.

The only, and often quoted, estimate of Arab rural indebtedness was made by the Johnson-Crosbie committee, appointed by the government of Palestine in the aftermath of the Arab riots of 1929 to investigate the conditions of the country's agriculturists. The committee's report points to a total debt of P£2 million in 1930, which amounts to 67 percent of the value added generated by Arab agriculture that year. This ratio lies well within the "heavy-burden" range of rural indebtedness, identified by Tun Wai in his classic surveys of financial markets in underdeveloped countries (1957–58, 1977), as accounting for more than 50 percent of annual agricultural income.

The interest rates faced by Arab borrowers in the unorganized financial market ranged from 6 percent to 12 percent annually on government and other institutionally provided (including by banks) rural credit, to 30 percent and more charged by moneylenders (*Survey*, 1946, vol. I, pp. 348–68; Kamen, 1991, pp. 240–55). Not surprisingly, this range and composition of interest charges by lender type are quite similar to the rates observed in a number of traditional rural economies after World War II (Tun Wai, 1957–58, 1977; Bell, 1988; Fry, 1988).

As for organized financial instruments such as commercial banks, these served the modern, largely urban segments of Arab economic life, including that of "capitalist" citrus farming. However, the partial financial backing provided by Palestine's commercial banks (chiefly the British Barclays Bank) to rural credit and saving societies and to the Agricultural Mortgage Company, and the provisions enabling the banks since the mid-1930s to extend seasonal credit against collateral of future crops, were major bridges linking the organized and the unorganized financial markets serving the Arab peasant community (*Survey*, 1946, vol. I, pp. 348–68).

These links gained in importance during the war, when the high and stable demand for Palestine's agricultural produce, coupled with extended financial subsidization by the government and the debt-eroding inflation, increased rural income, reduced the indebtedness of Arab peasants, improved their creditworthiness, raised the accessibility and utilization of organized financial instruments, and narrowed interest rate differentials (*Survey*, 1946, vol. I, pp. 348–68; Kamen, 1991; Gross and Metzer, 1993). The swift wartime expansion of commercial Arab banks operating in Palestine (the Arab Bank and the Arab National Bank) provides strong indirect evidence supporting these developments. The deposits and credit outstanding of these two banks combined grew more than twenty-six- and fourteen-fold, respectively, between 1939 and 1946, much faster than any other financial institution in Palestine at the time (*Survey*, 1946, vol. II, p. 559; *Supplement to Survey of Palestine*, 1947, p. 79).

In the relatively advanced Jewish economy, however, the weight of unorganized financial instruments seems to have been negligible. Its substantial inflow of capital and (mainly private) domestic savings were collected and transferred to investors by commercial and mortgage banks, and by quasi-bank credit cooperatives. In addition, with the inflow of immigrants from Nazi Germany and the arrangements facilitating the transfer of their capital in the 1930s (see chapter 3), a slowly evolving securities market emerged, allowing for the domestic recruitment of equity and debenture capital by domestic establishments. Between 1933 and 1937 new securities amounting to P£7.1 million were issued by local establishments (95 percent by Jewish bodies). Half of this sum was raised in the domestic securities market and the other half in London (Sarnat, 1966). Since total Jewish fixed capital formation (including land) amounted to P£45 million in these five years, it follows that the funds raised through the securities markets could have accounted for at most 15 percent of Jewish investment in the 1930s.

As for the entire flow of Jewish investable funds, some of them were mobilized through financial intermediaries by the Zionist Organization – fulfilling "nation building" tasks and public-sector functions in the Jewish community, including the provision of low-cost loanable funds to Jewish farmers. Note that the Zionist national institutions were directly responsible for about 20 percent of all Jewish investments in the inter-war years, including land purchases (see table A.23; Gross and Metzer, 1978, tables 10, 11). The rest were allocated partly by the quasi-public *Histadrut* sector and its enterprises, *kibbutzim* and other collective and cooperative entities, but mostly by private businesses and households (see also chapter 6).

Considering the institutional component of the country's financial markets as a whole, the Mandatory period can be divided into two distinct sub-periods. In the first, extending from the beginning of the Mandate to the early 1930s, a small number of foreign banks dominated the industry – a structure similar to that of the late Ottoman period and of other colonialized countries in the Middle East and elsewhere, which owe the development of their banking industry to the penetration of foreign (Ottoman and/or European) institutions (Ali, 1957–58).

The major foreign banks operating in Mandatory Palestine were the British Barclays Bank (Dominion, Colonial & Overseas) acting as agents for the Palestine Currency Board in London and as the government's banker; and the Ottoman Bank, headquartered in London. In addition, three other foreign banks conducted small volumes of business in the country: the Italian Banco di Roma (up to 1940), the Dutch Holland Bank Union, and the Polish Post Office Saving Bank (Michaelis, 1986). Note, however, that the London-incorporated and registered Anglo Palestine Bank (APB), established by the World Zionist Organization in 1902 to serve as a commercial bank for Palestine's evolving Jewish national community, was also formally a foreign bank, and was classified as such in the official banking statistics. Unfortunately, systematic records pertaining to banking activity are not available prior to 1936, but fragmentary assessments suggest that the foreign banks, excluding the APB, may have held, as late as 1931, at least 60 percent of all the funds deposited in Palestine's banks and credit cooperatives combined (Halevi, 1977, p. 185).

The second interval began in 1932–33 and spanned the rest of the Mandatory period. Its early phase (1933–36) was closely associated with the financially skilled, entrepreneurship-rich, and capital-abundant Fifth Aliya (see chapter 3; Gelber, 1990; Niederland, 1996). It was typified by the fast-rising weight of the APB and mushrooming local banks, whose number rose from twenty-two in 1931 to seventy by mid-1936, including the two Arab banks mentioned above (*Survey*, 1946, vol. II, p. 553). Contemporary estimates indicate that as early as 1933, the APB held 44 percent of the country's deposits (compared to 28 percent two years earlier), with the combined share of local banks and cooperative societies rising from 10–12 percent in 1931 to 19 percent in 1933, and that of the foreign banks declining from 60 percent to 37 percent between these two years (Halevi, 1977, p. 185).

Up to 1936, banks were established and operated in Palestine under the provisions of the 1921 Banking Ordinance, which stipulated only that "no banking business should be transacted, except by a company registered under the provisions of the Companies Ordinance" (*Survey*, 1946, vol. II, p. 553). Keeping the entry to the industry essentially unrestricted and its structure and operation unregulated, the government allowed virtually free and (officially) unprotected banking.

Besides the general expansion of business and the growth of economic activity toward the mid-1930s, this (non-) regulatory environment reduced the costs of banking and provided another stimulus to the proliferation of the industry. On the other hand, the risks, particularly those faced by small, capital-poor banks, were certainly non-trivial in such an uncontrolled, but also unsecured, setting. And indeed, the mild run on the banks in reaction to the outbreak of the Ethiopian crisis in September 1935 – a prelude to the closing phase of Palestine's banking history – revealed that many smaller banks did not have a sufficiently solid financial base to withstand the crisis; in the absence of a central bank, they had to resort to the industry's leading institutions (Barclays and APB) as lenders of last resort.

Just as governments of the depression-afflicted countries tightened financial controls in the early 1930s (Fry, 1988), the government of Palestine was led by the financial instability and economic decline of the mid-decade to amend the banking ordinance and introduce new regulatory mechanisms (once in March 1936 and again in October 1937). The amended ordinance required all local banks to have minimal volumes of subscribed and paid-up capital (P£50,000 and P£25,000 respectively), and to submit periodical financial statements to the newly established office of the examiner of banks. The examiner was also authorized to oblige local banks to maintain liquidity ratios no lower than 35 percent (Michaelis, 1986).

One byproduct of the new inspection mechanism was the systematic collection and publication of data on banks and credit societies by the examiner. These statistics reveal a continuous decline in the number of local banks (all but two of which were owned by Jews), from a record high of seventy in 1936, to thirty-two by the end of 1939, and to twenty by the end of 1946. A similar, but milder pattern of decline is also observed in the number of credit societies (most of which were also Jewish owned) from ninety-three in 1936 to eighty-two in 1946.

The declining number of local banks did not, however, cause a similar reduction in their relative weight, which remained (excluding the APB) roughly unchanged at 16 percent of all deposits and about a quarter of the credit outstanding, between 1936 and 1946, while that of foreign banks shrank substantially in the last decade of the Mandate (from 28 percent to 17 percent of all deposits, and from 19 percent to 11 percent of the industry's total credit). The relative decline of the latter was certainly affected in part by the country's shrinking international businesses during the war.

This pattern was accompanied by rising concentration in the banking industry, with the share of the APB – the largest single bank operating in Palestine – growing from 37 percent of deposits and 26 percent of the credit outstanding in 1936, to 47 percent and 34 percent respectively in 1946. Adding the two Arab banks, which were the two largest locally registered banks in the mid-1940s, shows that these "big three" combined held in 1946 55 percent of the country's bank deposits and 52 percent of all the financial institutions' outstanding credit (*Survey*, 1946, vol. II, pp. 554–56; *Supplement to Survey of Palestine*, 1947, p. 77; Halevi, 1977, pp. 184–85).

The reduction in the number of banks, coupled with their growing concentration, reflects an adjustment process to the changing economic and regulatory conditions. Prominent among these were: declining profitability during the slump of 1936–39; the increasing costs of banking caused by the new regulations; and a possible rise in the optimal size of a single banking firm. The latter may have been partly due to the regulatory capital requirements, and partly to other, independent factors, shaping the oligopolistic structure of the industry.

Compared to the relative competitiveness of banking in the industrialized countries, oligopolistic financial markets are typical in most contemporary developing countries (Fry, 1988). In Mandatory Palestine, however, the oligopolistic structure may have been enhanced, among other factors, by the special positions occupied by the APB and the two Arab banks in their respective communities. The APB, being the "Zionist" bank, which supported private and public undertakings in the context of building the Jewish "National Home," attracted sizable funds, and enlarged the scope and duration of credit and direct investments beyond those of typical commercial banking; it was also lender of last resort (i.e., a quasi-central bank) for some of the local Jewish banks (Halevi, 1977). Similarly the ethno-national considerations attached to the foundation and purpose of operation of the Arab bank (established in 1930), most notably the Arab National Bank (established in 1933), made them a "natural" solution for Arab savers, more and more of whom sought an institutional banking outlet for their assets in the 1940s.

As far as the size and economic significance of Palestine's banking industry are concerned, the two standard parameters – the ratio of demand deposits to total money (currency in circulation plus demand deposits), measuring banking development, and the ratio of banks' overall claims (loans, advancements and investments) to national income, indicating the extent to which banks are used to finance economic activity (Tun Wai, 1956–57) – were quite high in Mandatory Palestine. Demand deposits constituted about 68 percent of the country's money supply in 1936–39, slightly higher than the average ratio of five major developed countries (France, the Netherlands, Switzerland, the UK, and the USA) in 1938 (67.2 percent), and substantially higher than the average ratio in twenty-seven less-developed countries in that year (47 percent). Among Middle Eastern countries, the largest share of deposits to total money supply was observed in 1938 in Iran (54 percent), and the second largest in Egypt (51 percent), both figures much smaller than in Palestine (Tun Wai, 1956–57). The extent of overall monetization, as measured by the ratio of total money to national income, was also quite substantial in Palestine in the late 1930s (59 percent in 1936–39), and much larger than in the most monetized Midddle Eastern countries in 1954 (Lebanon: 51 percent, Egypt: 42 percent, and Iraq: 31 percent; Ali, 1957–58).

Similarly, the ratio of bank claims to Palestine's total product – 45 percent in 1936–39 (*SAP*, 1937–38, 1939, 1940; *Survey*, 1946, vol. II, pp. 555–57) – was higher than the claims-to-income ratio in five out of eight developed countries recorded by Tun Wai (1956–57) for 1938, and far higher than his recorded ratios for the (three) less-developed countries the same year, ranging from 5 percent to 8 percent (Tun Wai, 1957–58). In addition, Palestine's claims-to-income ratio in the late 1930s was appreciably higher than those reported by Ali (1957–58) for Egypt (18 percent), Syria (27 percent) and Turkey (26 percent) in 1954 (ratios for earlier years were not recorded for the countries in the region). Moreover, if the loans made by credit cooperatives, accounting for 22 percent of all the institutional credit (banks and credit cooperatives, combined) in 1936–39, are added to Palestine's banking claims, the claims-to-income ratio rises to 55 percent, further improving Palestine's comparative position.

The questions that this record raises in the context of Palestine's divided economy is to what extent was the organized financial market segregated along ethno-national lines, and what role did it play in the economic lives of Arabs and Jews. No data are available on the ethno-national distribution of deposits and claims at the single banking firm level, but according to the existing impressionistic and qualitative evidence (see, for example, *Twenty Five Years of Service to the Arab Economy*, 1956; Halevi, 1977; Michaelis, 1986; Gross and Greenberg, 1994), it is likely that while the major foreign banks may have served the population and businesses of Palestine rather indiscriminately, the local Arab banks and credit cooperatives collected deposits from and extended credit primarily to Arabs, and the Jewish institutions (including the APB), largely to Jews.

Nor are data available on the allocation of overall bank credit between Arabs and Jews, but some indications of the weight of the banking system (including credit cooperatives) in their respective economic lives can be obtained from scattered estimates of total bank deposits by depositors' ethno-nationality, as reported by Abramowitz and Guelfat (1944) and by Waschitz (1947) for the mid-1930s, and by the Mandatory government (*Survey*, 1946, vol. II, p. 557; *Supplement to Survey of Palestine*, 1947, p. 77) for the mid-1940s. Taking deposit-to-output ratios as indicative of the banks' economic significance in the two communities, it is observed that in the Jewish sector they ranged from 63 percent to 70 percent and in the Arab sector from 23 percent to 28 percent. Moreover, even if we were to take, for the Arab community, the ratio of deposits to non-agricultural output (assuming that Arab agriculture was served chiefly by the non-institutional segment of the unorganized financial market), the highest ratio would be 43 percent, substantially lower than the lowest Jewish ratio of deposits to net output. These discrepancies, which are compatible with the developmental gap between the two sectors, may partly reflect disparities in monetization and economic complexity, and partly differences in the means and patterns of savings and investment.

Labor

In examining labor as a factor of production, two distinct but related aspects should be considered. One is the pre-market (supply-determining) profile of the labor force; the other is the structure and functioning of the labor market and the factors shaping the demand for labor and its effective market supply. Naturally, we should start our examination with the first aspect by reviewing comparatively the age structure of Arabs and Jews, their respective labor force participation patterns, and their occupational compositions.

Size and characteristics of the labor force

The basic age profile of Arabs and Jews is presented in table 4.3. The table also reports the standard "dependency ratio" (the ratio of people younger than fifteen and older than sixty-five to those aged fifteen to sixty-four), which serves as a crude measure of the economic burden borne by working-age adults who support the non-working segment of the population.

Fertility differences between Arabs and Jews and the high proportion of prime working ages among Jewish immigrants were principal determinants of the major disparities between the age structures of the two communities. These disparities are most pronounced in the share of the principal working-age bracket, twenty to forty-four (in which Palestine's Jews held the world record for the inter-war period: see *The Aging of Populations*, 1956, table III), versus the proportion of the pre-working-age brackets in the population, under fourteen. The superiority of the Jews in the former and of the Arabs in the latter created a strong Jewish productive advantage. And since the share of the elderly (sixty-five and above) in both populations was roughly the same, this advantage was clearly reflected in a large (and rising) dependency-ratio gap which, in turn, had a direct bearing on income-per-capita differentials. It can easily be shown that even if labor productivity were identical in the two communities, the age-structure disparity alone would have caused income per capita in the Jewish community to be 15 percent higher than in the Arab community in 1931 and 25 percent in 1944.

Note, however, that since school enrollment in rural societies is typically quite low, the average rural working age (especially of males) may begin earlier on in life. Similarly, the tendency of old men to remain economically active in rural communities may extend their effective working age well beyond sixty-five (see Durand, 1953). Consequently, the ordinarily calculated dependency ratio in pre-modern populations may

Table 4.3. *Age structure and dependency ratios: Palestine, 1931, 1940 (%)*

age group	1931	1940	1944	1947
Arabs				
1. 0–14	40.8	43.0	42.4	
2. 15–19	7.0	10.1	11.2	
3. 20–44	36.2	30.2	29.7	
4. 45–64	11.7	12.4	12.6	
5. 65+	4.4	4.3	4.1	
6. all ages	100.0	100.0	100.0	
7. dependency ratio[a]	82.5	89.8	86.9	
Jews				
1. 0–14	32.7	27.4	28.3	29.5
2. 15–19	7.8	8.6	8.0	8.0
3. 20–44	43.8	46.2	44.7	43.4
4. 45–64	11.5	13.3	14.2	15.0
5. 65+	4.2	4.5	4.8	4.1
6. all ages	100.0	100.0	100.0	100.0
7. dependency ratio[a]	58.5	46.8	49.5	50.6

Note:

$$a \left(\frac{1.+5.}{2.+3.+4.} \right) \times 100.$$

Sources: Survey (1946), vol. III, section 1, table 1; Sicron and Gill (1955), table 1; Bachi (1977), table A13; McCarthy (1990), table A4–5

overstate the actual burden on employable persons. To correct for these possible biases, the Arab dependency ratios for 1931 and 1940 were recalculated, assuming that only half the people aged between ten and fourteen and over sixty-five could not be counted as potential breadwinners. The resulting Arab ratios (0.637 and 0.634 respectively), while significantly lower than those of table 4.3, are still higher than those for Jews.

The proportion of a population's working-age segment accounts for the potential size of its labor force (defined as employed persons and persons who are unemployed but actively seek employment). But the extent to which this potential is realized depends on the labor-force participation rate (i.e., the percentage of working-age people actually belonging to the labor force).

The enumeration of Palestine's population by employment characteristics in the 1931 census enables an estimation of the labor force by ethno-nationality and sex, though not by age. The participation rates in table 4.4 were calculated using these estimates. They are presented as percentage shares of the population aged over ten and over fifteen, in

Table 4.4. *Labor-force participation rates, 1931 (% of population)*

	Arabs		Jews	
	excluding persons living on income[a]	all	excluding persons living on income[a]	all
% of population aged 10+				
males	72.2	74.1	76.8	78.9
females	6.8	7.9	23.4	24.7
total	39.5	41.1	50.2	51.9
% of population aged 15+				
males	83.0	85.2	87.0	89.4
females	8.1	9.4	25.6	27.0
total	45.0	46.7	55.8	57.7

Note:
[a] Persons who were recorded in the census as living on property income and on remittances from abroad are excluded in this column from the labor force.
Source: Census of Palestine (1933), vol. II, table XVI

compliance with the observation that in a good number of semi-industrial and agricultural countries a sizable segment (between 20 percent and 60 percent) of boys aged ten to fourteen were economically active in the inter-war period (Durand, 1953).

The relative size of the Jewish labor force in 1931 was between ten and eleven percentage points higher than the Arab labor force.[11] Most of this wide gap was caused by the difference in women's labor-force participation rates: the rate for Jewish women was about three times higher than that for Arab women. It should be pointed out, however, that the labor-force estimates for women, which typically exclude housewives, may be downward biased, especially in rural societies. Rural women, elsewhere classified as housewives, are often engaged in the family's farm production. Their exclusion may, therefore, underestimate the "true" size of the labor force, and hence the contribution of women (and in our case especially of Arab women) to measured output.

Nonetheless, the estimated labor-force participation rates of Arab women (7.9 percent of the over-ten and 9.4 percent of the over-fifteen age group in 1931) were very small by any standard, including comparison

[11] Presumably reflecting the wartime economic prosperity, the overall labor-force participation rate in 1945 was 3–3.5 percentage points higher than in 1931 in both communities, leaving the gap virtually unchanged (see table A.4).

with other traditional societies in which one would expect to find low labor-force participation of women. In spite of the uneven quality of the female labor-force data in the inter-war years and the caveats imposed on comparing them internationally (Durand, 1953), the fact that only Mexico's rates (7.3 percent and 6.1 percent for the two age groups, respectively) were lower than those of Arab women in Palestine clearly stands out. Jewish women's substantially higher participation in the labor force (24.7 percent of the over-ten and 27 percent of the over-fifteen age brackets) was within the international middle range, similar to developed Western countries such as Norway, the Netherlands, Belgium, the USA, Australia, and New Zealand (*Demographic Yearbook 1948*, tables 4, 10; and *The Aging of Populations*, 1956, table III).

As for the labor-force participation of men, the calculated rate of 78.9 percent for Jews, which placed them twenty-fifth among forty countries (with participation rates ranging from 90.2 percent to 71 percent in the over-ten age group: *Demographic Yearbook 1948*, tables 4, 10; and *The Aging of Populations*, 1956, table III), seems to be accounted for by their high school enrollment. But the observed participation rates of Arab men remain somewhat puzzling. With low school attendance, and possibly also late retirement, their recorded participation (74.1 percent) appears too small in comparison with both the Jewish and the "world" rates (the Arabs placed thirty-fifth among the forty countries). This rather low rate suggests that the census returns may have underreported the extent of Arab labor, especially regarding men.[12] Nonetheless, the wide gap in female participation would probably have left the basic finding – a higher labor-force-to-adult-population ratio in the Jewish community – intact, even if "true" measures of labor-force participation in the Arab community could have been taken into account.

Although the distinction between "occupation" and "industry" is somewhat blurred in the population census, its classification of earners (gainfully employed persons) and working dependents by type of employment within industries is detailed enough to allow for at least a crude

[12] Some support for this conjecture is provided by the relatively small number of Arab males aged under seventeen who were classified in the 1931 census as working dependents (i.e., persons employed within the household, whose work did not constitute an independent source of income, either in money or in kind). Even if all these individuals were assumed to be younger than fifteen, they would constitute no more than 3.2 percent of the Arab male population aged ten to fourteen. This very small percentage provides some indication of the low labor-force participation rate implied by the census for this age group. Note, by way of comparison, that the recorded labor-force participation rates among males in the ten-to-fourteen age group in agricultural countries such as Turkey and Egypt reached 48.7 percent in 1945 and 63.4 percent in 1937, respectively (Durand, 1953).

Table 4.5. *Arab, Jewish, and American civilian labor force by occupation (%)*

	Palestine (1931			Jews (1945)	USA (1940)
	Arabs	Jews	Jews as % of all workers		
all workers					
managers, officials and clerks	3.1	14.9	58.0	13.7	16.9
technical and professional	2.7	11.8	56.2	11.4	7.5
sales personnel	7.8	12.0	30.7	15.8	6.7
other (skilled and unskilled)	86.4	61.3	17.0	59.1	68.9
all: %	100.0	100.0	22.4	100.0	100.0
'000	227.1	65.6		215.5	51,742.0
non-agricultural workers					
managers, officials and clerks in:					
finance business	1.2	2.9	59.7	4.2	
public administration	3.2	1.5	22.3	6.1	
others	3.6	13.5	69.0	4.8	
total	*8.0*	*17.9*	*57.4*	*15.1*	*20.5*
technical professional	6.9	14.7	56.2	12.9	9.1
sales personnel	20.3	15.0	30.7	17.7	8.1
other (skilled and unskilled)	64.8	52.4	32.8	54.3	62.4
all: %	100.0	100.0	37.6	100.0	100.0
'000	87.6	52.7		191.5	42,747.0

Sources: Palestine – 1931: *Census of Palestine* (1933), vol. II, table XVI, for all occupations except manufacturing workers; table XXI for manufacturing. The table presents the occupational breakdown in "organized industry." Based on the *Census of Jewish Industries and Handicrafts* of 1930 (*Report of the Censuses*, 1931), it was assumed that Jewish workers in "organized industry" constituted two-thirds of all the Jews employed in manufacturing in 1931. For Arabs, a share of 50 percent was taken. For 1945, "Occupational Structure of the Jewish Population" (1946). USA – *Historical Statistics of the USA* (1975), part I, series D 182–232

occupational breakdown of Arab and Jewish labor in 1931. This is done in table 4.5, which also presents estimates of the Jewish occupational structure in 1945 (no similar figures for Arab labor are available for that or any other year except 1931), and, for comparative purposes, the occupational composition of the American labor force in 1940.

The occupations listed in table 4.5 can be roughly divided into the following categories. A skilled white-collar category ("managers, officials and clerical workers," and "technical and professional workers"); an in-between category ("sales workers");[13] and a blue-collar category (consisting of skilled, unskilled, and "other workers"). The outstanding feature of the distributions is obviously the comparatively high skill intensity of the Jewish labor force. In 1931, 26.7 percent of all Jewish workers held white-collar occupations, compared with only 5.8 percent of the Arabs. Because of the intercommunal differences in the industrial composition of labor (see chapter 5), this disparity narrows considerably when only non-agricultural workers are considered, but it remains substantial nevertheless (32.6 percent of non-farm Jewish workers versus 14.9 percent of the Arabs were engaged in white-collar pursuits).

Jewish labor was more heavily engaged in typical white-collar activities such as financial, business, technical, and professional services. Furthermore, the share of white-collar occupations in "other industries" (including manufacturing, construction, transportation, and communications) was higher in the relatively more advanced Jewish economy. Only in public administration, whose scale of activity was more closely linked to community size, was the proportion of white-collar occupations among Arab workers higher than among Jews. Note, too, that more Jews than Arabs were engaged in the major white-collar occupations, not only in percentage terms but in absolute numbers too. It is remarkable that the Jews, who in 1931 constituted about 22 percent of the entire labor force in Palestine and 38 percent of all the non-agricultural labor, held no less than 56 percent of the country's white-collar occupations. Table 4.5 also demonstrates that the skill-intensive composition of Jewish occupations, which changed very little between 1931 and 1945 (despite the relatively high skills of immigrants in the 1930s) stands out not only *vis-à-vis* the largely traditional Arab community but also in comparison with an economically advanced labor force such as that of the USA on the eve of World War II.

These observations are consistent with the socio-economic differences between the two communities. Viewed from the supply side, they reflect the skill and educational advantages of the Jewish population and its labor force, and – from the demand side – the skill requirements of the relatively modern and more complex Jewish economy, and the emphasis on developing and maintaining high levels of education and health services within the Jewish community. An additional possible factor operating on the demand side might have been the demand of non-Jews for professional

[13] Although in the standard occupational classification "sales workers" are viewed as belonging to the "white collar" category (see, for example, *Historical Statistics of the US*, 1975, part I, series D 182–232), the large number of hucksters and peddlers, which, in the case of Palestine, could not be separated from other sales workers, warrants the separation.

services, to which some Jewish professionals were able and willing to respond.

Moving now to the labor market, two major issues are addressed: the nature and operation of the labor market in the context of Palestine's ethno-national divide, and the macro-economic mechanisms linking the rapidly growing Jewish population (and labor supply) with the demand for labor and the level and pace of aggregate economic activity.

The labor market

Data pertaining to Palestine's labor market in general, and to its Arab component in particular, are quite limited in scope and quality, which imposes serious constraints on our ability to describe it systematically. The principal features of the market in terms of wages, patterns of employment, and labor organization can, however, be crudely outlined.

The most prominent characteristic of wages was the persistent differential along ethno-national lines. Throughout the entire Mandatory period Jews earned higher wages than their Arab counterparts in virtually all industries and occupations. As shown in table 4.6, the differences ranged from a few percentage points to extremely large gaps of about 300 percent (see also Sussman, 1974).

Note that most of the reported figures are daily wages, and since the working day was longer in the Arab sector than in the Jewish sector (eight to ten as opposed to mostly eight hours in manufacturing and construction, for example, see *Wage Rates Statistics Bulletin*, no. 4, 1937), the wage gap in hourly terms was even wider. Similar gaps are also observed in public-sector employment at the central government level (be it departmental regular staff, contract, or casual labor), although not in all municipalities.

Conceptually, one would expect that in a "frictionless," fully competitive market, with uninterrupted and costless labor mobility, only heterogeneous workers who are not perfect substitutes for one another in production would earn different wages. Labor heterogeneity could reflect variations in personal abilities, productivity differences due to variations in age and education, and/or dissimilarities in occupation-specific skills and know-how among workers. The existence of a "frictionless" labor market, though, does not necessarily prevent possible frictions in other segments of the economy from affecting the distribution of human capital, labor productivity, and hence the dispersion of wages. Take, for example, the high costs and often poor quality of education and health services provided in traditional-rural (or otherwise deprived) sectors, thus reinforcing segmented socio-economic structures, which are

Table 4.6. Jewish-Arab wage differentials

A Non-public employment; lowest (L) and highest (H) Jewish/Arab ratios of daily wages (Arab wage=1) across occupations in each year

	1931	1935	1939	1945
masons	(L) 1.100	(L) 1.182		
weavers	(H) 3.750	(H) 3.182		
fitters (metal industry)			(L) 1.177	
workers in soap factories			(H) 2.946	
citrus wrappers				(L) 1.050
plowers				(H) 2.500

B Public employment; lowest (L) and highest (H) Jewish/Arab wage ratios (Arab wage=1), by category

	1934/35	1935/36	1944/45
government employment			
regular staff	(H) 3.180		(L) 1.264
contract labor	(H) 2.918	(L) 2.542	
casual labor		(L) 1.775	
		(H) 2.683	
municipalities			
Jerusalem			(L) 0.921
Tel-Aviv		(H) 3.141	

Sources: Memoranda (1937), p. 141; *Wage Rate Statistics Bulletin*, no. 1, 1937, table 3, no. 9, 1940, table 4; *Survey* (1946), vol. II, pp. 773–80; *Supplement to Survey of Palestine* (1947), p. 92

identified, among other features, by inter-sectoral labor productivity gaps (see the discussion of organizational dualism in chapter 1). The effect of the disparity between the self-provided public services (primarily educa-tion and health) in the Jewish community, let alone the immigrants' rela-tively high stock of human capital, and those utilized by Arabs (see chapters 2 and 3) on the attributes of the labor force in the two communi-ties are cases in point.

However, differences in labor-force characteristics between otherwise distinguishable ethnic and socio-economic groups may contribute to observed wage gaps, even within the same occupations and skill cate-gories. Such an outcome is possible when it is costly to obtain information on the qualifications of workers, and potential employers economize on the cost of search by resorting to signals derived from applicants' group identity as a substitute for screening and individual selection. Under these circumstances, workers belonging to groups generally perceived to be of low labor productivity may be paid lower wages than their marginal productivity even in a competitive labor market, thereby creating "unjustifiable" wage gaps between employees who possess comparable labor market skills. A reinforcing implication of the signaling-produced wage differential may be a self-fulfilling supply response by members of "inferiorly" signaled groups, who may be discouraged from investing in education, because they expect low returns.

On the other hand, it can be argued that, in the context of a dual economy, workers with work experience in the modern sector, even if otherwise unskilled, cannot be perfectly substituted by seemingly identical "raw labor" from peasant agriculture, which needs to be trained and adjusted to regular (usually non-farm) wage employment. It follows that in a (distortionless) dual labor market, firms in the modern sector would benefit from paying a wage premium to a stable and experienced labor force, thereby economizing on high turnover and adjustment costs (Myint, 1985; Taubman and Wachter, 1986). From the workers' point of view, such a premium, reflecting genuine productivity disparities, would also serve as a differential, compensating them for the psychological cost of migrating from the village to the city, and for the higher cost of living in the city.

With due respect to those attributes of "organizational dualism" (à la Myint) that provide an economic rationale for wage gaps in competitive and undistorted labor markets, there remain gaps that cannot be explained away by labor heterogeneity, geographic factors, or information and search costs, and these reflect labor-market distortions. Such gaps include, among others, the exploitation of market power by employers or labor unions, institutionally determined (minimum) wages, restrictions on migration, and various discriminatory attitudes leading to entry barriers and differential labor-market practices (either voluntarily or socially and institutionally imposed), adversely affecting certain groups.

Wage differentials may also be caused, or reinforced, by factors external to the labor market *per se*; for example, constraints on inter-sectoral capital mobility (see the discussion in the section on capital, above), which could hinder capital movements from labor-scarce (and probably capital-abundant) sectors to labor-abundant (and probably capital-scarce) ones, thereby inhibiting inter-sectoral wage convergence. Another case in point could be the negative effect of ethnic residential segregation on labor mobility, confining residentially restricted groups to local labor markets in which they may raise the supply of labor and reduce wages (see Lewin-Epstein and Semyonov, 1992, 1993, on economic inequality between Arabs and Jews in Israel).

The common structural manifestation of all these factors is a segmented labor market, in which wages and employment are determined separately (possibly by different rules) within each segment, although not independently of one another, especially insofar as the supply response of labor is concerned. For instance, the economic development literature that dwells on the dual economy variant of the segmented labor market (modern or "primary" versus traditional or "secondary" sectors) tends to emphasize the pull effect of high wages in the modern sector on rural labor. Workers from the traditional sector are attracted by higher earning prospects in the modern sector, and tend to queue for high-paid urban jobs as long as the (present) value of their expected earning (taking into account the cost of waiting) in the modern sector is larger than that of their forgone earnings in the traditional sector. These patterns contribute to the widely observed phenomenon of rural emigration coupled with urban agglomeration and unemployment in developing countries (and often enough in developed economies characterized by segmented labor markets, as well). However, when urban jobs are available on a casual basis, or where distances are not too large, it is not always necessary to exit from the rural sector in order to realize non-farm earning prospects; workers can take up mixed rural-urban employment, queuing for jobs is less onerous and unemployment is diminished, while wage gaps are maintained (Harris and Todaro, 1970; Tidrick, 1975; Taubman and Wachter, 1986; Dickens and Lang, 1992).

Returning to the labor market of Mandatory Palestine equipped with the list of commonly suggested causes of persistent wage differentials, what we should ideally have done is empirically to have isolated the factors "responsible" for the observed wage gaps between Arabs and Jews and quantitatively assessed their respective weights. Differentiation between labor heterogeneity, general attributes of market segmentation, and Palestine-specific features should have been particularly illuminating in this respect. The paucity of data precludes such a systematic examination of Palestine's wage determination, and we are left with a "second-best" option of reviewing, rather impressionistically, the fragmented evidence available and discussing its implications.

As already mentioned, the large discrepancies in educational attainment and composition of skills may explain a good part of the disparities in the occupational structures of Arabs and Jews, and hence some of the overall differences in their labor earnings. The same factors may well explain some of the wage gaps in government employment, which was ethno-nationally reported by type of employment (regular, casual, or contractual) but not by occupation. Moreover, the literacy and schooling advantage of the Jewish labor force could also have induced a labor-productivity edge within occupations, including those requiring only plain (unskilled) labor; this possibility was pointed out in contemporary observations and in later interpretations (see Sussman, 1974).

However, since no breakdown of labor-force characteristics is available at the occupational level, it is impossible to determine how much of the intra-occupation wage gap can be attributed to possible productivity differences between Arab and Jewish workers, and how much to the structure of the labor market. Nonetheless, in view of the large recorded wage disparities, especially in low-skill occupations, it seems safe to suggest that Jews earned appreciably higher wages than did Arab workers of comparable productivity (see also Sussman, 1974). This implies that a major – possibly *the* major – part of the wage gap between the workers of the two communities should be accounted for by structural and institutional factors segmenting the labor market.

Some of these factors were undoubtedly of a general nature, reflecting the attributes of "ordinary" economic dualism characterizing Palestine's ethno-national divide. Reference is here to: (a) "hidden" productivity differences between laborers of peasant origin and the more experienced, even if unskilled, urban work force, and the related demand side response to distinguishing signals preserving the "modern"-"traditional" wage gap; (b) "pull" effects of comparatively high-wage urban jobs coupled with demographic pressure on rural resources and additional factors (such as capital-market dualism) "pushing" peasants out of traditional agriculture; (c) institutional constraints (such as union power) barring clearance of the urban labor market, thus inducing "time-sharing" of non-farm jobs by workers moving between village and town, and possibly also queuing for urban jobs, causing unemployment among rural emigrants.

A comparison of Arab agricultural product per worker in the 1930s (P£20 in 1931, P£33 in 1935, and P£25 in 1939 – chapter 5) with the *lowest* recorded non-farm annual wages earned by Arabs, namely, unskilled construction workers (P£31, P£35, and P£27 on the basis of 250 yearly work days in 1931, 1935, and 1939, respectively: *Wage Rate Statistics Bulletin*, 1927–35, 1940), shows that the income of urban labor was definitely higher than the value added per worker in Arab agriculture. Moreover, since the value-added figures include income accruing to agricultural land and capital, this means that urban earnings were higher than the opportunity costs, not only of Arab agricultural wage laborers, but of the average landowning peasant as well. Only the steep increase in demand for agricultural produce during World War II raised the level of product per worker in Arab agriculture fast enough to substantially reduce, in the first half of the 1940s, the wage advantage of non-farm occupations.

The observations of the relative attractiveness of non-agricultural pursuits are compatible with the decline in the relative share of Arab agricultural employment, from 64.1 percent in 1922 to 54.1 percent in 1935 (in the late 1930s, during the depression which affected mainly non-farm production, the share rose again, to 58.2 percent in 1939, see table A.5). Likewise, they are consistent with evidence on non-agricultural use of labor within rural areas (largely by the government's Public Works Department) and on Arab internal migration, primarily from the hill country to the coastal plain's urban localities (Bachi, 1977; Kamen, 1991). However, regardless of the labor-supply response to the farm/non-farm income differentials, their persistence indicates that the adjustment process may have been sluggish and incomplete. This inference is supported by fragmentary government figures, suggesting that Arab unemployment – about 7–10 percent of the labor force – was high relative to unemployment among Jews – 2–4 percent at least in the early 1930s (*Sikumim*, 3–5, 1931–33).

This picture represents typical (often slow) patterns of inter-sectoral reallocation of labor in developmentally divided dual economies, which may well have evolved in Palestine even if the ethno-national split had never existed (although not necessarily in the absence of economic growth, which was nourished by Jewish immigration and capital inflow), with the Arab-Jewish economic divide playing an intensifying role. Outside the labor market, one could point to the contribution of the unilateral land transactions between Arabs and Jews to the declining land-labor ratio in the Arab rural sector and to the rising supply of Arab wage labor. Similarly, the ethno-nationally segregated nature of the capital market may also have added impetus to the increasing supply of Arab labor seeking employment outside the economic domain of the Arab community.

But the major contributing factors in this regard were undoubtedly the ethno-national features of segregation within the labor market itself. The exclusion of (mainly unskilled) Arab wage labor from the Jewish economy in general, and from its agricultural industry in particular, as epitomized by the notion of *avoda ivrit* (Jewish labor), was a basic tenet of Zionist ideology and policy of economic nationalism. Indeed, the Zionist Organization used persuasion, socio-political pressure, and the limited coercive means at its disposal – for example enforcing the "Jewish labor only" rule on lessees of "national land" – to further its aims (Metzer, 1978; and chapter 6).

Preventing "cheap" Arab labor from competing with Jewish workers was to be instrumental in keeping Jewish wages high enough to attract potential immigrants to Palestine and induce newcomers to turn to agriculture and other blue-collar, manual occupations. This outcome was to have provided the necessary ingredients for a Jewish territorial entity founded on agriculture to develop, while preventing it from becoming a colonialist-type settlement that relies on hired indigenous labor. In addition, by maintaining labor "self-sufficiency," the necessary conditions for turning the immigrating Jews into an occupationally well-balanced community and a territorial nation in the making was to have been secured (Metzer, 1978, 1979; and chapter 6).

The segregation postulate required Jewish employers to self-impose voluntarily, or involuntarily adhere to restrictions on hiring Arab workers, thereby causing a misallocation of resources in the Jewish economy. The resulting output loss could therefore be interpreted as the "price" paid for fulfilling Zionist national goals in the economic sphere, which itself could conceptually be viewed as a public good, generating non-pecuniary psychological income to be derived from the success of the nation-building endeavor and accruing to the entire Jewish population of Palestine (on nationalism as a public good see Breton, 1964; Breton and Breton, 1995; and for the application to Palestine see Metzer, 1978).

However, as argued by Breton (1964) and by Breton and Breton (1995), the public-good attributes of nationalism are generally not sufficient to explain investment in it; for a full explanation one has to resort to its distributional aspects in terms of material income. The interference with frictionless allocations of resources caused by nationally motivated economic discrimination typically generates gains in pecuniary income to be captured by those groups who benefit materially from the discrimination, besides their psychological income gains. These material gains, however, are a transfer from the rest of the national community, since the net output effect of economic nationalism is negative (at least in the short run). It follows that investment in economic nationalism may be the result of the dominant political position of groups that stand to gain from it materially and of the ability of such groups to convince the rest of the national community to substitute non-pecuniary gains of nationalism for material income.

In the labor scene of Palestine, Jewish workers would be the major material beneficiaries from an Arab-excluding Jewish labor market, whereas Jewish employers, primarily owners of labor-intensive citrus groves, were to be its great losers. This brings into the picture the Zionist labor movement and its unified organizational and political organ, the *Histadrut* (see chapter 1), which were obviously chief advocates of ethno-national segregation in the labor market.

As Breton's model of economic nationalism predicts, the Jewish labor movement operated on two fronts in attempting to bar Arab unskilled labor from the Jewish labor market. One was the "public opinion" front: it stressed national arguments for labor-market segregation that were largely advocated by most Zionist leaders and factions, and claimed that the non-pecuniary "social" gains of promoting Jewish nationality outweighed any pecuniary private loss that may arise (Sussman, 1973; Metzer, 1978, 1979). The second front was "organizational." Using its dominant position in the Jewish labor market, the *Histadrut* utilized the standard means of organized labor – strikes, aggressive picketing, and various forms of arm-twisting – to deter Jewish (private) employers from hiring "unorganized" manual workers in general, and Arab workers in particular (see Shapira, 1977). Needless to say, in the *Histadrut*'s own productive establishments the exclusiveness of Jewish labor was strictly maintained.

This struggle can also be looked at in the context of the *Histadrut*'s attempts to institutionalize a minimum wage safety net for unskilled Jewish workers and make it compatible with its basic goal of securing and expanding employment in the Jewish economy. Being fully aware of the cost in terms of rising unemployment that could result from an effective minimum (above the market-clearing) wage, the *Histadrut* aimed at containing its potentially adverse effects on Jewish employment by striving to prevent labor from being hired at a lower wage. To this end, and in addition to its efforts to segregate the labor market along ethno-national lines, the *Histadrut* pushed for a country-wide minimum wage legislation, and also sought to promote unionization among Arab workers so as to raise their minimum supply wage and reduce their substitutability for Jewish workers.[14] These endeavors failed on both counts (Sussman, 1974; Taqqu, 1977; and chapter 1). Particularly noticeable was the low level of Arab unionization: according to the government's estimates, only 15,000–20,000 Arab workers belonged to any labor union in 1945 (*Survey*, 1946, vol. II, chap. 17). Taking the total number of Arab employees in the mid-1940s to be 140,000–150,000, of whom 100,000 were non-farm workers (Taqqu, 1980), it follows that union membership accounted for no more than 10–15 percent of all Arab wage earners: Even if we assume that all Arab union members were non-farm workers, the proportion of organized workers among the latter would not have exceeded 20 percent, a far cry from the extent of unionization in the Jewish community.

In 1935, before the Arab revolt halted most inter-war Arab-Jewish economic relations, 12,000 Arabs – more than in any other year – were esti-

---

[14] For interpretations of these issues, policies, and outcomes based on various sociological approaches to segmented labor markets, see Kimmerling (1983a); Shafir (1989); Grinberg (1991); Shalev (1992); Bernstein (1996).

mated to have been employed by Jews, 7,000 of them in (mostly citrus) agriculture – 1,800 each in manufacturing and construction, and 1,400 in services. They accounted for about 5 percent of the entire Arab labor force, and for about 8.5 percent of all persons employed in the Jewish economy that year. The latter percentage, while lower than the analogous shares of 14 percent and 10 percent in 1921 and 1931 respectively, was quite large (table A.5; BMZ, table A5).[15]

Given the possible substitution between self-employment and wage labor, which is largely determined by the opportunity cost of labor in terms of (actual or imputed) wages, it is indeed the size of the relevant labor force, or the volume of total employment, that should be taken as the denominator of the compared ratios. But when considering the profile of wage earners in a particular sector, the appropriate basis for comparison should be the total number of employees in that sector.

Viewed thus, the weight of Arab labor hired by Jews in the inter-war period becomes even more significant. In 1931, before the massive immigration of the 1930s, the 7,000 Arabs estimated to have been employed by Jews constituted some 20–23 percent of all wage earners in the Jewish economy (*Census of Jewish Workers*, 1926; Sussman, 1974). In 1935, at the peak of Jewish immigration, the 12,000 Arabs working in the Jewish sector constituted 15–17 percent of all the wage earners in the Jewish sector (*Census of Jewish Workers*, 1937; Sussman, 1974). Assuming, on the basis of the assessments made by Sussman (1974) and Taqqu (1980), that the share of all self-employed Arabs was between 30 percent and 40 percent of the Arab labor force (totaling 227,000 and 255,000 in 1931 and 1935 respectively; table A.4), employment in the Jewish sector in 1931 was between 8 percent and 10 percent of all Arab wage earners, and in 1935 11 percent to 15 percent.

These figures clearly demonstrate that the unskilled labor market was far from segregated. Moreover, Sussman (1973) has shown that wages in the Jewish economy were largely market determined and not institutionally set, and that the supply of unskilled Arab labor imposed an effective ceiling on the wages of unskilled Jewish labor, creating a fairly large wage differential between skilled and unskilled Jewish employees. Nonetheless, the Arab-Jewish wage gaps shown in table 4.6 strongly suggest that the labor market, if not segregated, was definitely ethno-nationally segmented. The wages earned by Arabs in the Jewish economy, though apparently higher than the alternative wage in the Arab economy, were *ceteris paribus*, lower than the wages earned by Jews (Sussman, 1974).

---

[15] Note, for comparison, that Arab workers from the West Bank and Gaza combined did never account for more than 6 percent of all employed persons in the post-1967 Israeli economy (Metzer, 1988).

It follows that although failing to exclude Arab (unskilled) labor from the Jewish labor market (Anita Shapira even chose the title *Futile Struggle* for her 1977 book on the Jewish labor controversy in inter-war Palestine), the ideological and organizational efforts in that direction seem to have imposed enough pressure and non-pecuniary costs on Jewish employers to limit the entry of Arab workers into the Jewish labor market, thus inhibiting wage convergence. Jewish employers of Arab labor may also have been tempted to recoup part of these costs (à la Gary S. Becker's *Economics of Discrimination*, 1971) by offering lower wages to Arab employees than to their Jewish counterparts. All in all, these Palestine-specific attributes evidently reinforced the more general factors in maintaining the wage gaps in Palestine's dual labor market.

The labor market was characterized not only by an Arab-Jewish wage gap, but also – and probably mainly – by the fact that regardless of the significant weight and wage effects of Arab labor supply and employment in the Jewish sector, most of the labor services supplied by Arabs and Jews were allocated and utilized within their respective ethno-national confines. For example, even if we added the largest number of Arabs employed by the government in the inter-war period (32,000 in 1939) to those employed by Jews in 1935 (12,000), we see that out of an Arab labor force of 255,000 in 1935 no less than 211,000 (83 percent) were either self-employed or employed by other Arabs – individuals or institutions. Going through the same exercise for the Jewish community, at most 5 percent of the Jewish labor force (7,000 out of 130,000) could have been employed by non-Jews in 1935 (Metzer and Kaplan, 1990, chap. 5; tables A.4, A.5).

The Arab labor scene, as already sketched, was largely shaped by responses to pressures and opportunities generated by population growth, changes within the rural sector (including the consequences of land sales to Jews), and external demand. Its main features were a rise in wage labor within and outside agriculture, commuting of rural labor, and exit from the village on a seasonal, temporary, and even permanent basis (see also Taqqu, 1980). Some of these adjustments, reallocations, and, possibly, displacement were externally forced upon Arab labor as kind of a "second best" or even "least worst" response, but others certainly reflected new economic opportunities, particularly during the boom years of the 1930s and the wartime high demand. On the whole, however, the growth of Arab productivity and output per capita (chapter 1) rules out the possibility that the changes involving Arab labor had a net adverse effect on the average standard of living in the Arab community. This does not mean, however, that a particular group (or groups) may not have experienced a decline, or a slower than average rise, in material well-being. Moreover, it is quite possible that, while the economic vigor of the rapidly growing Jewish community may have provided an impetus for the secular growth of Arab income, this growth might have been faster were it not for the constraints imposed on the labor market (and on other factor markets) by considerations of Jewish economic nationalism.

Labor and economic activity in the Jewish community

Turning now to the Jewish sector, the major issues in view of the massive – albeit fluctuating – immigration-induced increments to the labor force are the functioning of the labor market itself, and the mechanisms linking its supply-and-demand components to the level of and changes in aggregate production. Considering the operation of the labor market, one should certainly attempt to explore the dynamics of labor absorption by addressing such questions as: were wages and/or employment opportunities affected by work seekers' length of residence in the country? How was employment allocated in instances of excess supply of labor? What was the nature and pace of the adjustment of newcomers – occupation and earnings wise – to conditions in the local labor market?

As for wages, the scattered information on their structure and determination, as documented and interpreted by Sussman (1974), suggests that they were generally determined in a decentralized manner, being negotiated at the local and even single-establishment level by employers and rather autonomous *Histadrut* local "Workers' Committees." This process and its outcomes seemed to approximate quite closely the mechanism of wage determination in an unorganized competitive labor market, except, probably, for the widely adhered to, predetermined minimum wage paid to unskilled Jewish labor, which the *Histadrut* insisted upon.

But apart from securing an "accepted" wage level, a major concern of the *Histadrut* in formulating its labor policy was the allocation of available employment, at least in the short run, among Jewish "organized labor" – constituting about 75 percent of all Jewish wage earners since the early 1930s. The *Histadrut* played a key role in the placement of workers through its labor exchanges, especially when in temporary and seasonal jobs. The practice it followed, particularly in periods of excess labor supply, was to ration the scarce temporary employment offerings among as large a number of work seekers as possible. In so doing, the number of allotted (weekly or monthly) working days per worker was used as a means for achieving distributive equity of job opportunities, possibly at the expense of allocative efficiency (Sussman, 1974, pp. 85–86; BMZ, p. 161).

Another concern for equity was embodied in "wage-lists" by occupations, which the *Histadrut* circulated as guidelines for collective bargaining, aimed at achieving a regime of equal pay for equal work. While not binding in any way or form, these lists indicate that inter-occupational wage differentials existed between and within industries. Note, specifically, that in some of these lists (for example, occupational wages in construction in 1933), the suggested daily wage of "newly arrived" immigrants was about 20 percent lower than that of unskilled workers (Sussman, 1974, p. 69). Does this imply the existence of a labor productivity gap of exactly 20 percent between unskilled veterans and new immigrants? Not necessarily; but the possibility of an initial productivity gap, which may have narrowed in time, as immigrants adjusted to the local economy, should come as no surprise, and is supported also by the finding of secularly rising overall productivity in the Jewish economy.

Unfortunately, the lack of appropriate micro-data – for instance, wages earned by individuals that could in principle be matched with their demographic and socio-economic attributes – precludes any further systematic examination of the labor market's operational features. We are left with a few sporadic quantitative sources (mainly on employment and occupational adjustment), on which to base some speculative and tentative suggestions. One of these sources is the records of the Jewish Agency's "Recruitment Committees," which operated during World War II (see chapter 3); they contain some information on the employment status and labor market characteristics of about 5,000 males. An estimated logistic model fed by 3,467 observations from these records suggests that the chances of a Jewish male to have been employed in the mid-1940s were higher the older and more educated he was, and the longer he resided in Palestine.[16] There is obviously no basis to claim representativeness of the sample from which these findings were drawn, and any generalization based on them would be sheer guesswork; yet the conjecture that education and experience of both a general and Palestine-specific nature may have improved one's standing in the labor market seems convincing enough.

Another aspect of the adaptability of immigrants to Palestine's labor

---

[16] Of all the individual observations, only 3,467 contain information on age, year of immigration, and schooling in three discrete categories (primary, secondary, and higher education). The estimated logit regression for employment (EMP) as a dependent variable (value *one* for unemployed individuals, and *zero* for employed), and for age (AGE), years of residence in Palestine (RSP), and education (ED) as independent variables, is as follows (numbers in parentheses are standard errors):

$$\text{EMP} = 0.1032 - 0.0443\text{AGE} - 0.0223\text{RSP} - 0.3175\text{ED}.$$
$$\quad\;\;(0.2389)\;\;(0.00812)\quad\;(0.00917)\quad\;(0.0761)$$

conditions, besides mere experience, was their occupational suitability and adjustment. Some information on the retention and change of occupations can be obtained from the *General Census of Jewish Workers* which the *Histadrut* conducted in March 1937, following the peak years of the Fifth Aliya, 1933–35. The census cross-classified, among other enumerations, about 104,000 foreign-born wage earners and members of *kibbutzim* and *moshavim* by their occupations abroad and in Palestine. These workers constituted about 64 percent of the entire Jewish labor force – 163,000 in 1937 (table A.4); hence, although it did not record self-employed persons, the census covered a large enough proportion of the immigrant worker population.

The *Census* reports that of the workers who had known occupations in Palestine (101,500 in total), 83.4 percent held gainful jobs, or at least were listed as holding a certain occupation in their countries of origin; 16.3 percent were pupils or students prior to immigration; and the rest (3.3 percent) were listed as not having worked abroad at all. Of those who held a known occupation in 1937 and were gainfully employed before immigration, only 22 percent retained their pre-migration occupations; the remaining 78 percent changed them in Palestine, at least temporarily.

Note that when roughly dividing the range of occupations into two groups, "blue- collar" (consisting of material production, services, transportation, and plain labor) and "white collar" (clerical jobs, teaching, medicine, and other professions), it turns out that of the foreign-born workers who were gainfully employed abroad, 81 percent held "blue collar" jobs in Palestine and 19 percent held "white collar" jobs, whereas in the countries of origin the occupational composition of the same group of people was 73 percent and 27 percent respectively. This implies that about 90 percent of the immigrants' occupational changes occurred within each of the two broadly defined occupational groups, and only about 10 percent shifted from "white" to "blue collar" jobs. Note, too, that in responding to the question about occupations abroad, some of the respondents may have referred to occupations they acquired in pre-immigration-preparatory programs sponsored by the Zionist Organization and youth movements. It therefore follows that the occupational adaptation process of Jewish immigrants may have been even more extensive than implied by the 1937 census.

But occupational change and allocative shifts inside the labor market, substantial as they may have been, are only part of the complex process involving both micro- and macro-economic effects of – and adjustments to – immigration-induced changes in labor supply. At the aggregate level we may ask, with respect to the long run, what the growth implications of the steep rise in the supply of labor were; and, considering the short run, what was the mechanism linking the cyclical patterns of overall economic activity to fluctuations in immigration and labor. Fortunately, compared to the disaggregate components of the labor market and the economy at large, better data are at hand regarding their aggregate aspects, allowing, as done by Beenstock, Metzer, and Ziv (BMZ) for a rather systematic examination of their interplay.

It has already been shown that immigration, being well endowed with human capital, was accompanied by a substantial inflow of physical capital, thereby enabling the rapidly growing labor force to be supported by an even faster increase in the supply of capital. These patterns led to a secular rise in total output, which by its very nature could be facilitated only by the growth of inputs and/or total factor productivity.

BMZ found that productivity in the Jewish economy was rising, among non-identifiable determinants, due to endogenously accumulated experience; this could be attributed, at least in part, to the increase in productive capacity of labor while "learning by doing." It could thus be argued that the massive increase in the supply of Jewish labor, besides accounting directly for the rise in output, contributed to the growth process indirectly as well, via the probable realization of economies of scale (at the aggregate level), and long-run advances in productivity.

In the short run, the direct link between immigration and total factor productivity that has been econometrically established by BMZ demonstrates that, other things being equal, swings in immigration induced fluctuations in similar directions in the *level* of measured productivity. This finding suggests that immigration may have exerted a beneficial, temporary effect on productivity. It was as if an extra "national effort" was made by the resident population and by immigrants, when immigration intensified, to stretch the economy's productive capability so as to absorb the newcomers.

While a complete explanation of this empirical phenomenon is difficult to come by, it may, at least in part, be understood in terms of variations in the intensity of resource utilization. These may reflect, to some extent, the stretching of short-run overall production beyond the long-run sustained capacity at a given technology, as an initial supply response to positive demand shocks, caused in our case by upward swings in immigration (see Fischer, Dornbusch, and Schmalensee, 1988, chap. 31, for the general argument; and Ben-Porath, 1986a, for Mandatory Palestine and Israel).

This phenomenon enabling the incremental demand generated by the upsurges of immigration to be partly met by short-run extra efforts of non-idle resources and partly by the rise in the immigration-driven supply of labor, led to an immediate increase in employment and output. However, BMZ also found (somewhat counter-intuitively) that the intensification of immigration was reflected by an immediate rise in real wages and a decline in unemployment. This suggests that, notwithstanding the increase in labor utilization and supply caused by the upturn of immigration, it was the increase in the demand for labor, derived from its induced rise of aggregate demand for output, that dominated the labor-market scene in the short run.

Likewise, the slowing down of immigration and capital inflow did have an adverse effect on aggregate demand and caused a decline in the derived labor demand, probably to a larger extent than the downturn in productivity and labor utilization at ongoing wages. This allowed the lagged effect of the immigration-driven growth in the supply of labor to take its toll in the form of cyclically rising unemployment, coupled with a fall in real wages (for a similar argument in a more general context involving immigration to the state of Israel see Ben-Porath, 1986a). Moreover, BMZ show that the above-discussed *Histadrut* policy of labor rationing introduced an element of productive inefficiency, thereby intensifying the immigration-linked cyclical swings of productivity and output.

It follows, rather paradoxically, that the hot political issue regarding the limits of Palestine's absorptive capacity (which, from an economic point of view, could be framed only in short-run static terms, see also Halevi, 1979, 1983) may have grown more acute in instances of immigration downswings and not, as one might have thought, in instances of extensive influx of people.

5 Production and trade

As a natural sequel to the account of Palestine's productive resources, we turn in this chapter to the "output and trade" side of their utilization. The first part of the discussion considers production and productivity in the aggregate, and across and within industries; the second part addresses some issues concerning the scope and structure of foreign and inter-communal trade.

Production

Structure and dynamics

The available estimates of inputs – annual series of capital and employment in the Jewish economy and a few benchmark figures of labor and capital in the Arab economy – combined with our newly constructed output series allow for a crude summary description of aggregate production in the two sectors (see tables A.4, A.22–A.26; BMZ, tables A4–A6). This is done within a "growth-accounting" framework[1] in table 5.1, which suggests orders of magnitude for the growth rates of labor and reproducible capital, for their combined contribution to the expansion of output, and for the "residual" growth of output, not accounted for by the increase in inputs.

---

[1] When labor (L) and capital (K) are assumed to be the only (long-run) variable factors of production, the combined contribution of their growth rates ($L^\star$ and $K^\star$ respectively) to that of output ($Y^\star$) is calculated under the assumption of constant returns to scale in production (i.e., an increase of all inputs by a certain rate generates a rise in output by the same rate) as:

$$aL^\star + (1-a)K^\star.$$

It follows that the "residual" growth of output ($A^\star$) is given by:

$$A^\star = Y^\star - [aL^\star + (1-a)K^\star].$$

The "a" coefficient stands for the output share of labor (which, assuming competitive factor markets, is typically approximated by the ratio of the overall costs of labor to total output) and $(1-a)$ is the output share of capital.

Table 5.1. *Palestine's growth accounting, 1922–47*

		Arabs		Jews
annual rates of change (%)				
(1) NDP		6.5		13.2
(2) labor		2.6		8.8
(3) capital		4.2		11.6
	I[a]		II[a]	
(4) TFP	2.9		3.6	3.5
contribution to NDP growth (%)[b]				
(5) labor & capital	55.4		44.6	73.5
(6) TFP	44.6		55.4	26.5

Notes:
[a] Possible TFP growth rates for alternative factor shares were calculated as follows:

$\quad$ (I) = (1) − [0.4×(2) + 0.6×(3)]

$\quad$ (II) = (1) − [0.8×(2) + 0.2×(3)] .

[b] (5) = 100×[(1)−(4)]/(1); (6) = 100−(5).

Sources: all rates of change in the Jewish sector: BMZ, table A6; annual rates of change of NDP, labor, and capital in the Arab sector from tables A.4, A.22, A.25

If production is correctly specified and accurately quantified, the derived "residual" may be viewed as a reasonable approximation of the growth of overall productivity, which is interpreted as a change in the flow of output per combined unit of utilized inputs. Hence the term "total factor productivity" (TFP) used in the growth-accounting literature for the "residual." However, it is quite clear that by its very nature, the size of the residual is highly sensitive to misspecifications and to empirical omissions and errors in measurement. For example, not accounting for increasing returns to scale in production when they are present, failing to correct the quantity of labor for differences in the endowment of human capital among employed persons, or not adjusting for possible changes in the extent of factor utilization all affect the size of the residual, even if, when properly measured, TFP did not change at all. Having said that, and keeping all the reservations in mind, the empirical growth literature nevertheless takes the residual-type measure of TFP as a rough indication, particularly on a comparative basis, of the extent to which the growth of output is generated by other than conventionally measured factors of production (see, for example, Maddison, 1995).

Viewed thus, the numbers in table 5.1 suggest that a substantial advance in productivity may have been an integral component of overall growth in the Arab and Jewish economies, and that their average growth rates of TFP were of similar orders of magnitude (but since the growth of total output in the Jewish economy was much faster than in the Arab economy, the relative contribution of TFP to the increase in output was substantially higher in the latter; see the discussion in chapter 1). Moreover, if the proportion of such land transferred from Arabs to Jews that was economically utilized either prior to and/or after the transfer could be assessed and incorporated in our growth-accounting exercise, the extent of output growth ascribed to the bundle of increasing inputs would have been larger in the Jewish sector and smaller in the Arab one. This implies that, other things being equal, the rates of change in TFP reported in table 5.1 should be taken as upper-bound estimates of the rates of productivity growth for the Jewish economy and as lower-bound estimates for the Arab economy.

Another factor working in the same direction relates to our inability, for lack of appropriate data, to account for the human capital attributes of labor. In view of the Jewish advantage in educational attainment (chapter 2), it is highly likely that incorporating a separate human capital input in our growth accounting would have further reduced the TFP element of Jewish economic growth, leaving a smaller unexplained residual.

As for the "genuine" productivity attributes of Palestine's growth record, some of them were certainly external to one or both ethnonational sectors. Take, for example, the government-built physical and administrative infrastructure, providing external economies to Arab and Jewish producers, or the intense economic activity in the Jewish sector, which may have generated some externalities, positively affecting productivity in the Arab domestic economy.

Other mechanisms enhancing the secular growth of productivity evolved internally, partly as a response to external effects. Besides improvements in the technology of production generally associated with time, one can think of the following features in the context of Mandatory Palestine: (a) adjustment of Jewish immigrants to their new economic environment, which increased their productive capacity and overall productivity (see chapter 4); this mechanism is closely linked to endogenous elements of secular productivity and output growth, embodied in learning-by-doing and accumulation of experience, as emphasized in the new-growth literature, and found to have raised TFP in the Jewish economy;[2] (b) adoption of improved methods of production, derived from government extension programs and from applied research and various kinds of

---

[2] For a review of the recent growth literature, see "New Growth Theory" (1994), and the references cited there. For the Jewish economy, see BMZ.

technological spill-overs and demonstration effects, which were generated primarily by modern Jewish agriculture (see below); (c) increasing
utilization of productive resources and their gainful reallocation in
response to external changes in demand; for example, the utilization and
reallocation effect of rising demand for exported citrus fruit from the
mid-1920s to the mid-1930s, of increasing Jewish demand for Arab
goods and services up to the mid-1930s, and of growing British (and
Allied) demand for Palestine's output during World War II.

However, plausible as these suggested mechanisms are, an empirical
assessment of their contribution to overall productivity is practically
impossible in view of the extremely speculative and highly aggregate
nature of key quantities in our estimated growth-accounting scheme.
Moreover, the accounting in table 5.1 – illuminating as it may be in quan-
tifying the contribution of inputs and productivity to aggregate economic
growth – provides only limited information on the structure of production
in the Arab and Jewish economies. For further insight into the structural
features, their change, and the ingredients of productivity advance, one
must examine the industrial composition of employment and production,
and the activity within single industries in a comparative framework.

In examining the industrial breakdown of table 5.2, the most conspicu-
ous observation that stands out clearly is the substantial and persistent
disparity between the industrial structures of employment and output in
the two economies, especially evident in the relative shares of agriculture
and manufacturing. This dissimilarity is consistent with, and serves an
integral component of, the socio-economic profiles, developmentally distinguishing between the two communities within a generally dualistic
context (see also chapter 1).

The reported structures are also roughly compatible with the two
sectors' respective positions on the international comparative scale,
linking the industrial structure of production and employment with the
level of income per capita. But for Arabs and Jews alike, the observed proportion (both employment and output wise) of agriculture and material
product generally was lower in the mid-1930s and that of non-agricultural industries – primarily services – higher than predicted by their
respective income levels (see Ofer, 1967; Syrquin, 1986; Metzer, 1992).

Possible explanations for the relatively high share of services in the Arab
sector could turn, in part, on demand factors associated with Palestine's
"location" at the traditional crossroads of long-haul commerce and
transit trade in the eastern Mediterranean, and on its being a destination
for multi-religion pilgrimage (Abramowitz and Guelfat, 1944). A similar
effect could have been generated by the demand of the Jewish sector for
transport, commercial, and personal services produced by Arabs.

Table 5.2. *Industrial composition of domestic product and employment (%)ᵃ and relative labor productivity in the Arab and Jewish economies*

	Arabs			Jews		
	NDP	employ-ment	RLPᵇ	NDP	employ-ment	RLPᵇ
1922						
agriculture	39.4	65.5	0.602	12.9	26.7	0.483
manufacturing	5.2	4.8	1.083	19.7	16.7	1.180
construction	1.8	1.6	1.125	12.5	13.3	0.940
services	53.6	28.1	1.907	54.9	43.3	1.268
total	*100.0*	*100.0*	*1.000*	*100.0*	*100.0*	*1.000*
1931						
agriculture	33.9	63.2	0.536	14.6	26.1	0.559
manufacturing	10.7	8.2	1.305	21.4	20.3	1.054
construction	3.2	2.3	1.391	6.7	8.7	0.770
services	52.2	26.3	1.985	57.3	44.9	1.276
total	*100.0*	*100.0*	*1.000*	*100.0*	*100.0*	*1.000*
1939						
agriculture	30.1	58.2	0.517	9.7	22.2	0.437
manufacturing	10.8	7.5	1.440	24.2	22.7	1.066
construction	1.3	1.4	0.929	3.9	3.0	1.300
services	57.8	32.9	1.757	62.2	52.1	1.194
total	*100.0*	*100.0*	*1.000*	*100.0*	*100.0*	*1.000*
1945						
agriculture	38.9	54.5	0.714	10.7	12.9	0.829
manufacturing	10.3	8.8	1.170	33.1	30.9	1.071
construction	2.4	5.0	0.480	6.0	4.3	1.395
services	48.4	31.7	1.527	50.2	51.9	0.967
total	*100.0*	*100.0*	*1.000*	*100.0*	*100.0*	*1.000*

Notes:
ᵃ Employment refers to persons employed in the domestic economy. Hence, Arabs employed by Jews are included in Jewish composition, but not in Arab composition of employment.
ᵇ RLP (Relative Labor Productivity) is defined for each industry as the ratio of its product to employment share, with aggregate relative productivity being equal to one by definition.
Sources: tables A.5, A.19, A.20; BMZ, tables A2, A5

As to the Jewish economy, following Ofer (1967) it may be suggested that the excess proportion of services was facilitated by three major characteristics: one was the large inflow of capital, which permitted a substantial surplus of imported over exported goods (see below) to induce some substitution between services and goods in the composition of domestic production (this argument applies in part to the Arabs as well). Moreover, part of the imported capital was unilaterally transferred to the Zionist public sector, providing the Jewish community with free resources that were used for the extensive self-provision of public services (see also Michaely, 1963; chapter 6). This mechanism was supply-linked to the second characteristic, namely the relatively large Jewish demand for education and health services (see chapter 2). Finally, one can point to the labor-supply effect of the service-oriented skill and occupational composition of the Jewish (immigrant) labor force, which, regardless of Zionist ideology emphasizing material production (see chapters 1, 3, 4, and 6), channeled labor to the relatively flexible service industry.

Looking at the structure of employment within each sector, separately, we observe that although not radically altered, it changed somewhat in the inter-war period. One prominent change was the continuous decline in agricultural employment. In the Arab economy, the steadily shrinking employment share of agriculture throughout the entire Mandate period reflected primarily the secular (albeit mild) exit from farming, as discussed earlier; in the inter-war Jewish economy, it was mainly a manifestation of the largely urban inclination of immigrants, most of whom were absorbed in towns. The major shift of Jewish labor from agriculture to manufacturing, however, occurred in the war years. Note, also, that the employment share of Jewish agriculture remained higher than that of manufacturing until the mid-1930s (21.8 percent versus 20.6 percent of Jewish workers only, and 24.9 percent versus 20.1 percent of all employed persons in the Jewish economy in 1935; table A.5).

The decline of labor-intensive citrus production in the second half of the 1930s, and its collapse during the war, which was only partly compensated for by the increasing wartime demand for locally produced foodstuffs (see below), contributed to the sharp relative and absolute reduction in agricultural employment; 37,000 persons were employed in Jewish agriculture in 1939 and 30,500 in 1945.[3] The considerable rise in the employment share of manufacturing was also mostly a response to the rising demand for manufactured goods generated by the Allied forces in the Mediterranean and by regional and local demand for import sub-

---

[3] These numbers were estimated by applying the labor-force shares derived from table A.5 to the figures of total employment from BMZ, table A5.

stitutes in the war-related regime of declining international trade (see Gross and Metzer, 1993, and the discussion below).

The Arab economy, on the other hand, while maintaining a secular declining trend in the employment share of agriculture throughout the war, was not sufficiently affected by the exogenous changes in demand to experience an absolute reduction in agricultural employment (the number of employed persons in Arab agriculture rose from 163,000 in 1939 to 186,000 in 1945: table A.5).

Generally, labor productivity in agriculture was relatively low in both the Arab and the Jewish economies (see the ratios of relative productivity by industry in table 5.2), and shifting labor away from agriculture to non-agricultural production should have contributed to an overall rise in output per worker. Indeed, over the entire period inter-industry reallocation of labor accounted for about 8 percent of the rise in aggregate NDP per employed person in the two economies (which grew by a factor of 1.15 in the Arab economy and of 1.263 in the Jewish economy between 1922 and 1945). In the Arab sector the effect of labor reallocation on productivity was primarily a pre-war phenomenon (making for 13.3 percent of the rise in NDP per employed person in 1922–39, but only 1.5 percent in 1939–45), but in the Jewish sector, not surprisingly in view of the figures in table 5.2, the labor reallocation effect was noticeable mainly during the war (contributing 13.5 percent in 1939–45 versus 4.6 percent in 1922–39 to the increase in total NDP per worker).[4]

---

[4] Utilizing the estimates of production and employment by industry, the change in NDP per employed person over a given time period was derived according to the following break-down:

$$y^* = (y_i/y)t_0(L_i/L)t_1y^*_i + (y_i/y)t_0[(L_i/L)t_1 - (L_i/L)t_0] \, ,$$

where: y =   aggregate product per employed person
          y^* = percentage growth of aggregate product per employed person
          y_i = product per employed person in the i-th industry
          y^*_i = percentage growth of product per employed person in the i-th industry
          L =   total employment
          L_i = number of employed persons in the i-th industry
          t_0 = base year
          t_1 = end year

The Arab employment figures by industry are from table A.5; the Jewish figures were generated by applying the percentages of the labor force's industrial breakdown in table A.5 to the total employment estimates in BMZ, table A5. The product estimates by industry in constant (1936) prices were generated, for the industries of material production in 1922–39, from the output figures in constant prices (tables A.11, A.14, A.16), to which their respective product-output ratios in current prices were applied; and for services, as a residual, subtracting from the NNP estimates in constant prices (table A.22) the value added of material production. The product figures by industry in 1945 were calculated for both sectors on the basis of the (possibly somewhat strong) assumption that the industrial structure was percent-wise the same for NNP in current prices and in 1936 prices.

However, significant as the reallocation of labor between industries may have been, the reported orders of magnitude reveal that as far as the growth of aggregate production and labor productivity are concerned, most of the "action," both in the Arab and Jewish economies, remained within industries. Let us therefore take a closer look at some of the attributes of structure and change in the two major industries of material production: agriculture and manufacturing.

Agriculture

Taking the period as a whole, agriculture, despite its decreasing employment and output share and its relatively low labor productivity, was obviously not a declining or even a stagnant industry in either sector. Rather, according to our estimates, net farm product in constant prices grew at a healthy 6 percent per annum in 1922–45 in the Arab economy (identical to the rate at which Arab aggregate product grew), and at an extremely rapid rate of 12.6 percent annually in the Jewish economy, only slightly lower than total Jewish product (13.3 percent).

Moreover, combined with the comparatively slow increase in farm employment, these growth rates were high enough to cause output per worker in agriculture to rise faster than in any other industry over the entire period, and thereby diminish the relative inferiority of agricultural (labor) productivity in both sectors. In the Arab sector, agricultural product per worker grew at an average rate of 4.1 percent annually in 1922–45, compared with 3.4 percent for total product per worker; in the Jewish sector, the respective growth rates were 6.1 percent and 3.6 percent.

While agricultural production expanded more or less steadily over the entire period, the citrus-dominated inter-war growth patterns are clearly different from those of the war years. Palestine's pre-war citrus industry, being almost completely dependent on external markets (between 80 and 90 percent of the citrus crops were exported), responded to changes in export prices by adjusting its productive capacity (figure 5.1). The high, and slightly rising, (moving) average prices in the first half of the 1920s[5] induced fast and continuously rising investment between the mid-1920s and the mid-1930s, increasing the area of citrus groves more than tenfold from 1924 to 1937 (figure 5.2). Similarly, by gradually adapting expectations to the declining prices of the 1930s, and interpreting them as indicating a long-term fall in demand, Palestine's (Arab and Jewish) citrus

[5] They reflected the post-World War I acceleration in European demand for citrus fruit, largely due to consumers' enthusiasm for the newly discovered vitamins contained in them; see Gross (1984a) and the references cited there.

growers reduced investment in this industry from the mid-1930s onward, bringing the expansion of planted areas to a halt by 1937 (figures 5.1, 5.2).

Note, however, that since it takes about six years before a newly planted grove starts producing marketable quantities of fruit, the substantial investments undertaken before the mid-1930s led to an uninterrupted increase in citrus productive capacity. Given the competition prevailing in the field, this capacity turned into a continuous rise in output and volume of exports throughout the decade (figure 5.2).

Over the inter-war period as a whole (1922–39), the volume of citrus output grew thirteenfold, by far surpassing the twofold increase in non-citrus farm output, and raising the weight of citrus (both crops and investments in young groves) in the country's total agricultural output from 11 percent in the first half of the 1920s to an average 50 percent in 1932–35. And although the citrus share of aggregate farm output declined to 41 percent in the second half of the 1930s, it remained the largest single agricultural branch on the eve of World War II (tables A.9, A.12).

The expansion of citrus was impressive not only in terms of domestic farm production, but also *vis-à-vis* the world market, where Palestine's s*hamouti* (Jaffa) oranges were much appreciated and, at least partly, demand-differentiated from other brands. In 1932 Palestine accounted for 11.3 percent of the world total export of citrus, and in 1935 for no less than 20 percent. Moreover, unlike other major citrus-exporting countries, in which citrus exports reached at most 26 percent of the dollar value of total merchandise exports (Spain in 1933), in Palestine citrus contributed 46 percent of all merchandise exports by 1932, reaching a peak of 84 percent in 1935, and ending the decade with a proportion of 74 percent in 1939 (Hazen, 1938).

Requiring large amounts of labor and capital inputs for husbandry, citrus production was a highly intensive undertaking, generating extremely high yields per unit of land relative to non-citrus crops. Note that in 1939, the year in which the largest pre-war volume of citrus was picked, citrus fruit accounted for no less than 54 percent of Palestine's overall crop output in value terms, whereas citrus groves covered only 5 percent of the country's total cultivated area (table A.6; Abramowitz and Guelfat, 1944, pp. 48–50; Gurevich and Gertz, 1947, pp. 46–60).

The substantial weight of citrus in farm output was particularly noticeable in the Jewish sector. Citrus already accounted for 36 percent of the entire Jewish agricultural output (produce and investment) in the early 1920s; the share peaked at 75 percent in the mid-1930s, declining to about 65 percent on the eve of the war. In the Arab economy, the

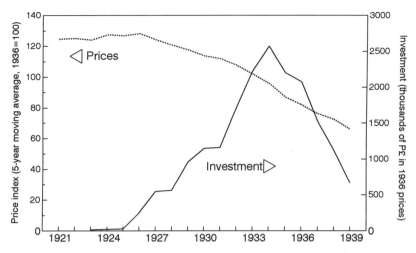

Figure 5.1 Index of citrus export prices and citrus investments in Palestine, 1921–39
(sources: tables A.7, A.8)

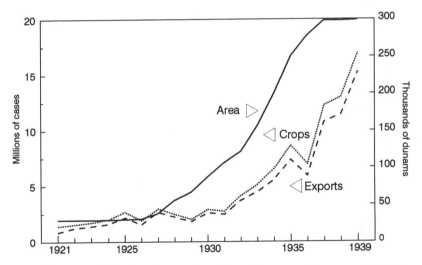

Figure 5.2 Palestine citrus: planted area,* crops, and exports, 1921–39
(source: table A.6)
* beginning of year

respective orders of magnitude were 6 percent, 35 percent, and 26 percent (table A.12).

Although citriculture played a relatively minor role in Arab agriculture, groves owned by Arabs had generated more than half (63 percent) of Palestine's citrus crop in the beginning of the Mandate period. Over the years massive Jewish investment in the field, which were almost twice as large as those of the Arabs (P£12,000 versus P£6,700 in 1936 prices between 1922 and 1939), enabled Jewish planted area and crops to catch up with those of the Arabs in the early 1930s, and then surpass them. By the end of the decade the initial proportions had been reversed, and Jews produced about 62 percent of all citrus fruit (tables A.6–A.9; Metzer and Kaplan, 1990, chapter 1).

Citrus was a capital- and labor-intensive cash crop commonly grown by private grove owners in both the Arab and the Jewish sectors. Furthermore, the available evidence, though largely impressionistic, suggests that the methods of production, too, did not differ much between Jews and Arabs. The relatively well-educated Jewish planters were able and willing to absorb and disseminate information about modern citriculture techniques (mainly those developed in California) through professional periodicals and other channels of communication. The diffusion of these techniques crossed sectoral boundaries and their (at least partial) adoption by Arab citrus growers provides a vivid illustration of technological demonstration effects (Gross, 1984a; Karlinsky, 1995).

Surveying the contemporary discussions in Jewish agricultural periodicals and in various reports, Karlinsky (1995) was able to show that modern technologies, which were based, *inter alia*, on electric energy for irrigation and on mechanized cultivation and packing, were not adopted indiscriminately. Given a variety of soil conditions, the size distribution of groves, the availability of productive resources, and the "path dependence" on time-honored methods of production, the choice of technique, including retention of "old techniques," seems to have been largely guided by perceived profitability. Moreover, in view of the rather narrow Jewish advantage in citrus yields per dunam relative to non-citrus crops,[6] it may be suggested that Jews and Arabs applied similar considerations in choosing methods and technologies, resulting in fairly similar productive performance.

---

[6] The Jewish-Arab average yield ratios were 1.12 for citrus (in 1921–39), and 2.74 for other field crops and fruit combined (in 1927 and 1937). Yields for citrus were calculated from sources to figs. 5.1 and 5.2, and for other crops from area and output estimates in Himadeh (1938), chap. IV; Abramowitz and Guelfat (1944), pp. 29–59; Kamen (1991), chap. 6; from the production series in Metzer and Kaplan (1990), chap. 1; and from table A.10.

Despite its importance and leading position in the inter-war growth of farm output, citriculture was in certain respects an atypical branch in both Arab and Jewish agriculture. In the Arab economy, its distinct nature was particularly eye-catching; the advanced, capitalistically managed cash-crop-type citrus growing was clearly set apart from the traditional, peasant, dry farming that dominated domestic agriculture. In the mid-to-late 1930s, citrus fruit covered only 2 percent of the 7.4 million dunams cultivated by Arabs, and they probably employed no more than 20 percent of the workers in Arab agriculture, while generating about 28 percent of its total output between 1935 and 1939 (tables A.6, A.12; Abramowitz and Guelfat, 1944, pp. 48–50; *Statistical Handbook*, 1947, p. 179).

In Jewish agriculture, given the much higher weight of citrus in farm output (68 percent in 1935–39), the respective proportions were obviously different; citrus groves accounted for 30 percent of the cultivated area (about 520,000 dunams in 1937), and between 40 and 50 percent of all agricultural employment (table A.5; Gurevich and Gertz, 1938; Metzer and Kaplan, 1990, chap. 1; BMZ, table A5). Moreover, citriculture was not uncharacteristically advanced compared with other pursuits in Jewish agriculture (see below), and its peculiarity stemmed from being run mainly (although not exclusively) by private planters on private land, using hired labor, of which Arab workers may have constituted between 55 and 60 percent (*Aliya*, no. 4, 1936; *Censuses of Workers in [Moshavot] Groves*, 1939).

These structural and organizational features contrasted with those of the largely self-employed, mixed-farming features that characterized production on Jewish public land, primarily by *kibbutzim* and *moshavim*. As such, citriculture ran contrary to the ideal Zionist model of Jewish husbandry, which was based on family and communal farming, on "National Land" by self-employed cultivators. This ideal structure of husbandry should have fostered individual and collective attachment to soil and territory by Jewish immigrant-settlers, thereby preventing the emergence of a colonialist-type plantation economy, which typically depends on indigenous hired labor (see Metzer, 1978, 1979; chapters 3, 4, 6).

Turning now to non-citrus farming, we have already mentioned that the growth of non-citrus output was appreciably slower than that of citrus before World War II. In the Arab sector, citrus output rose about five times faster than the rest of farm output between 1921 and 1939, and in the Jewish sector, about three times faster (table 5.3). Nonetheless, non-citrus cultivation underwent some noticeable changes – primarily in the Jewish farm economy and to lesser extent in the Arab peasant economy – and was undoubtedly far from stagnant.

Table 5.3. *Indices of farm output in constant prices (1921=100)*

	citrus	non-citrus (mixed farming)			total
		crops	other*a*	all	
Arabs					
1921	100	100	100	100	100
1927	354	132	125	130	147
1931	355	119	131	123	141
1935	841	191	122	166	218
1939	966	211	136	184	244
Jews					
1921	100	100	100	100	100
1927	468	280	333	297	370
1931	845	292	474	350	560
1935	2,028	417	974	593	1,201
1939	2,632	522	1,357	786	1,569

Note:
a Mainly livestock, poultry and dairy products.
Sources: tables A.10, A.11; Metzer and Kaplan (1990), p. 20

The most prominent change in Jewish non-citrus agriculture was the gradual shift from low-yield, extensive grain farming, typifying early Jewish rural settlements, to mixed farming in which livestock and dairy produce played a major role (see Gross, 1984a). The combined output of the two latter branches increased approximately fourteenfold over the period, raising their proportion in non-citrus output from 32 percent in 1921 to 55 percent in 1939 (Metzer and Kaplan, 1990, chap. 1). Another significant development was the expansion of irrigation, especially in growing fodder (which was naturally closely related to raising livestock) and vegetables, increasing the weight of irrigated non-citrus crops from about 4 percent of the cultivated area in the 1920s to 8 percent in the mid-1930s (Gurevich and Gertz, 1938).

The intensification and growth of Jewish non-citrus output (almost eightfold between 1921 and 1939) was backed by public (Zionist) and private investments and by agricultural research and extension services (established by the Zionist Organization as early as 1921), which fostered improved methods of production and high-quality hybrids. These facilitated technological advances in livestock, dairy, and crop farming, with veterinary and other services rendered by the government Department of Agriculture contributing as well (*Survey*, 1946, vol. I, chap. IX; Gross, 1984a).

In considering the adoption and diffusion of new technologies and the improvement of input and output mix, special attention should be given to farmers' education, which is believed to affect farm productivity positively. Besides enhancing the productivity of conventionally measured inputs (see above), numerous comparative studies suggest that education might reduce the cost of disseminating and internalizing information about improved production technologies, hence raising, other things being equal, expected returns to their adoption. Likewise, education might enable higher entrepreneurial sensitivity, and consequently faster response to changes in output and input prices aimed at increasing profits (see T. P. Schultz, 1988, for a summary of the relevant literature). In view of these observations, it seems highly likely that the high educational attainment of Jewish farmers was instrumental in the adoption of available agricultural improvements, and in generating demand for such improvements.

These suggested linkages are in line with the empirically accepted wisdom that well-educated workers, advanced technologies, and modern implements and machinery are complementary inputs in production (agricultural and otherwise). Complementarity of this nature certainly characterized the advance of Jewish farming, resulting in substantially increasing yields. Note, for example, that the annual yield of milk per cow on Jewish farms rose by 40 percent in 1927–41 (from 2,150 liters to 4,100 liters: see *Palestine Facts and Figures*, 1947, p. 132; Gross, 1984a). The rise in the yield of non-citrus crops is even more impressive: output quadrupled between 1921 and 1935 on an area that expanded by only about 6.5 percent over the same period (Gurevich and Gertz, 1938; Metzer and Kaplan, 1990, chap. 1).

Arab non-citrus farming expanded much more slowly. Livestock and dairy output grew by only 36 percent over the inter-war period and crop production just about doubled. As there is no indication of an overall rise in crop yields, it seems that growth in this case was primarily extensive, i.e., achieved by expanding the cultivated area. However, significant changes did take place in the produce mix, as demonstrated by the indices of table 5.4. Arab agriculture was also intensifying and moving toward marketable products (primarily vegetables, potatoes, fruit, and olives), leaving the extent of traditional extensive grain farming relatively unchanged. These patterns suggest that Arab peasants were responsive to changes in demand, a large share of which was generated by the increasing Jewish consumers' market (see below).

The shift toward more intensified farming also led to some modernization in production, as indicated, for example, by the spread of irrigation in vegetable growing (from 3,000 dunams in 1927 to 36,500 dunams in

Table 5.4. *Indicators of Arab (non-citrus) agricultural development*

	grains	tobacco	vegetables	olives	other fruit
A Indices of area size					
1922	—	100	100	100	100
1931	100	200	200	225	183
1935	134	—	367	395	373
1940	113	420	567	486	430
B Quantity indices of output, 1931=100 (average 1935–39)					
Total=158 96		—	818	147	415

Sources: area: Himadeh (1938), pp. 125–36, 158; Abramowitz and Guelfat (1944), pp. 32, 48–50; quantities: Samuel (1946), table 46a; Samuel (1947)

1939/40: Kamen, 1991, pp. 213–14), by increasing demand for better seeds produced by government extension services, and by wider use of modern agricultural implements and machinery. The latter development may also have reflected, to some extent, farmers' labor-economizing response to rising wages due to the growing demand for Arab labor in the early to mid-1930s (Abramowitz and Guelfat, 1944, pp. 50–51).

These developments were facilitated in part by government efforts directed at improving Arab peasant farming (in the form of professional support, demonstration plots, provision of seeds, and other extension services, and by the imposition of import surcharges, for example, on potatoes) and, most likely, also by the demonstration effects of the modern Jewish farm economy. But although these observed changes may be indicative of the willingness of Arab farmers to consider new crops and techniques, there were two interrelated obstacles inhibiting their widespread diffusion. One was the extremely low educational attainment of Arab peasants (see chapter 2); the second (partly derived from the first) was the high, largely uninsurable risks involved in the investments required for the adoption of suggested improvements (such as fertilization, expansion of fodder crops, extension of irrigation and introduction of various improved seeds: see Kamen, 1991, for an extensive discussion on the subject). Consequently, only a relatively small part of Arab husbandry became modernized, thus preventing the convergence of Arab-Jewish agricultural productive performance. Indeed, Jewish-Arab technology and yield gaps in non-citrus farming remained rather large throughout the period. For instance, in 1940, of the 500 tractors operating in Palestine, Arabs owned and used only 50, and Jews 450 (Kamen, 1991, pp. 220–21). Likewise, Jewish-Arab yield ratios in 1937 were 3.1 for non-citrus crop output per dunam, 6.8 for milk per cow, and 2.5 for eggs per hen (*Palestine Facts and Figures*, 1947, p. 132).

Another revealing observation is the difference between the two sectors in the proportion of value added (defined as the value of total output produced *minus* that of purchased inputs) in farm output. Unlike citrus, where the value added-output ratio was virtually identical in Arab and Jewish groves (averaging 52.4 percent in 1921–39), in non-citrus farming the ratios differed substantially (reaching 74 percent on average in the Arab economy between 1921 and 1939, but only about 54 percent in the Jewish economy; see tables A.9, A.10, A.13). These numbers support the inferences derived from the yield differentials, namely, that the production of citrus was equally advanced in the two sectors, which utilized purchased inputs to the same extent, whereas modern Jewish mixed farming, relying heavily on purchased inputs, differed appreciably from Arab peasant agriculture which, like any other traditional farm sector, depended extensively on self-produced inputs.

The dynamics of Palestine's pre-war agriculture was obviously citrus driven, but the outbreak of World War II changed everything. Farming had to adjust to two exogenous developments resulting from the curtailment of shipping in the Mediterranean. One was the crumbling citrus export market (citrus exports declined from 15 million cases in 1938–39 to a mere 170,000 cases in 1940–41, rising to only 2.75 million cases in 1944–45); the other was the substantial growth in domestic and regional demand for locally produced farm produce. In part, this fast-growing demand was generated by the need to substitute imports (in 1939 no less than 41 percent of the food consumed in Palestine was imported and in 1943–44 only 30 percent); in part it reflected net growth (for example, domestic food consumption rose by 8 percent between 1939 and 1944), fueled *inter alia* by the demand of the Allied forces in the region and of the neighboring countries, who sought regional sources of agricultural produce (Gross and Metzer, 1993). All in all, the increasing demand for foodstuffs made for fast growth of non-citrus produce, enough to compensate for the sharp decline in citrus production.[7]

Interestingly enough, the mechanisms of Arab and Jewish agricultural growth differed in the war years quite markedly from their respective inter-war patterns. In Jewish farming, although intensification contin-

---

[7] Farm (non-citrus) output grew 1.3-fold in the Arab sector and 2.4-fold in the Jewish sector between 1937 and 1945. Drawing on the output figures generated by Samuel (1946, 1947), Gurevich and Gertz (1947), and quoted in table A.10, it is estimated that the total volume of agricultural output (in constant prices) by the end of the war remained roughly unchanged from that of 1939 (to be precise, it was 1.3 percent larger).

ued,[8] expanding the area under cultivation was a substantial factor in the wartime rise of agricultural production. Total tilled area in the Jewish farm economy expanded by about 26 percent during the war, with land allocated to non-citrus crops rising by 45 percent. This increase, coupled with the spread of irrigation, and probably with further technological improvements, may have been instrumental in the 70–80 percent rise in labor productivity.

The mechanics of Arab wartime agricultural growth, accounting for 72 percent of the total increase in the country's non-citrus produce at the time, was quite different. Contrary to the inter-war years, it came about with essentially no expansion of land under cultivation. But the 14 percent increase in agricultural employment, and the continuing intensification and spread of irrigation (in 1944–45 Arabs cultivated 107,000 dunams of irrigated vegetables compared with 36,500 dunams in 1939: Kamen, 1991, chap. 6), suggest that the growth of Arab farm output and yields during the war was generated by rising labor-land ratios, and most probably by advancing total productivity in farming as well (Gross and Metzer, 1993).

Manufacturing

We have seen that agriculture remained the largest single Arab industry throughout the Mandate period in terms both of employment and of output, with manufacturing a distant second, not exceeding 10 percent of either employment or value added. In the Jewish economy, manufacturing was the largest industry in output terms from the start, and has maintained first place ever since, although (as mentioned above) employment in manufacturing surpassed that of agriculture only toward the end of the 1930s. Moreover, Jews generated about half of the country's manufacturing value added by the early 1920s. Their share rose to about 60 percent in the early 1930s, reaching 72 percent in 1933–39 thanks largely to the massive inflow of people and capital at the time of the Fifth Aliya, and climbing further to 80 percent during the war-induced industrialization phase (tables A.19, A.20; Gross and Metzer, 1993). All of this indicates that the dynamics of manufacturing in Mandatory Palestine was primarily, although definitely not exclusively, a Jewish story.

In accounting for the intra-industry attributes of manufacturing, our primary data sources are the government censuses of Arab and Jewish manufacturing in 1928, 1940, and 1943, and those for Jewish manufac-

---

[8] For example, the irrigated area in mixed farming grew from 10.7 percent of the entire non-citrus cultivated area in 1941 to 17.5 percent in 1945 (Gurevich and Gertz, 1947).

turing conducted by the Palestine Economic Society (PES) in 1921/22, and by the Jewish Agency in six other years (1923, 1925, 1926, 1930, 1937, and 1943). The government censuses should have contained the necessary building-blocks for a comparative examination of the long-run development of manufacturing in the two sectors, but unfortunately their partial and non-uniform coverage enables only some restricted cross-sectional comparisons between Arabs and Jews (see *SAP*, 1944/45; Gross, 1979).

The first comparison is based on the 1928 *First Census of Industries* (referring to productive activity in 1927) in which the government endeavored to include all factories and workshops, regardless of size, that produced for the market (excluding only producers of custom-made items). The census working sheets record data on Arab and Jewish factories and workshops separately, but the government, in an attempt not to further aggravate the already tense Arab-Jewish relations following the riots of 1929, prevented their separate publication. The findings of the census were therefore published in 1929 in an aggregate country-wide form, and it took another fifty years before the original ethno-nationally divided figures were finally made public in 1979 (Eliachar, 1979; Gross, 1979; see also the discussion in the appendix on the census' coverage problems).

A capsule summary of the census of 1928, based on its 1979 republication (and of the 1943 census as well: see below), appears in table 5.5. The manufacturing figures differed between the two communities in two major respects: output mix and establishment size. In the Arab sector, manufacturing was largely traditional, concentrating on processing agricultural produce and turning it into food, drink, and tobacco products, which accounted for 71 percent of all the industry's output. Moreover, no less than 79 percent of the output of Arab manufacturing was produced in 1927 by only four single branches: flour milling (36 percent), tobacco products (21 percent), soap (15 percent), and olive and sesame oil (7 percent).

Jewish manufacturing, on the other hand, although hardly a typical well-developed manufacturing industry of that era's industrialization standards, was more heterogeneous and concentrated somewhat less on the production of foodstuffs and final consumer goods. As such, it was distinctly more modern than Arab manufacturing. Food, drink, and tobacco, for example, accounted for only 45 percent of Jewish manufacturing output in 1928; another 23 percent was generated by metal, wood products, and building materials, with textile and leather goods contributing an additional 17 percent. The composition of output by a single branch was also much more diversified. The largest four branches combined produced only 39 percent of total Jewish industrial output, compared with Arabs' 79 percent (in Jewish manufacturing it took sixteen separate branches to produce 79 percent of output).

As for plant size, the census of 1928 reports that the number of employed persons in Jewish establishments was larger than in Arab ones across all aggregated minor branches. In total, the Jewish-Arab ratio was more than 2:1 (6.9 vs. 3.2 employed persons per establishment). Moreover, while most of the Jewish handicrafts and factories were of small and medium size (out of a total of 2,475 establishments in 1929, 1,854 [75 percent] employed between one and three workers each, 425 [17 percent] had between five and nine workers, and 166 [7 percent] had between ten and forty-nine employed persons), seven plants employed more than a hundred workers per plant, and the cement factory Nesher employed around four hundred workers by 1927 (*Report of the Censuses*, 1931). Similarly, the stock of capital per establishment was four times higher in Jewish than in Arab manufacturing in the second half of the 1920s.

The next government census, recording in 1940 the state of the industry in 1939, was confined to productive activity considered by the government to be strategically relevant to the war effort. Furthermore, being restricted to establishments employing at least five persons, it was particularly biased against Arab manufacturing and thus ill suited to inter-sectoral examinations. These deficiencies were partly remedied in the 1943 census (reporting the state of manufacturing in 1942), whose purpose was purely statistical and whose coverage was widened accordingly (*SAP*, 1944–45, pp. 48–61), allowing for Arab-Jewish comparisons that exhibit disparities similar to those found in 1927 (table 5.5). Note than in addition to the differences in establishment size and capital, Jewish manufacturing utilized on average twelve times as much horsepower (generated by steam and internal combustion engines and electric motors) per enumerated establishment as its Arab counterpart, suggesting a wide divergence in means and techniques of production between the two manufacturing industries by the end of the period.

Considering the evolution of Jewish manufacturing over the period as a whole, table 5.6 reports some illuminating measures, derived from the Jewish industrial censuses and from the output series of table A.14. The numbers show that along with the growing flow of output per establishment, manufacturing in the Jewish sector exhibited a steady rise in the size of the typical establishment and a continuous increase in its utilization of motor power. In support of the latter finding observe the growing ratio of electric power (in kwh) used to output produced (in 1936 prices) in all of Palestine's manufacturing, from about 0.5 in the early 1930s to 2

Table 5.5. *Comparative indicators of Arab and Jewish manufacturing in 1927 and 1942ᵃ according to the government censuses of industry*

A Composition of manufacturing output by branch (%)

	1927		1942	
	Arabs	Jews	Arabs	Jews
food, beverages, and tobacco	71.0	45.5	57.4	39.6
soap and chemicals	15.3	3.4	8.3	7.0
textiles and leather	5.0	17.3	24.2	21.9
metal, wood, and building materials	7.2	22.7	7.7	18.3
paper and printing	0.7	5.6	0.8	1.8
electricity	0.1	4.3	—	—
others	0.8	1.3	1.6	11.4
total	100.0	100.0	100.0	100.0

B Total manufacturing industry – quantities per establishment

	Arabs	Jews	Jewish–Arab ratio
1927			
number of workers	3.2	6.9	2.156
capital (P£)	482.8	1,862.0	3.857
output (P£)	898.8	1,561.8	1.738
1942			
number of workers	5.7	19.8	3.474
horse power	2.4	30.1	12.542
capital (P£)	1,368.0	6,341.9	4.636
output (P£)	3,631.7	15,228.5	4.193

Note:
ᵃ The data for 1942 do not include the industrial establishments granted government concessions for the exploitation of natural resources and the provision of public utilities by Jews and Arabs whose census records could not be separated. (These were the Jewish Palestine Electric Corporation, Ltd., Palestine Potash Ltd., and Palestine Salt Co., accounting for 90% of the output of these establishments, the Jerusalem Electric and Public Service Corporation, Ltd., and Shukri Deeb Ltd. (Salt) making for the remaining 10%.)
Sources: 1927: re-publication of Palestine's *First Census of Industries* (see text) in Eliachar, 1979; 1942: summary of the *Census of Industry, 1943* in *SAP* (1945), pp. 50–61.

Table 5.6. *Indicators of the development of Jewish manufacturing quantities per establishment*[a]

	1921–22	1930	1937	1943
number of workers	2.6	4.3	5.1	8.8
horse power	0.4	2.5	5.1	9.5
output (P£ in 1936 prices)	356.8	1,162.0	1,412.7	2,800.9

Note:
[a] The differences between the orders of magnitude reported here and in table 5.5 are due to the fact that the quantities in this table include handicrafts while those of the previous table do not.
Sources: number of establishments, number of workers, and utilized horsepower in 1921–22, 1930, and 1937: *Palestine, Facts and Figures* (1947), p. 156; horsepower in 1943: *Statistical Handbook* (1947), p. 210; for output: table A.14.

on the eve of World War II and to 2.6 in 1945.[9] These patterns point to an apparent increase in optimal plant size, possibly inducing a more extensive use of relatively high-fixed-cost machinery, and implying the realization of scale economies in production, most likely engendered by the growing market. In the inter-war years, it was generated mainly by the immigration waves of the mid-1920s and mid-1930s (see chapter 3); and during the war, by the soaring military and regional demand.

The significance of the wartime industrial changes lies not only in the quantitative indicators of intensified growth and mechanization of Jewish manufacturing, but also, and maybe more so, in the production of new, technologically advanced products, fostered by the war-caused demand. These include machine parts, electrical equipment, optical and precision instruments, chemicals, medical instruments, vaccines, and various pharmaceutical products. Their production was enabled by the scientific and technical infrastructure of the Jewish institutions of research and higher learning, and by the professional and highly skilled immigrants of the 1930s, who had been underutilized before the war (see Gross and Metzer, 1993).

The story of the war-driven developments in Jewish manufacturing

[9] The kwh figures were taken from *Statistical Handbook* (1947), p. 232 and from *Survey* (1946), vol. I, p. 513. The manufacturing output figures for the inter-war period are those of table A.14. The output estimate for 1945 was derived from the all country percentage distribution of NDP in current prices (tables A.19, A.20), assuming that it adequately represented the industrial composition of production in prices of 1936. The product of manufacturing, thus calculated, was turned into an output figure by means of the 1939 value added-output ratio for the country as a whole (tables A.14, A.19, A.20).

would not be complete without mentioning the newly established diamond-cutting industry. In the 1930s, about 90 percent of global diamond cutting and polishing was done in Belgium, Holland, and Germany: With the occupation of the Low Countries by Germany in May 1940, the established diamond industry was cut off from its markets and sources of supply, and alternative production centers developed in New York, Palestine, South Africa, and Brazil; the first two were run mainly by Jewish refugees from Belgium. By 1943, Palestine's thirty-three diamond-cutting and polishing shops employed 3,500 workers (8 percent of all employed persons in Jewish manufacturing at the time), twice as many as in the United States. Practically all the workers had to be locally trained and the machinery domestically built. In responding to external demand, the Jewish diamond industry in Palestine managed to compete successfully in the world market, establishing itself as a major production center on a global scale and as a prime export branch, during and after the war (Gross and Metzer, 1993). The flourishing diamond-cutting industry demonstrates, as did inter-war citriculture, the close links between Palestine's economy and the outside market, a characteristic that leads us naturally to the next subject: the country's external trade.

Trade

Given the distinction between the Arab and Jewish economies, Palestine's external trade should be regarded as comprising two distinct components: one is trade with the rest of the world, and the other goods and services (including factor services) exchanged bilaterally between Arabs and Jews.[10]

An aggregate view

Considering outside trade first, a summary of the annual changes in Palestine's and in global inter-war merchandise trade (imports *plus* exports) is provided in figure 5.3. It is seen that the two patterns diverged considerably from one another, largely because of the fast-growing volume of Palestine's trade in the first half of the 1930s, when international commerce suffered its depression-related setback. Moreover, table

---

[10] In principle, government purchases of goods and services (including labor and other factor services) from Arabs and Jews, and government-paid services sold to them, should also be considered as external trade of the two sectors. Data limitations, however, preclude the application of this distinction on a continuous basis. Moreover, serving as a public sector for both communities, the economic activities and functions of the Mandatory government affecting each one of them might also be viewed as internal to their economies (see further discussion in the appendix).

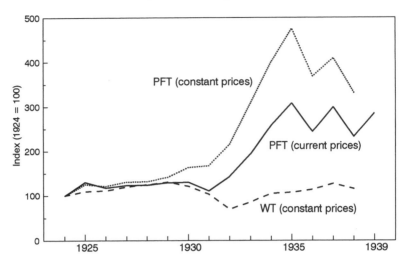

Figure 5.3 Trade indices: Palestine foreign trade (PFT) and world
trade (WT), 1924–39
(sources: for world trade: *Review of World Trade*, 1939, pp. 60–61;
Maddison, 1962, pp. 169–172, and 1995, table I–4; for Palestine's
trade: *Survey*, 1946, vol. I, p. 462 for imports and exports. The latter
were adjusted by replacing the official figures for the value of citrus
export [*SAP*, 1940 table 77] by our revised figures [calculated from
table A.6 cols. 5 and 6]. Palestine's trade figures in current prices were
deflated by the implicit price index of world trade derived from
Maddison, 1995, tables I–3 and I–4)

5.7 reveals that the countries of the Middle East, except for Palestine, followed the shrinking pattern of world trade in those years, leaving the
latter as a clear outlier both globally and regionally.

Dividing Palestine's merchandise foreign trade into its import and
export components, figure 5.4 demonstrates that the size and changes in
the volume of trade were determined primarily by imports. The influx of
capital (see chapters 1 and 4) facilitated a massive flow of imports which
could be kept persistently and substantially larger than exports throughout the inter-war years, thus dominating the country's trade scene.[11]

Over the inter-war years the value of Palestine's imported merchandise

---

[11] Of all the imports of 1923–39 about a quarter consisted of food, beverages, and tobacco
products (FBT), and another 8 percent were raw materials (*Statistical Handbook*, 1947,
pp. 238–39); a more detailed breakdown constructed by Halperin (1954) for 1932–39
indicates that raw materials in those years accounted for 6 percent of total imports,
capital goods for 20 percent, FBT for 24 percent, and the residual 50 percent was
assumed to consist of other consumption goods.

Table 5.7. *Merchandise foreign trade of Middle Eastern countries in constant prices (volume indices; 1928=100)*

	1928	1933	1938
Egypt	100	53	89
Iran	100	62	120
Iraq	100	74	156
Palestine	100	234	252
Syria and Lebanon	100	70	99
Turkey	100	60	156

Sources: volume indices calculated from trade figures in current prices and from the world trade price index. Trade figures: Palestine – see sources to Palestine's trade in figure 5.3 and *Statistical Handbook* (1947), pp. 238–39; other countries – Issawi (1982), pp. 26–27; price index: Maddison (1962), pp. 127–95; (1995), tables I-3, I-4

was on average 3.4 times larger than its exports – a ratio unmatched by any other net importing country at the time. Similarly, the ratio of imports to Palestine's (Arab *plus* Jewish) net domestic product (NDP_p), reaching about 45 percent on average in 1922–39, was also extremely high. In 1929, the peak inter-war year of world trade, only one country (Belgium) out of forty had an imports-income ratio that was (slightly) higher than that of Palestine (46.8 percent versus 46.3 percent), and in 1939, none of the fifty-two countries for which data are available surpassed Palestine's ratio of 48.4 percent. In Egypt and Turkey, for example, the import-income ratios in 1939 were only 11 percent and 6.9 percent, respectively. While Palestine's export intensity (13 percent of income on average) was much more modest in comparative terms, the uncharacteristically large imports made the weight of total trade (imports *plus* exports) in Palestine's economy (58 percent of NDP_p on average over the entire period) one of the highest observed trade intensities between the two world wars.[12]

[12] The comparative trade income ratios were derived from data contained in the following sources: *Review of World Trade*, various years; Mitchell (1982, 1992, 1993); Maddison (1995), and table B.1. In 1929, twenty-one out of forty economies had an export-income ratio higher than Palestine's 12.9 percent. In 1939, Palestine's proportion of 18.7 percent was exceeded by seventeen out of fifty-two economies. Of the recorded economies, six (out of forty) had a trade-income ratio higher than Palestine's 59.2 percent in 1929, and in 1939 only two (out of fifty-two) exceeded its ratio of 67.1 percent. The two other Middle Eastern countries lagged far behind in 1939: Egypt, with a trade volume of 21.8 percent of income, ranked thirty-eighth among the fifty-two countries, and Turkey, with a trade-income ratio of 14.3 percent, occupied the forty-eighth place.

Figure 5.4 Palestine's foreign trade in merchandise, 1922–39
(in current prices)
(sources: the same as the sources for Palestine's trade in figure 5.3)

In economies whose trade is not administratively constrained one typically observes a positive association between domestic product and imports, reflecting the utilization of imported inputs in domestic production and the income-induced demand for consumption of both locally and foreign-produced goods. The government of Palestine used import duties as a major revenue-generating device and increasingly also as a means of protecting domestic production. It exercised, in accordance with the Mandate (the famous Article 18), a generally nondiscriminatory and unrestricted trade policy (except for a few bilateral trade agreements, notably with Syria, see below).[13] This enabled imports to flow into the country fairly smoothly throughout the inter-war period, which indeed they did, following roughly the cyclical pattern of income growth (chapter 1).

Since Jewish capital inflows constituted 90 percent and more of the country's imported capital before the war (Halperin, 1954), and the available estimates suggest that Jews bought around 70 percent of total imports in the mid-1930s (see below), it is not surprising to find that Palestine's imports were more closely associated with Jewish product than with that of the country as a whole.[14] Particularly remarkable is the

[13] For documentation, discussions, and critical evaluations of government commercial policies see *Survey of Palestine* (1946), vol. I; Halperin (1954); Morag (1967); Smith (1993).

[14] The coefficients of correlation between the rates of change of Palestine's total merchandise imports and those of domestic product are 0.650 for Jewish domestic product and 0.558 for the domestic product of the country as a whole.

rapid rise of imports between 1931 and 1935. The well-known influx of people and capital to Palestine in these years, besides inducing imports indirectly, via the growth of income, also affected them directly through the tendency of immigrants – availing themselves of the "transfer" (*ha'avarah*) agreement with Nazi Germany (see chapter 4) – to bring in their capital in the form of durable consumer and producer's goods, which accounted for about a quarter of all imports in 1934–35 (Halperin, 1954, p. 146).

The substantial increase in Palestine's imports in the first half of the 1930s, although running contrary to the falling trend of world trade, may have been aided by the policies of the depression-inflicted countries attempting to increase their exports and reduce their imports. But the capital inflow, enabling Palestine to maintain a persistently large import surplus, saved the country from the typical depressionary beggar-thy-neighbor effects of such "unemployment exporting" policies.

Interestingly enough, we find that the volume of exports from Palestine also exhibited a rising trend throughout the period including the depression years (figure 5.4). The explanation for this pattern rests entirely on the expansion of citrus exports, possibly reflecting a relatively elastic demand facing Palestine's citrus industry whose supply was growing continuously, while investment in new groves was gradually adjusting downward to the declining citrus prices in the export markets (see above).

Citrus accounted on average for 54 percent of the value of Palestine's merchandise exports in 1922–30, rising to 77 percent in 1931–39. The dominant position of citrus in shaping the pattern of total exports is unmistakably demonstrated in figure 5.5. However, while citrus exports (and hence all exported merchandise combined) did not cease growing in the first half of the 1930s, non-citrus exports (composed primarily of soap, various manufactured products, watermelons, and grains: see *SAP*, various years) followed the expected path of decline at the peak years of the world depression.

In addition to the generally declining demand in those years (world export prices and quantity sank by 48 percent and 27 percent respectively between 1929 and 1932: Maddison, 1995), Palestine's (non-citrus) exports were also adversely affected by Egypt's imposition of highly protective tariffs in 1930. These tariffs sharply curtailed exports of soap and watermelons (accounting for about 32 percent of the country's non-citrus exports in the late 1920s) that had previously been destined mainly for the Egyptian market (*SAP*, various years; Halperin, 1954; Gross, 1984b).

The rapidly increasing volume of citrus sales, and to some extent also

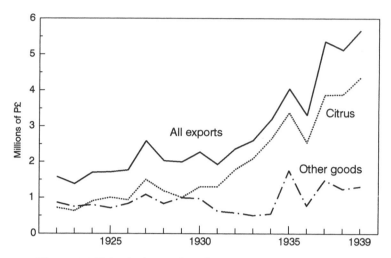

Figure 5.5 Palestine's merchandise exports, citrus and other goods, 1922–39 (in current prices)
(sources: the same as the sources for Palestine's trade in figure 5.3)

the shrinking Egyptian market, substantially changed the composition of Palestine's exports by country of destination. The weight of Middle Eastern countries declined from about 60 percent of the total in the mid-1920s to a mere 10 percent in the 1930s, and that of Europe rose from around 40 percent to 80 percent. The United Kingdom, where about 70 percent of all citrus exports were sold, became the destination of more than half of the country's exported merchandise in value terms. Likewise, the bulk of Palestine's imports originated outside the region: The Middle East supplied only 15–20 percent, Europe 55–60 percent, and the United States another 15 percent of all imports (*SAP*, various years). Taking the entire volume of trade (exports and imports combined), Palestine's intra-regional flows constituted no more than 26 percent of its total foreign trade as early as the mid-1920s, a percentage that dropped to about 14 percent in the 1930s.

Note, however, that Palestine's trade with Syria, the largest of its intra-regional flows (accounting for 52–60 percent of Palestine's intra-regional trade during the inter-war period), was practically free from custom duties and other constraints as per a comprehensive bilateral trade agreement (see *Survey*, 1946, vol. I, pp. 441–43). Other things being equal, Syria thus had an advantage over most other trading partners with whom Palestine's trade was duty-charged on both ends. Consequently, some trade may have been diverted from other partners inside and outside the region, but new trade may also have been created in both countries, sub-stituting imports from one another for domestic production, primarily of foodstuffs and textiles. This suggests that were it not for the trade agreement with Syria the weight of the Middle East in Palestine's trade may have been even lower than it actually was.

A similar pattern is observed for other Middle Eastern countries (Egypt, Syria, Iraq, Cyprus, and Turkey), whose intra-regional trade was rather limited in the late 1930s and has remained so ever since.[15] Possible explanations for this general picture may hinge on the lack of diversification of resource endowments within the region (Fischer, 1993) and on its close links (colonial and otherwise) to major European countries. For example, Cyprus, Egypt, Iraq, and Palestine conducted between 25 and 30 percent of their trade with the United Kingdom; Syria conducted 14 percent of its trade with France; and Germany accounted for 45 percent of Turkey's trade (*Statistical Handbook of Middle Eastern Countries*, 1945).

The direction of merchandise trade in the present-day and inter-war Middle East (Mandatory Palestine included) accords with the general observation that industrialized countries trade primarily among themselves, and developing countries mainly with industrialized ones, reflecting typical differences in economy size, income level, factor endowment, and supply of goods and services. Note, however, that most of the intra-regional trade in the present-day Middle East is conducted in labor services, not in merchandise (Fischer, 1993), and the flow of labor across borders may have played a significant role in the external trade of Mandatory Palestine as well. Unfortunately, lack of reliable data precludes any estimate of the magnitudes involved.

Moving to the war years, the major changes in Palestine's foreign trade provide a kind of capsule summary of the war-related effects on economic activity. On the one hand, the destruction of the European (continental) market and the disruption of the Mediterranean trade routes, coupled with limited shipping space, curtailed civilian interregional trade; citrus exports virtually collapsed (see above), and imports of goods were sharply

---

[15] Intra-regional trade in the late 1930s ranged from 24 percent of total trade in Syria, to 2 percent in Turkey (the only exception being Trans-Jordan, 61 percent of whose trade was conducted intra-regionally), see *Statistical Handbook of Middle Eastern Countries* (1945). Note that the trade patterns of the countries in the region have not changed much. The extent of intra-regional trade in goods accounted for only 6.2 percent of the region's entire merchandise trade in 1983 (Fischer, 1993), and the intra-regional export in the Middle East and North Africa (7.7 percent of total regional export) was the lowest of all the world's regions in 1990–94; the largest intra-regional proportion of trade in goods of any single Middle Eastern country is Syria's, 13.6 percent in the early 1990s (El-Erian and Fischer, 1996).

reduced (they declined by 63 percent in constant prices between 1939 and 1940, and remained low thereafter; their level in 1945 was 3 percent lower than in 1940; Gross and Metzer, 1993).

On the other hand, Britain's logistical strategy of turning the Middle East into a major supply center for the Allied forces in the area and of making the region as economically self-sufficient as possible[16] had an appreciable effect, although only temporarily, on the scale and mix of Palestine's exports. In responding to the rising Allied demand (sales to whom accounted for 60 percent of the country's total exports of goods and services in 1940–45), to the expanding Middle Eastern market for locally produced output, and to world (mainly American) demand for cut diamonds (see above), Palestine's exports of goods and services in constant prices grew 2.3-fold between 1939 and 1943 (Gross and Metzer, 1993).

This growth was accompanied by substantial compositional changes. For example, in 1939, citrus fruit accounted for about 75 percent of the value of Palestine's merchandise exports, and manufactured products for another 21 percent. But in 1943, cut diamonds constituted 35.5 percent of all exported goods,[17] other manufactured products 58 percent, while citrus declined to a mere 4.3 percent of merchandise exports (Gross and Metzer, 1993). Likewise, the share of the USA in the country's exports of goods grew, thanks to the diamond industry, from 3 percent in 1939 to 24 percent in 1945, and the Middle East became the major destination for Palestine's merchandise sold abroad (48.5 percent of the total in 1945, compared to 11 percent in 1939: *SAP*, 1944/45, and *Supplement to Survey*, 1947).

On the balance-of-payments and monetary front, the substantial rise in exports and the decline in imports turned the inter-war current-account deficit, amounting to about 29 percent of the country's NDP in 1936–39, into a wartime surplus of about 20 percent of NDP in 1940–45. But as soon as the war ended the deficit in the current account was "back in place," reaching about 11 percent of NDP by 1946 (Gross and Metzer, 1993).

The above-mentioned surplus in the current account, combined with the continuous inflow of capital and unilateral transfers, led to a buildup of foreign-exchange reserves against which domestic money was issued by the Palestine Currency Board in London.[18] Since Palestine's sterling reserves were frozen, and opportunities to utilize them for purchases

---

[16] Note, in this context, that among other factors, the oil pipe between Mosul and Haifa and the completion in 1939 of the British-owned oil refineries in Haifa rendered Palestine and the neighboring countries practically independent of sea-borne fuel supplies.

[17] Note, however, that the value added in the diamond-cutting process of (imported) rough diamonds was only about 10–20 percent.

[18] This was the officially appointed issuing body of Palestine's currency at a constant exchange rate of P£1 to £1: see chapter 6.

abroad were in any case minimal, the accumulated reserves were automatically transformed into domestic monetary expansion. Indeed, Palestine's money supply grew about sevenfold over the war years, causing the domestic price level almost to triple between 1939 and 1945.

The post-war revival of international trade, with its renewed import surpluses, largely facilitated by the rapidly increasing inflow of capital, provided an added supply response to rising domestic demand. This enabled the economy to continue growing in the last two years of the Mandate in a significantly milder inflationary environment than that of the wartime expansion (Gross and Metzer, 1993).

External and bilateral trade, Arabs and Jews

Up to this point, the external trade of Mandatory Palestine has been looked at in the aggregate, an approach dictated by the nature of the trade data which, except for the exports of citrus, were available on a continuous basis only for the country as a whole. Nonetheless, contemporary and later scholars have utilized various sources of information on differential consumption patterns and production mix in an attempt to ethno-nationally disaggregate the export-and-import data at various points.[19] Some results are reported in table 5.8, panel A, for two key years; 1922 (the beginning of the period) and 1935 (the year ending the pre-war interval of fast growth, just before the economic decline of the second half of the 1930s set in). Being highly conjectural, however, the trade figures in the table should be taken only as suggestive of likely orders of magnitude, and certainly not as firmly constructed estimates.

In view of the widening income gap between Arabs and Jews, and the massive influx of Jewish capital, it is hardly surprising to find that the Jewish volume of foreign trade (in current prices) grew much faster between 1922 and 1935 than it did in the Arab economy, and that such trade played a substantially larger role in Jewish economic life. Likewise, given the ethnonational breakdown of merchandise trade (derived from Gaathon's [1978] percentage distributions) reported in table 5.8, panel B for 1935, it is suggested that the two sectors may have differed from one another not only in volume and intensity, but in the composition of trade as well.[20]

---

[19] For relevant pieces of information and references related to various attempts to break down Palestine's foreign trade into sectoral components see Abramowitz and Guelfat (1944); Gaathon (1978); Metzer and Kaplan (1985).

[20] The paucity of data necessitates reliance on one single year for the disaggregated trade picture; the shortcomings of this procedure are obvious. Nonetheless, it seems that 1935 is quite representative of the period of relatively uninterrupted internal and external trade in Palestine at the peak of its inter-war economic growth.

Table 5.8. *Comparative characteristics of Arab and Jewish merchandise foreign trade (%, current prices)*

A Palestine's merchandise foreign trade, by sector, 1922, 1935

	1922			1935			annual growth rate, 1922/35	
	Arabs	Jews	total	Arabs	Jews	total	Arabs	Jews
distribution of trade by sector								
imports	61.4	38.6	100.0	28.0	72.0	100.0	2.8	14.5
exports	62.5	37.5	100.0	38.7	61.3	100.0	3.5	11.5
all trade	61.6	38.4	100.0	30.0	70.0	100.0	2.9	14.0
ratios of trade components to NDP								
imports	33.7	88.1	44.2	33.2	65.2	51.4		
exports	9.6	24.0	12.4	10.4	12.6	11.6		
all trade	43.3	112.1	56.6	43.6	77.8	63.0		

B Composition of merchandise foreign trade by sector, 1935

	Arabs	Jews	share of Arabs
imports			
goods for consumption	42.1	27.6	37.5
durables and fixed capital	6.0	21.2	10.0
intermediate goods (inputs)	36.5	37.0	27.9
governmental and unspecified			
imports	15.4	14.2	30.0
total imports	*100.0*	*100.0*	*28.0*
exports			
farm products			
citrus	90.7	79.1	42.0
other farm products	5.6	1.5	70.2
all farm products	96.3	80.6	43.0
manufacturing			
processed farm products	1.8	4.6	20.0
other manuf. products	1.9	14.8	7.5
all manufacturing	3.7	19.4	10.7
total exports	*100.0*	*100.0*	*38.7*

Sources: Abramowitz and Guelfat (1944), pp. 97–99; *Survey* (1946), vol. I, p. 462; Metzer and Kaplan (1985); Gaathon (1978), tables VI, VII; and sources for Palestine's trade in figure 5.3

On the import side, Arabs and Jews differed primarily in the import weights of current consumption and capital goods (including consumer durables). About 42 percent of the goods imported by Arabs in 1935 were for consumption purposes, compared with 28 percent of Jewish imports, while the proportion of capital goods was 6 percent and 21 percent in Arab and Jewish imports respectively. A similar picture is revealed for the country as a whole: Arabs consumed 37 percent of all the goods imported for consumption, but utilized only 10 percent of Palestine's imported durable and capital goods, while their share in total imports (and in the imports of intermediate products used in production) was about 28 percent.

Part of the Jewish "advantage" in the importation of durable and capital goods in the mid-1930s was due to the *ha'avarah* arrangements, facilitating the extraction of Jewish capital from Nazi Germany in the form of German products (see chapter 3), of which capital and durable goods constituted a substantial component (the *ha'avarah* transfers may have accounted for no less than 50 percent of the value of durables and capital goods imported by Jews in 1936: see Gaathon, 1978; Halperin, 1954). In part, however, this "advantage" reflected structural differences between the two sectors, discussed above, in relative capital intensity in production, and in consumers' wealth and demand for durable goods.

On the export side, citrus dominated the scene in both sectors in 1935, generating 90 percent of total Arab merchandise exports and 94 percent of their agricultural component. The corresponding Jewish proportions were 80 percent and 98 percent respectively. Moreover, even as early as 1921, before the large expansion of citriculture, and prior to the constraints imposed (in 1930) by Egypt on imports of farm produce from Palestine, which primarily affected exports of watermelons and soap by Arabs, citrus constituted about 69 percent of Arab, and 83 percent of Jewish agricultural exports (Metzer and Kaplan, 1985).

Unlike citrus, however, manufacturing exports played a very uneven role in the two sectors, comprising in 1935 about 19 percent of Jewish exports, but merely 4 percent of Arab exports. Note, also, that 89 percent of Palestine's exports of manufactured goods originated in the Jewish sector (only a quarter of which were processed agricultural goods), compared with 61 percent of total merchandise exports. These observations, which reflect the different comparative advantages of the two sectors, are consistent with the disparities in the industrial structure of their domestic products.

The volume and characteristics of merchandise foreign trade provide, however, only a partial account of external trade at the sectoral level. In order to complete it, one must add the bilateral trade of Arabs and Jews, as well as their imports and exports of services. This is attempted in table 5.9, which reports conjectural estimates of the components of all-inclusive external trade of Arabs and Jews in 1935, thereby providing a comparative perspective on their bilateral trade, just before it was brought to a halt by the Arab revolt and the Jewish response to it in 1936–39.

The revealed structure of Arab-Jewish trade seems to have been characterized by a mixture of attributes; some might generally be expected of inter-sectoral trade in a developmentally disparate "dual economy," and others were of a Palestine-specific nature. The former are exemplified by agricultural produce and (mainly unskilled) labor services that Arabs sold to Jews, partly in exchange for manufactured goods and various services, and the latter by three noteworthy components of Jewish purchases from Arabs: first and foremost, the acquisition of land, making for one-third of the entire volume of Jewish purchases from Palestine's Arabs in 1935. The second is rentals of Arab-owned dwellings, primarily in mixed towns such as Jerusalem, Haifa, and Jaffa, which accounted for another 17 percent of Jewish "imports" from Arabs (without land; 11 percent with land). The third feature was the relatively large proportion of manufactured goods, constituting a fifth of sales by Arabs to their Jewish neighbors (without land; 12 percent with land). About two-thirds of these manufactured goods were quarry products and other building materials, used as inputs in the booming construction industry of the growing, immigration-absorbing Jewish community of the mid-1930s.

The question that comes to mind is: how significant was the bilateral component in each sector's external trade and economic activity? Taking the entire volume of trade (imports *plus* exports), a clear difference is observed between the two economies: the flow of Jewish foreign trade in 1935 was more than twice as large as that of the Arabs, so that the weight of inter-sectoral trade was substantially higher in Arab than in Jewish overall external trade (inter-sectoral trade accounted for 37 percent of external trade in the Arab economy, and 30 percent of its net-of-land volume, compared with 21 percent and 16 percent, respectively, of Jewish trade).

Examining the import and export segments of each sector's external trade separately, it is seen that in terms of the breakdown of imports into their "Palestine" and "world" origins, the two sectors were quite similar. Purchases from Jews comprised about 18 percent of Arab total imports, and purchases from Arabs around 20 percent of Jewish (including land) imports. But unlike the Arab sector, whose imports from Jews and from foreign countries alike were dominated by manufactured goods, the composition of Jewish imports from foreign sources (86 percent of which

Table 5.9. *Composition of overall external trade of Arabs and Jews in 1935 (%)*

A Imports

	Arabs				Jews			
	from abroad	from Jews	all	share from Jews	from abroad	from Arabs	all	share from Arabs
goods								
agriculture	6.0		4.9		2.0	16.5	4.9	67.3
manufacturing	75.0	74.1	74.8	17.8	86.0	12.3	71.3	3.5
all	81.0	74.1	79.7	16.7	88.0	28.8	76.2	7.6
final services	19.0	25.9	20.3	23.0	12.0	8.2	11.2	14.6
factor services								
labor						14.8	3.0	100.0
dwellings						10.6	2.1	100.0
land						37.6	7.5	100.0
total imports	100.0	100.0	100.0	17.9	100.0	100.0	100.0	20.0

B Exports: Arabs

	destination			Jewish share	output share of export[a]	
	abroad	Jews	all		abroad	Jews
goods						
citrus	63.5		24.1		65.9[b]	
other ag.	3.9	16.5	11.7	87.3	2.0	13.5
manuf.	2.6	12.3	8.6	88.6	1.7	13.4
all goods	70.0	28.8	44.4	40.2	15.7	10.5
services						
final	30.0	8.2	16.5	30.9	7.3	13.3
labor		14.8	9.2	100.0		
dwellings		10.6	6.6	100.0		
all services	30.0	33.6	32.3	64.7		
land		37.6	23.3	100.0		
all exports	100.0	100.0	100.0	62.0		

Table 5.9. (*cont.*)

C Exports: Jews

	destination			Arab share	output share of export[a]	
	abroad	Jews	all		abroad	Jews
goods						
citrus	52.2		38.4		64.1[b]	
other agriculture	1.0		0.7		3.6	
manufacturing	12.8	74.1	29.0	67.5	5.6	11.6
all goods	66.0	74.1	68.1	28.7	19.5	7.9
final services	34.0	25.9	31.9	21.5	12.0	3.3
all exports	100.0	100.0	100.0	26.4		

Notes:
[a] The production aggregate used for goods is output (i.e., value added *plus* purchased raw materials and intermediate inputs), and that for services is product (i. e., value added).
[b] The percentage of citrus exports reports its weight in total output of citrus (including its investments component); the export share of crop output is estimated at 85 percent in 1935 for both Arabs and Jews (Metzer and Kaplan, 1990, chapter 1).
Sources: the reported percentages were derived, with minor adjustments, from the estimates of Gaathon (1978), chapters IV, XII, tables VI, VII, XIX; Metzer and Kaplan (1985, 1990); table A.18.

were manufactured merchandise) was obviously quite different from the diversified make-up of imports from Arabs.

It can thus be inferred that from the Arab point of view the neighboring Jewish economy may, by and large, not have been distinct from the rest of the world as a source of imports, except, probably for its proximity, providing some Jewish manufacturing with a comparative advantage over more distant competitors. But for the Jewish community, the types of goods and services (let alone land) that were bought from Arabs seem largely not to have substituted for, or competed with, world imports.

Turning to exports, it was here that sales between the neighboring peoples played a substantially different role in the Arab and Jewish economies. The figures in table 5.9 suggest that the Jewish market may have provided a destination for about 62 percent of all Arab (land-inclusive) exports, for no less than 50 percent of the net-of-land total, and for as much as 87 percent of Arab non-citrus farm exports in 1935. On the other hand, only 26.4 percent of all Jewish exports were destined for the Arab community (although the Arab sector was the major outlet for the export of Jewish manufactured products, comprising 29 percent of the entire flow of Jewish exports; Arabs bought about two-thirds of it).

Considering the proportion of net-of-citrus material output exported, Arabs sold about 13 percent of their manufacturing output in the Jewish market in 1935 and a similar percentage of their non-citrus farm output. Moreover, since no more than about half of Arab agricultural (non-citrus) output was produced for the market (and was not consumed by peasant-producers themselves), it turns out that at least a quarter of Arab marketed non-citrus farm output was sold to Jews (Metzer and Kaplan, 1985). Sales abroad added another 2 percent to the exported proportion of output in each of the two industries, making for an overall export share of Arab non-citrus material production of about 15 percent. No less than 88 percent of these exports were sold to Jews.

Interestingly, in the Jewish economy too, the proportion of non-citrus material output exported to all destinations was about 15–16 percent, of which two-thirds was sold to Arabs. But unlike the Arabs, whose farm products comprised 57 percent of their merchandise exports, in the Jewish economy non-citrus merchandise exports consisted almost exclusively (98 percent) of manufactured products. As indicated above, practically all Jewish-produced merchandise sold to Arabs consisted of manufactured goods, accounting for about 12 percent of Jewish manufacturing output in 1935.

Unlike the output share of the exports of goods, the product share of services sold by one economy to the other differed considerably. Only about 3 percent of the Jewish product of services were sold to Arabs, as against about 13 percent of the (national) product of Arab services which were sold to Jews. Of the latter, three-quarters (10 percent of the Arab product of services) consisted of labor and dwelling services, and the rest of final trade, transport, and other services.

Note that contrary to the exported goods and services that were produced domestically, and were therefore part of the exporting sector's domestic product, factor services (labor and dwellings) exported by Arabs were not used as inputs in Arab domestic production. As such, the income accruing to these factors from Jews who used them was obviously not included in the domestic product of the Arab community; it was, however, an integral component of Arab national product, composed, by definition, of Arab domestic product *plus* the net flow of income from Arab factors of production utilized externally. By the same token, the income derived from Arab factors of production employed by Jews was included in the domestic, but not in the national, product of the Jewish community (for further elaboration see the appendix).

Serving as a distinct component of the various output aggregates of the

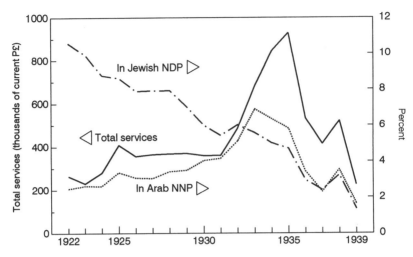

Figure 5.6 Arab labor and dwelling services used by Jews: total and
product shares 1922–39
(sources: tables A.18–A.20)

two economies, the net value of bilaterally traded factor services between
Arabs and Jews was estimated on an annual basis as part of the recent
reconstruction of Palestine's national accounts (table A.18). Drawing on
these (highly conjectural) estimates, some notions of the extent and
pattern of the contribution of the exported (imported) factor services to
Arab national (and to Jewish domestic) product may be offered.

This is done in figure 5.6. The annual flow of Arab factor services utilized by Jews was on the rise, until the outbreak of the Arab revolt in 1936,
and declined thereafter. Their weight in Arab NNP also rose until 1933,
suggesting that the fast-growing (albeit fluctuating) Jewish demand for
Arab labor and dwellings made their exports grow faster than the Arab
NNP. Likewise, the shrinkage of Arab-Jewish trade in the second half of
the 1930s seems to have been sharper than the downturn of Arab economic activity, causing the weight of factor services in Arab NNP to
decline in those years.

Even at its peak, however, in 1933, the contribution of income from the
export of factor services to the Jewish economy did not exceed 7 percent
of Arab NNP. To gain some perspective on these orders of magnitude,
note that exported labor services (mainly to Israel) from the West Bank
and Gaza between 1968 and 1986 generated on average no less than 25
percent of the two territories' combined national product. Similarly, the
extent of exported Arab labor, which in 1935 reached at most 5 percent of

the Arab labor force, constituted in the West Bank and Gaza between 35 percent and 40 percent of their joint labor force in the mid-1980s (table A.5; Metzer, 1988).

In terms of employment in the labor-importing economies, however, the comparative proportions were quite different. At the beginning of the Mandate Arabs may have comprised around 14 percent of all employed persons in the Jewish economy, a share that declined to about 8 percent in 1935. But in Jewish citrus groves Arab workers may have accounted for a substantial 60 percent of all employed persons in 1935, and in Jewish agriculture at large for no less than 42 percent (table A.5; BMZ, table A5). In post-1967 Israel, workers from the West Bank and Gaza, substantial as their number was *vis-à-vis* the territories' total labor force, constituted no more than 6 percent of the total employment in the Israeli economy (their largest concentration was in construction, where they accounted for 35 percent of total employment in 1984, while in agriculture they made for "only" 15 percent of all employed persons: Metzer, 1988).

Returning to the Mandate period, figure 5.6 demonstrates that unlike their weight in Arab economic activity, the contribution of Arab factor services to Jewish NDP declined continuously from a moderate 10 percent at the beginning of the Mandate period to 5 percent in the mid-1930s, and down to about 1 percent by the end of the decade. This declining path may have reflected the fact that the growing Jewish community and economy, while usually generating a rising demand for Arab labor and housing services, gradually managed to provide an increasing portion of these services from its own resources. To this one should probably add the Jewish self-imposed constraints on hiring Arab labor (see chapter 4), which may have contained part of the growth of its role in Jewish domestic economic activity.

Finally, lumping all the export components together, the total value of goods and services sold by Jews to Arabs reached about 7 percent of Jewish NDP in 1935, with sales to the rest of the world adding another 19 percent, thus making the Jewish all-inclusive exports to NDP ratio a healthy 26 percent. The product ratio of Arab net-of-land exports to Jews (14 percent of Arab net national product) was twice as high as the Jewish equivalent, thanks mainly to the sale of labor and dwelling services. But the smaller extent of Arab exports to foreign countries (14 percent of NNP) made for an Arab ratio of overall net-of-land exports to NNP of about 28 percent (or 37 percent when land sales to Jews are included). In other words, the two developmentally diverse economies, while differing markedly in the composition of their total exports, were quite similar in the product intensity of their overall export trade.

6   Public sectors in Palestine's economic life

The roles played by the Mandatory government and by the organized Jewish community's public institutions in shaping the economy and its dualistic nature were discussed in chapter 1 in general terms, and referred to in passing throughout this volume. The present chapter seeks to supplement the above discussions, primarily by putting the economic functions of Palestine's government and (Jewish) non-government public sectors in a quantitative perspective.

The government

The scholarly literature on the British rule in Palestine, to which a number of significant additional contributions have been made in the past two decades, deals at length with the complex and conflicting factors underlying the modus operandi of the Mandatory government both as ruler and as public sector.[1] Although they do not necessarily reach a common assessment and interpretation, the scholars working in the field seem to agree on the basic considerations that guided Britain in molding its rule and in formulating its economic institutions and policies in Palestine as a colonial power and as the League of Nations' Mandatory.[2] These considerations are commonly identified as being derived from

---

[1] The literature on British rule in Palestine is obviously vast. A representative short list of relatively recent contributions dealing with government economic policies and management and with related political considerations and implications includes the following: Gross and Metzer (1978); Hattis-Rolef (1979); Kayyali (1979); Wasserstein (1979); Baer (1980); Metzer (1982); Biger (1983); Halevi and Klinov-Malul (1968); Halevi (1983); Gross (1984b, which provides a comprehensive and highly insightful survey of the economic policy of the Mandatory government in Palestine); Miller (1985); Reuveny (1993); and Smith (1993). The extensive bibliography in Smith (1993) covers most of the relevant literature, old and new.

[2] Since we are here interested primarily in the actual outcomes of policies, we will not dwell on the frequent differences that arose between the British government in London (notably the Treasury and the Colonial Office) and the Mandatory government in Jerusalem regarding matters of economic policy, or on the mechanisms of resolving them. For an elaboration on these issues see Gross (1984b).

imperial interests in a colonial and geopolitical context, coupled with liberal (laissez-faire) attitudes in the economic sphere, on the one hand, and guided by various Palestine-specific concerns, on the other (Gross, 1984b; and chapter 1).

Britain's interests as a colonial empire led it to establish in Palestine a smoothly functioning colonial-style government based on a modern administrative, legal, and fiscal system, as well as on indigenous structures and customs. The same interests also called for government initiative and finances in developing the country's physical transport and communication infrastructure, while in other respects minimizing government intervention in economic affairs, and conducting an "open door," largely non-discriminating, external trade policy (see chapter 5). The liberal approach of non-intervention in economic matters, and the retention of traditional socio-economic structures (primarily in the rural Arab community), fitted in well with the colonialist posture of maintaining socio-economic stability in colonized areas and encouraging their continued concentration on the production of primary products, thereby providing for colonial economic activity complementary to (and not competing with) the industrial "mother country" (see Meredith, 1975; Gross, 1984b; Smith, 1993).

These broad contours of governance were reinforced by the unique situation of Palestine. Zionist aspirations for the formation of a Jewish commonwealth (National Home), assisted, as stipulated in the Mandate, by the British government (see chapter 1), naturally called for the constitution of a modern state administration and active government involvement in infrastructure construction and the promotion of economic development. Likewise, the general colonial policy of government non-intervention in local social and economic affairs was enhanced in Palestine by the ethno-national conflict between the Arab indigenous community and the Jewish immigrating settlers' community.

The sensitivities surrounding the delicate and always unsatisfactory – to one party or another – attempts by the government to abide by its dual obligation to the Zionist cause and the Arab case meant that any government move that could be interpreted as assisting one community (say, granting concessions to natural monopolies, devising schemes of protective tariffs, or any other area of public policy) was perceived, for that very reason, by the other community as harmful. In the words of the 1937 *Palestine Royal Commission Report* (*RCR*, 1937, p. 169): "The removal of an Arab grievance creates a Jewish grievance and vice versa." Add to this the unavoidable distributional effect of almost any fiscal measure, on either the revenue or the expenditure side, due to the wide socio-economic differences between Arabs and Jews (see below), and one gets strong incentives, indeed, for the Mandatory government to minimize intervention in intra- and intercommunal socio-economic matters.[3]

On the whole, the economic activity of the Mandatory government was to be bound by the general principle of British colonial administration, dictating conservative fiscal management in colonial and Mandated areas so as to avoid imposing a fiscal burden on the "mother country." Public expenditures in Palestine were therefore constrained over time by local tax revenues and by the funds the Mandatory government was able to borrow internally and in the British capital market (Gross and Metzer, 1978; Gross, 1984b).

While generally adhering to these constraints, British rule was at first (1920–23), and not surprisingly, characterized by large public investments and deficit financing (under the development-oriented leadership of the first high commissioner, Sir Herbert Samuel). This policy changed to fiscal conservatism in 1924–35 and then switched back to expansionism and deficit creation when excessive (relative to tax revenues) government expenditures were made in the years of political upheaval and economic decline (1936–39) and during the inflationary years of World War II (Gross, 1984b; Gross and Metzer, 1993).

On the monetary front, Palestine became part of Britain's common colonial currency system in 1927, whereupon a special Currency Board became responsible for issuing Palestine's currency against its sterling reserves, which were, in turn, invested by the board in British securities. The system provided for free sterling convertibility of the Palestine pound (which replaced the Egyptian pound as the country's legal tender in 1927) at a 1:1 exchange rate.[4] Barclays Bank in Jerusalem was the issuing agent for the Palestine Currency Board (Halperin, 1954; Ottensooser, 1955). According to this monetary scheme, Britain provided Palestine with a common currency in return for sterling credit extended by the Palestine Currency Board to Britain by investing its sterling reserves in British government and colonial securities. However, the scheme also prevented the Mandatory government (as it did all governments of British-controlled areas operating under the same monetary rules) from conducting an independent monetary policy, since the local money

---

[3] One example is the government's non-intervention in labor affairs, especially in Jewish attempts to segregate labor along ethno-national lines. For a discussion of these government policies see, for example: Morag (1967); Metzer (1982); Smith (1993); and Lockman (1996). See also the detailed discussion in Smith (1993) on the political implications of the government concessions granted to (mostly Jewish) industrial establishments for the provision of public utilities (electricity) and the extraction of minerals.

[4] Free convertibility was suspended during World War II, when the sterling reserves of the Palestine Currency Board were administratively frozen by the British government (Gross and Metzer, 1993).

supply was endogenously determined by its very nature. Likewise, the system left no room for a central bank to operate in the country (nor did it allow for an officially designated "lender of last resort" to the commercial banking industry). These built-in restrictions implied that the government of Palestine could not use such instruments as nominal interest rates or the domestic quantity of money to act counter-cyclically, or resort to monetary expansion for (inflationary) financing of budgetary deficits.[5]

Note, however, that the avoidance of fiscal deficits and the selective use of public borrowing were not typically colonial administration directives; they were policy guidelines commonly practiced by many governments in the post-hyperinflation and pre-Keynesian era, when the role of government in economic life was still rather modest. It is therefore not surprising that the weight of government outlays in inter-war Palestine (averaging about 18.5 percent of the country's combined Arab and Jewish NNP for all central government expenditures and 15 percent for their non-business component) lay well within the range observed in a good number of European countries at the time.[6]

It follows that while mere size is not necessarily a distinguishing feature of a "colonial" public sector, the composition of government outlays in Mandatory Palestine was "colonial" indeed. Reference here is to the predominance of general administration and public safety, which typically accounts for 50 to 60 percent of the expenditures of colonial governments, followed by economic and environmental services (another 20 to 25 percent), with social services in third place, usually accounting for about 10 percent (and rarely exceeding 20 percent) of all outlays of (central) government in colonial and mandated territories in the inter-war years (Gross and Metzer, 1978, table 18).

The allocation of government expenditures in inter-war Palestine between these three broad categories is clearly compatible with the "colonial" makeup, and – as shown in table 6.1 – stands in sharp contrast to the (Western European-style) composition of government domestic outlays in the UK.[7] The main difference between the distribution of

---

[5] The wartime inflation was fueled by the increase in Palestine's money supply (caused by the country's export surplus, see chapter 5), which at the time could not be used to finance imports or otherwise be sterilized. The inflationary spiral of World War II could therefore be viewed as largely exogenous (Gross and Metzer, 1993).

[6] Non-business expenditures are calculated by subtracting, from total outlays, the capital and current expenditures on government-owned and -operated railroads, post, telegraph, and telephone services (Gross, 1984b, tables 1–3). The ratios of government outlays to national income between 1925 and 1935 were about 20 percent in the UK and Ireland, 19 percent in Greece, and 17 percent in Italy (Mitchell, 1992, tables G5 and J1).

[7] The quantitative account here and in the rest of the chapter is based largely on the inter-war period, because of the unrepresentative nature of the war years with respect to "ordinary" public-sector activity in Mandatory Palestine.

Table 6.1. *Public civilian expenditures: governments of Palestine (1920–40) and of the United Kingdom (1926–35) (%)*

	Palestine (1920–40)	United Kingdom (1926–35)
administration and public safety	60.3	11.3
economic outlays	27.2	22.3
social services	12.5	66.4
all	100.0	100.0

Source: Gross and Metzer (1978), tables 17, 19. In calculating Palestine's composition of government expenditure, I have allocated the outlays on public works (constituting 12.1 percent of the total) to the three categories as follows: 20 percent to administration and safety; 70 percent to economics; and 10 percent to social services.

government expenditures in the UK and in British colonially adminis-tered territories (Palestine included) lies in the relative weights of social services *vis-à-vis* administration and public safety. This discrepancy demonstrates how Britain's perceptions of the government's socio-eco-nomic functions at home differed from its views on the proper role of the (government) public sector in the colonies and mandated areas (Gross and Metzer, 1978). It also points to the central place occupied by the pro-vision of administration and security services in the operation of colonial government; in the case of Palestine, the public safety implications of the Arab-Jewish conflict generated an extra component of demand for such services.

Interestingly, the difference in the budgetary share of economic and environmental expenditures is fairly small, with Palestine leading Britain by five percentage points (table 6.1). This suggests that the construction and provision of economic infrastructure and other services were taken to be essential tasks of the public sector both at home and in the colonies. Palestine's lead may be explained by imperial-strategic considerations underpinning a good number of governmental projects (such as the extension of Palestine's railroad system and its links to the Middle Eastern regional network, the harbor in Haifa, and some of the newly constructed roads), and by the need for substantial overhead investments, primarily in transport and communication, in view of the poor economic state of the country after World War I and of the developmental tasks undertaken by Britain as Mandatory for Palestine (Gross, 1984b).

Unlike the functional distribution of government expenditures, which remained relatively stable throughout the period, the income component of the fiscal system underwent significant compositional changes over

Table 6.2. *Composition of taxes collected by the central government (%)*

	1921–33	1934–41	1942–47
direct taxes			
output and property taxes			
tithes, *werko*, and livestock tax	24.2	2.5	1.1
urban and rural property taxes		8.9	8.0
income tax			18.7
all direct taxes	24.2	11.4	27.8
indirect taxes			
customs	47.4	57.4	38.9
other indirect taxes	28.4	31.2	33.3
all indirect taxes	75.8	88.6	72.2
all taxes	*100.0*	*100.0*	*100.0*
direct/indirect tax ratio (%)	31.9	12.9	38.5

Source: Metzer (1982), table 1

time. These were concentrated in the makeup of direct (output, property, and income) taxes and their relative share in total tax revenue of the central government *vis-à-vis* that of indirect (customs, transaction, and excise) taxes (table 6.2).

Within the direct tax category, the most prominent changes during the inter-war period were: (a) the (gradual) abolition of the tithe – the traditional Ottoman tax on gross farm output – which by its very nature discriminated against low-value-added produce and against producers who suffered from declining yields; and (b) the replacement of the Ottoman land and buildings tax (the *werko*), based on property assessments from the early 1890s (except for property that changed hands after that, and was reassessed at the time of transaction), by modern, newly assessed property taxes. The new taxes on urban property were imposed in 1929, and on rural property in 1935. The imposition of the rural property tax, classifying land by actual cultivation and average yields, followed the recommendations of the renowned Johnson-Crosbie committee, which was appointed by the high commissioner in 1930 to examine the economic conditions of (primarily Arab) farmers and to recommend fiscal measures to increase equity within the agricultural sector and between it and the rest of the economy (Morag, 1967, chap. 1; Metzer, 1982).

The most significant change in the tax structure, however, was the introduction of a general progressive income tax in 1941, largely as a move to offset the reduction in the war-induced decline in revenue from import duties. In its imposition, the government finally implemented the major recommendation of the Johnson-Crosbie committee, which, because of Jewish objections (fearing that Jews would pay a disproportionate share of the income tax; see, for example, Ruppin, 1932), had to wait until the war before it could be acted on (Morag, 1967, chap. 1; Metzer, 1982).

The alterations in the composition of direct taxes, coupled with variations in the direct-indirect tax ratio (reported in table 6.2), closely resemble the typically development-induced patterns of change in tax structure observed and empirically generalized by Hinrichs (1966). These may be summarized as follows: in pre-modern economies, government revenues are derived primarily from traditional direct taxes on land, livestock, and gross agricultural output. With the onset of economic development, the weight of these taxes diminishes and that of indirect taxes on foreign trade and domestic transactions rises. As income continues to grow and economic activity diversifies, modern direct taxes on property and income gradually replace traditional levies; and in the indirect tax category the proportion of taxes on foreign trade declines. With further development direct taxation (now modern) occupies center stage again, thereby completing the U-shaped path of the direct-indirect tax ratio that is secularly associated with growth and modernization (Hinrich, 1966; Metzer, 1982).

While some of the changes in Palestine's tax structure that fit Hinrich's scheme were partly or wholly exogenous (for example, the exogenous factors facilitating the Jewish buildup in Palestine, or the relative decline in customs duties during World War II), a good number of them (not only property taxes, but also the new income tax) were, at least in part, endogenous, and could be linked to the enlargement of the market and to economic development in general. Although the timing of its introduction in 1941 was exogenously determined, the economic conditions favoring a general income tax were largely derived from the country's growth of income per earner and from the spread of modern economic activities (Metzer, 1982).

However, substantial as the changes in the tax structure may have been, import duties remained the single largest source of tax revenue throughout the period. Being relatively easy to collect, generally imposed customs were used by the Mandatory government as a major fiscal tool. By moving from the Ottoman *ad valorem* to specific duties, the government further improved the efficiency of collection and secured (*ex post*) an effectively rising tax rate in the inter-war era of generally declining prices.

In Palestine, uniformly imposed import duties (especially on goods for final use) had the additional advantage of not raising too many general or factional objections. Such objections were saved, however, for the Mandatory nondiscriminatory commercial policy (particularly as the flow of international trade came under administrative restrictions in an increasing number of countries during the depressionary 1930s) and for the various protective considerations, which were playing an ever more important role in the country's tariff structure (Morag, 1967, chap. 1; Gross, 1984b).

Motivated by "infant industry" arguments, and yielding to specific pressures for protection and support, the government ultimately exempted most raw materials and inputs used in material production from import duties, and imposed varying protective tariffs on almost all domestically manufactured goods (and on quite a few farm products as well).[8] These policies deviated somewhat from the colonial model of "mother countries" encouraging their colonies to maintain a comparative advantage in the production of primary products. They were partly driven by adaptations to conditions unique to Palestine, and were the basis of the government's endeavors to fulfill its dual obligation to promote the economic development of the modern Jewish settler community while caring for the economic well-being of the indigenous Arab population, within a general imperial developmental context (Smith, 1993, p. 46).

The non-uniform nature of the protective measures had an uneven effect on firms, industries, and consumers, whereupon the government's tariff and commercial policies came under attack from all factions concerned. Moreover, the industrial-structure and socio-economic differences between the Arab and Jewish communities led the Arabs, quite naturally, to push for the protection of agriculture (and to object to the exemption of agricultural inputs from import duties), whereas Jews emphasized the need to support manufacturing and foster modern farming by allowing customs-free imports of agricultural implements and inputs (Morag, 1967, chap. 1).

Thus, the issues involved in devising protective tariff schemes in Palestine are a vivid example of the difficulties faced by the government in attempting to pursue policies of least resistance, let alone to fulfill its "dual obligation."[9] These attempts were obviously not limited to

---

[8] Note, however, that Palestine's free trade arrangements with Syria somewhat offset the effect of the agriculture-protecting commercial policies (Morag, 1967, chap. 1).

[9] Smith (1993), for example, views the British tariff policy that evolved in Palestine during the 1920s as essentially a scheme providing protection to Jewish industry, whose ties with the indigenous population were fairly meager. And although she concedes that "it is impossible, of course, to correlate the successes in the Jewish industrial sector with the manipulation of the tariff system" (p. 181), she views British policy as a contributing factor in the development of a Jewish industrial enclave and, as such, in the separatist tendencies of the Jewish economy. While I agree with Smith on the contribution of some British policies to Jewish-Arab economic separatism (largely enhanced by the attributes of Jewish economic activity), the claims that the prime beneficiaries of the tariffs in Mandatory Palestine were Jewish industrialists, and that these benefits were in any way consequential, are empirically unverified.

customs; they were part of the fiscal system as a whole, and of the entire range of activities undertaken by the Mandatory government in its capacity as public sector. In examining the attributes and outcomes of these policies it would therefore be illuminating to look at the incidence of government taxes and expenditures along Arab-Jewish lines.

In a detailed study conducted some time ago (Metzer, 1982), I estimated the incidence of the taxes collected from, and outlays made by, the central government on Arabs and Jews in two fiscal years: April 1, 1926 to March 31, 1927; and April 1, 1935 to March 31, 1936. These two years were similar in that they were non-violent by the standards of Arab-Jewish relations and thus did not require costly expenditures on security. In other important respects they differed from one another: 1926/27 can be seen as representing the consolidation that set in during the second half of the 1920s, following the formative years of the new regime and the end of the first large wave of Jewish immigration (see chapter 3), preceding the major changes in the structure of direct taxes; 1935/6 typified the economic maturity reached at the height of the mass immigration of the mid-1930s, which substantially raised the weight of the Jewish community, both in terms of population and in terms of output (in 1935/36 Jews accounted for 27 percent of the country's population and 53 percent of its NNP, as against 16 percent and 26 percent respectively in 1926/27). Drawing on these estimates and revising them according to our recently constructed output figures, table 6.3 presents some orders of magnitude describing the allocation of taxes and government expenditures between Arabs and Jews.

Considering the income side of the system, observe that in both years the proportion of total tax revenues paid by Jews was substantially larger than their share in Palestine's total income, let alone in the overall population. Moreover, the figures in the table show that this outcome was driven solely by the exceedingly large proportion of indirect taxes paid by Jews, whereas the share of direct taxes, though it rose appreciably (thanks to the introduction of property taxes), remained lower than the Jewish share in the country's total output in both 1926/27 and 1935/36.

This observation indicates that it was primarily the intensity of transactions and the relatively high propensity to import out of income (and resources) that characterized the richer and more economically versatile Jewish community, that made for the higher Jewish tax-income ratio and hence for a progressive tax system between the two communities.[10]

---

[10] A tax system is defined as "progressive" (in income terms) if it reduces the inequality of income distribution; it is "regressive" if it raises income inequality; and "neutral" (or "proportional") if it has no effect on income inequality. A tax-income ratio that rises with income therefore indicates a progressive tax structure, a constant ratio indicates a neutral one, and a declining tax-income ratio a regressive tax structure.

Table 6.3. *Fiscal incidence – Arabs and Jews: 1926/27, 1935/36*

A Taxes I. *Composition and incidence (%)*

			incidence		
		composition	Arabs	Jews	total
1926/27	direct	24.2	78.5	21.5	100.0
	indirect	75.8	57.0	43.0	100.0
	all (P£1,779,600)	100.0	62.2	37.8	100.0
1935/36	direct	9.2	52.3	47.7	100.0
	indirect	90.8	34.5	65.5	100.0
	all (P£4,787,100)	100.0	36.1	63.9	100.0

II. *Taxes per capita and NNP (resource) shares of taxes*

		Arabs (A)	Jews (J)	(J)/(A)
1926/27	taxes per capita (P£)	1.5	4.5	3.000
	share in Palestine's NNP (%)	73.7	26.3	0.357
	share of taxes (%):			
	in NNP	9.4	16.0	1.702
	in resources	9.4	8.2	0.872
1935/36	taxes per capita (P£)	1.8	8.8	4.889
	share in Palestine's NNP (%)	46.5	53.5	1.151
	share of taxes (%):			
	in NNP	11.0	16.9	1.536
	in resources	11.0	11.3	1.027

B Non-business expenditures

		Arabs	Jews
1926/27	expenditure incidence (%):		
	administrative and economic	75.8	24.2
	social services	86.2	13.8
	all expenditures (P£1,521,100)	77.5	22.5
	expenditure per capita (P£)	1.6	2.3
	expenditure share in NNP (%)	10.0	8.2
1935/36	expenditure incidence (%):		
	administrative and economic	52.9	47.1
	social services	79.8	20.2
	all expenditures (P£3,857,600)	56.8	43.2
	expenditure per capita (P£)	2.3	4.8
	expenditure share in NNP (%)	13.9	9.2

C Net fiscal incidence: resources transferred from Jews to Arabs

		1926/27	1935/36
total	'000 P£	271.8	864.3
Arabs	% of NNP (+)	2.3	5.5
Jews	% of NNP (−)	6.5	4.8
	resources (−)	3.3	3.2

Sources: Adapted from Metzer (1982), tables 2, 3, 8, 12, A1–A4, and table A.22

Similarly, official governmental estimates indicate that Jews probably contributed about 63 percent of the central government's total tax revenues in 1944/45, with Arabs accounting for the remaining 37 percent (*Survey*, 1946, vol. II, chap. XIV). These distributions closely resemble the shares found for the mid-1930s, making for a Jewish tax-income ratio of 9.2 percent, compared with an Arab ratio of 7.6 percent. It may thus be inferred that although tax progressivity was maintained, it was weaker in the mid-1940s than in 1935/36, suggesting that the newly introduced progressive income tax was not sufficient to offset the effect of the decline in the share of indirect taxes during the war (from 90.8 percent in of total tax revenue in 1935/36 to 56.2 percent in 1944/45) on the reduction of the relative tax burden on Jews.

Note, however, that the government did not pursue a deliberate redistributive tax policy (certainly not before the imposition of the general income tax in the early 1940s). Rather, it limited its equity goals, insofar as Arabs and Jews were concerned, to the proportionality of the tax system (Metzer, 1982). Incidentally, as a percentage of resources (domestic product *plus* net capital imports), the realized tax rates were indeed quite similar in the two communities, rendering the inter-war tax system quite proportional between Arabs and Jews in terms of their overall resources (table 6.3).

Whether the tax system was progressive or proportional, the considerable (and widening) Jewish lead in income and resources per capita meant that in the mid-1920s taxes paid by Jews were thrice those paid by Arabs, in per capita terms, and almost five times larger in the mid-1930s. But the same economic and developmental disparities also created a Jewish advantage in the per capita utilization of government outlays: according to our incidence estimates, the average Jewish inhabitant of Palestine utilized 1.4–2.1 times more public services and aid (as measured by total non-business expenditures of the central government) than did his Arab counterpart (table 6.3).

A similar picture is revealed at the local government level, whose services between the late 1930s and mid-1940s – financed by property and occupancy taxes – were about 15 percent of the volume of expenditures by the central government. In 1944, for example, in a total of fifty-eight urban localities (involving 85 percent of all Jews residing in Palestine and 39 percent of the country's Arabs), the level of municipal and local public expenditures per Jewish inhabitant was three times higher than per Arab resident (*Survey*, 1946, vol. I, chaps. IV, V).

Returning to the central government, since the intercommunity tax differential was larger than that of government's expenditures (as the incidence figures in table 6.3 indicate), the Mandatory fiscal system provided a net (involuntary, of course) transfer of resources from the high-income Jewish community to the low-income Arab community. The burden that this transfer imposed on the Jews did not change much in income terms between the two years, accounting for c.5 percent of Jewish NNP in 1926/27 and 4.8 percent in 1935/36.[11] The same transfer, however, added only a modest 2.3 percent to Arab NNP in 1926/27, reflecting the fact that the Arab economy's total output in the mid-1920s was still about three times larger than the Jewish output. But in the mid-1930s, with Jewish NNP 15 percent larger than Arab NNP, the weight of the net fiscal transfer rose to 5.5 percent of Arab NNP.

Apart from "natural" conflicts of interests regarding the composition of taxes and government expenditures, the political economy of Palestine's fiscal system is marked by sharp disagreements between Arabs and Jews over the basic premises and political implications of its redistributional mechanism. This mechanism, while reducing income inequality between Arabs and Jews, could be viewed as an implementation of the ability-to-pay principle that is standard practice in public-finance schemes run by central governments concerned with equity considerations. In our context, however, this principle implied (tacit) acceptance of the notion that Palestine was a single entity under the unifying rule of the British Mandate. In view of the non-separatist approach generally adopted by the country's Arab majority, it is no wonder that the Arab position favored ability-to-pay guidelines (see chapter 1), as summarized by Abcarius:

Now, assuming that it can be established beyond any doubt that Jews are contributing to public revenue more than the Arabs, what would this imply? Simply this: that the Jews are better off materially ... that their earnings are greater than those of the Arabs, and consequently they are better able to pay taxes. But the indubitable fact remains that they are not contributing a bean more than their *due share* ... So long as taxes are equitably distributed it matters not in the least who pays more. The wealthier classes in any well-ordered community pay more in taxes than their less fortunate compatriots, while governmental expenditure is so directed as to produce the greatest possible degree of well-being among the population as a whole. In the process, governmental expenditure achieves, in effect, a certain redistribution of the national wealth in favor of the poorer classes. (Abcarius, 1946, pp. 183–84; italics in original)

The separatist Zionist view point contrasted with the Arabs' unified approach to the relationship between the government and the inhabitants of Palestine, both as individuals and as members of two distinct ethno-national communities. According to the Zionist position, the "National

---

[11] In terms of net resources (NNP *plus* net capital imports), the burden of the fiscal transfer was practically the same in the two years (3.3 percent in 1926/27 and 3.2 percent in 1935/36).

Home" clauses of the Mandate required the government to provide Jews with public services commensurate with the level of taxes collected from them. In the introduction to the Jewish Agency's tax-incidence study of 1934/35 (prepared in order to provide empirical support for this claim), David Gurevich, the agency statistician, states:

While agreeing with the view that the burden of taxation borne by every *individual* should be in relation to his ability to pay, the Jewish Agency is of the opinion that the amounts contributed by the *Jewish community as a whole* should be taken in consideration with respect to some, or all the items of Jewish expenditure. (Gurevich, 1936, p. 3; italics in original)

Thus, while accepting the equitable ability-to-pay principle at the individual level, the Zionist position pushed for the implementation of the *pay according to benefits received* (the opposite criterion) at the intercommunity level.

In reviewing the matter, the Palestine Royal Commission of 1937 suggested the following possible interpretations of the Jewish approach:

It runs counter to one of the two principles. Either it repudiates the basic idea of public finance in the democratic world – that the rich should be taxed to meet the needs of the poor – or it denies or ignores the theory that Arabs and Jews are members of one Palestinian society. (*RCR*, 1937, pp. 119–20)

Indeed, it was the rejection of the latter theory, and its implied abandonment of the National Home postulate, that made the Zionists oppose the equity principle of fiscalism, and precisely the same reasons caused Arabs to support it wholeheartedly.

The government, for its part, generally advocated a unified, equity-oriented approach to taxation and public services for the country as a whole. On concrete matters, however, it would have been impractical for the government to disregard community-specific factors, or the constraints imposed on its "dual obligation" policies by the rivalry between Arabs and Jews. Consider, for example, postponing the introduction of income tax, or willingness to examine (in 1931) Jewish demands for a larger share of government employment, based on their relative contribution to tax revenues. Moreover, given the autonomous provision of public services by (and within) the Jewish community, it could be argued that equity considerations *per se* did justify various community-specific governmental measures, mainly on the expenditure side (Metzer, 1982).

Indeed, unlike generally imposed taxes, a sizable portion of government investment, services, and transfer payments were earmarked according to community criteria. In the economic sphere the earmarked part constituted about 12 percent of all government expenditures in the mid-1920s and no less than one-third in the mid-1930s. Prominent examples of community-specific economic outlays include roads constructed in ethno-national homogeneous regions, agricultural facilities and services installed in Arab rural areas and specifically provided by the government to Arab peasants, and various grants to Jewish agricultural research institutes and projects (Metzer, 1982).

Interestingly, though, close examination reveals that the Jewish share in the earmarked portion of economic services rose steeply, from about 12 percent in 1926/27 to 51 percent in 1935/36, and much more rapidly than the rise in their share of the non-earmarked component (which grew from 23 percent to 47 percent between these two years: Metzer, 1982, appendix). In general terms, these figures may reflect the government's response to the demand for publicly provided economic services generated by the growing and modernizing Jewish-led economy. But more specifically, it was probably more closely related to the effects of the increasing density of Jewish settlement and its geographic expansion on the spatial distribution of transport infrastructure – the major component of the economic services category. Note, in particular, the government's favorable response to Jewish demands for access roads to new settlements and newly settled regions, which were backed by participation of the settlers and the Zionist Organization in financing such projects (Reichman, 1971; Metzer, 1982).

It may thus be inferred that, being partly induced by development-generated demand for modern infrastructure, the allocation of some of the government's economic outlays was driven by considerations of complementarity with the Jewish community's own public efforts in the field. While other – primarily strategic and internal security – considerations did affect road construction, certainly from 1936 onward, the resulting picture was one of a large number of Arab villages not being served by paved roads until the end of the Mandate period (Reichman, 1971).

As for the earmarked provision of social services, primarily education, the government viewed the autonomous, self-financed Jewish school system, which had no equivalent in the Arab community, as a substitute for its own activity in the field. Consequently, it directed its efforts to establishing and directly running government public schools for the Arab population. It also attempted, at least in the early years, to establish health facilities in heavily populated Arab areas. In Jewish education (and to a lesser extent in Jewish health-care services) the government's earmarked involvement took the form of financial aid channeled through officially recognized Jewish national and communal institutions (see chapter 1 and Metzer, 1982); besides, Jewish schools and health-care establishments were obviously subject to government regulation and inspection (*Survey*, 1946, vol. II, chap. XVI).

In distributional terms, the community-specific differences are reflected in the finding that education was the only area in which Arabs received, by design or otherwise, a larger portion than Jews of government expenditures on a per capita basis (more than double in 1926/27 and 1.6-fold in 1935/36: Metzer, 1982). Moreover, contrary to the changes in the incidence of all other governmental services (including health), which raised the Jewish per capita utilization advantage between 1926/27 and 1935/36, the per capita edge of Arabs over Jews in benefiting from government outlays in education grew from 1.6 times in 1926/27 to 2.2 times in 1935/36.

With Jewish resources allocated to education and health so substantial (see below), the government's attempts to compensate for Arab deficiencies in the provision and utilization of social services fell far short of the resources needed to close the enormous Jewish superiority in per capita overall outlays in these areas (see also chapter 2). In the mid-1920s, for example, total expenditure per capita on education in the Jewish sector (government and Jewish own) were fourteenfold larger than the government expenditure on Arab education. Although the gap narrowed, it remained 8.6-fold in the mid-1930s (the corresponding differentials in health were 12.2- and 8.7-fold, respectively), leaving the Arab population lagging far behind the Jewish community with respect to the extent of schooling and health care.[12]

These remarks, stressing the importance of Jewish self-provided public services, lead us naturally to the next section, in which Palestine's non-government public sectors are taken up.

Non-government public sectors

Alongside the central and local governments, a variety of religious and secular not-for-profit organizations operated in Palestine, running schools, hospitals, and some welfare services (nowadays we would classify them as belonging to the "third," non-public and non-private, sector). In the Arab community these were rather diffuse organizations, unco-ordinated, and fairly limited in scope. Jews, on the other hand, were able to turn their officially recognized national institutions (the Zionist Organization and, from 1929 on, the enlarged Jewish Agency for

---

[12] These differentials may be upward biased, since Arab expenditures on own education were not taken into account. However, the available data imply that these expenditures were minor (in 1944 for example, the outlays of non-Jewish voluntary health services amounted to 12 percent of Jewish own-expenditures in the field; *Survey*, vol. II, chap. XVI), so that the Arab-Jewish gap in the provision of social services must have been sub-stantial.

Table 6.4. *Percentage distribution of Jewish (own) public expenditures: 1925/26 and 1935/36*

	1925/26	1935/36
administration and security	5.4	5.9
economic outlays		
immigration	10.8	4.7
agricultural settlement	30.0	19.2
urban settlement	3.9	2.1
labor	6.0	3.2
all economic outlays	50.7	29.2
social services		
education	18.4	25.7
health	25.5	34.5
welfare		4.7
all social services	43.9	64.9
total expenditures	100.0	100.0
('000 P£)	(784.4)	(1302.5)
total expenditures: per capita (P£)	5.8	3.7
as % of NNP	18.5	7.2
% of Zionist budget in total expenditures	79.5	49.2

Sources: Statistical Handbook (1947), chapters on culture and education, and health; Gross and Metzer (1978), table 8; Ziv (1996), part II, chap. 6.

Palestine) and the elected governing body (*va'ad leumi*) of their statutory (religiously defined) community into a quasi-governmental public sector. From the early 1930s on, the evolving division of functions between the Jewish Agency and the *va'ad leumi* made the latter responsible, in addition to religious and communal affairs, for the Jewish school system. Add to this the health-care services provided by the USA-based Zionist Women's Organization (*Hadassah*), and by the *Histadrut*'s sick fund (*Kupat Holim*), as well as welfare services generated by these and other organizations, and one gets a pretty comprehensive system of self-administered Jewish public services (*Survey*, 1946 vol. II, chap. XXII; Horowitz and Lissak, 1978, chap. 3; Gross and Metzer, 1978; Ziv, 1996).

Combining all the Jewish self-provided public services (table 6.4) with the Jewish share in government expenditures in the mid-1920s and mid-1930s (table 6.3) reveals that the former reached 72 percent of all the public services utilized by Jews in 1926/27 (44 percent in 1935/36). The total public expenditure-output ratio in the Jewish economy thus rose from 8 to 9 percent, for government outlays only, to 29 percent and 16 percent for both sources combined in the two years, respectively.

The major single item in the all-inclusive Jewish public sector was the "Zionist budget" – expenditures of the Zionist Organization (and, from 1929 onward, the Jewish Agency) in Palestine.[13] These were largely funded by contributions made by world Jewry to the fund-raising bodies of the Zionist Organization (primarily *Keren Hayesod*, the Foundation Fund), which accounted over the period for about 80 percent of the Zionist budget's income (net of the funds raised by the JNF for purchasing land); the rest originated domestically: from government grants, other contributions, service fees (mainly tuition), interest, and debt repayments.

Being heavily financed by unilateral transfers from abroad, the Zionist Organization could, on the one hand, provide the Jewish community with a substantial volume of "free" public services, but, on the other hand, the level of its yearly expenditures became highly dependent on largely exogenous sources of income. For example, Gross and Metzer (1978) found that unlike the domestically generated sources of Zionist incomes, which (not surprisingly) were positively correlated with the level of income per capita of Palestine's Jews, the major source of income – annual contributions by world Jewry – was negatively associated with this variable. In part, the negative association between contributions from abroad and the economic well-being of the Jews in Palestine may suggest a "natural" contributors' response to needs; but it may also have reflected the fact that the world's cycles in economic activity and well-being, with which the Zionist funds raised abroad were positively linked, ran counter in time to the fluctuations in Palestine's Jewish economy (mainly in the 1930s).

These linkages may explain the generally non-rising pattern of expenditures in the Zionist budget up to the mid-1930s (figure 6.1) and the general decline in Zionist outlays, both per capita (Jews only, figure 6.2) and as a percentage of Jewish income (figure 6.3), during the same period. Note, however, that the part of the Mandatory government's total and per capita outlays (serving all of Palestine's inhabitants) that was financed mainly by wealth- and income-associated domestic taxation did show a secularly rising trend, while the share of government expenditures in Palestine's total output (Arab and Jewish combined) shows no particular trend (figures 6.1 and 6.3).

The secularly non-rising Zionist budget brought about a reduction in

---

[13] The all-inclusive Jewish public sector was taken to include, in addition to the domestic outlays of the Zionist Organization, all the educational outlays of *va'ad leumi* schools; health services provided by *Hadassah*, the *Histadrut* sick fund, and other non-profit organizations; and all the institutionalized welfare services in the Jewish community. For the foundations of the Zionist budget in the pre-Mandatory years of British rule (1918–21) see Lavsky (1980). For later years see Gross and Metzer (1978).

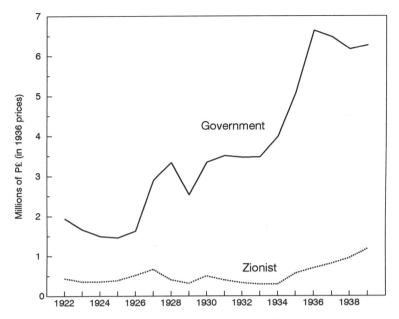

Figure 6.1 Public outlays: government and Zionist
(excluding land purchases), 1922–39
(sources: Gross and Metzer, 1978, tables 8, 14; Gross, 1984b, table 1)

the weight of its expenditures in the outlays of the extended Jewish public
sector, from about 80 percent in the mid-1920s to 49 percent in the mid-
1930s. A similar pattern can be seen in the decline of total Jewish public
expenditures per capita and as a percentage of Jewish income and
resources (table 6.4). However, on a disaggregate level, we see that health
expenditures per capita changed very little between the two years, and
education outlays per person aged five to nineteen even rose (in constant
prices). Both items, as well as total per capita Jewish public outlays on
social services, did increase between 1925/26 and 1935/36; the reduction
occurred mainly in economic services (Sicron and Gill, 1955; Gross and
Metzer, 1978).

These observations are consistent with the rising weight of domestic
sources in the financing of health and educational services as the Jewish
population and income per capita grew. The figures also suggest that
public expenditures on economic services – primarily preparatory training and immigrant absorption, land improvement and investment in agricultural settlements, and supporting rural (and, to a limited extent, also
urban) economic undertakings – were sensitive to variations in the

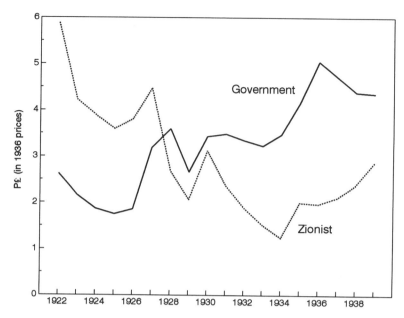

Figure 6.2 Public outlays per capita: government (total) and Zionist (Jews), 1922–39
(sources: Gross and Metzer, 1978, tables 8, 14; Gross, 1984b, table 1 for outlays; table A.1 for population)

Zionist inflow of funds. As conjectured above, some of these funds may have been "endogenously" responsive to absorption needs, a possibility that is also supported by the observed positive association between the patterns of immigration (lagged by one year) and of Zionist outlays on agricultural settlements (Gross and Metzer, 1978).

The composition of Jewish public expenditures, which was dominated by economic and social services (table 6.4), closely resembles the makeup of government outlays in the United Kingdom and in other developed European countries (Gross and Metzer, 1978, and above). Note, though, that the Jewish community was able to allocate most of its public resources to non-administrative purposes, thanks largely to the country-wide administrative and legal infrastructure provided by the Mandatory government.

Generally, the Jewish allocation of public outlays by function was motivated by – and reflected – the Zionist objective of establishing in Palestine a territorially based, occupationally balanced and socio-economically progressive Jewish national entity. In the realization of these goals, aimed

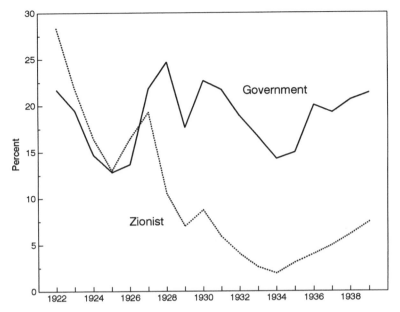

Figure 6.3 Income share of expenditure: government (in total) and
Zionist (in Jewish) NNP in current prices, 1922–39
(sources: Gross and Metzer, 1978, tables 8, 14; Gross, 1984b, table 1
for outlays; tables A.19 and A.20 for NNP)

at bringing about a Jewish majority in the country, agricultural settlement
was to play a major role. According to the standard Zionist "blueprint,"
the Jewish nation-building process in Palestine required first and foremost the transformation of immigrants in large numbers into agricultural
settlers, forming a Jewish labor-self-sufficient farm sector, whose spatial
boundaries (which were expected to expand by the continuous acquisition of land) were to determine the extent of the Jewish territorial base
(see chapters 1 and 4).

In addition, Zionist circles typically conceived of agricultural settlement as the most efficient means of absorbing immigration, requiring
smaller investments in physical capital and training, and a shorter gesta-
tion period than that of manufacturing. Similarly, the occupational
concentration in agriculture was expected to change the occupational
composition of Jews in Palestine from the typical Diaspora pattern, which
was heavily biased in favor of services, into a balanced industrial structure
that would emphasize material production. Moreover, farming (especially by self-employed farmers) was supposed to forge an emotional link,
a posteriori, between settlers and their land, above and beyond material

considerations. According to mainstream Zionist ideology, these attributes were to be essential factors in the transformation of the Jewish people into a "normal" territorial nation, with a physical (and not solely metaphysical) link to the land, and as such be instrumental in assuring the viability of Jewish colonization in Palestine.

Viewed thus, and notwithstanding the presumed efficiency advantage of agriculture over manufacturing in the absorption of immigrants, the promotion of agricultural settlement, relying exclusively on Jewish labor, and spatially located according to national and not necessarily economic criteria, was perceived by the Zionists as a national public good that should, at least in part, be collectively financed (see also chapter 4).

A complementary feature of this nation-building process was to be the renaissance of the Hebrew language and culture within a system of publicly initiated and maintained (although not freely provided) educational services. To complete the list of functions of the Jewish public sector there were the health and social insurance services facilitated by Jewish public and not-for-profit institutions, and utilized in practice, if not by design, almost exclusively by Jews (see chapter 2; and Metzer, 1977, 1978).

The public–private mix in the Jewish economy

As a direct corollary of the discussion so far one is logically led to ask what implications the Zionist design of a Jewish National Home (or state-to-be) had for the desired nature of the economic regime and the public-private mix in the Jewish community. In view of the high national priority accorded to labor-self-sufficient Jewish farming, reinforced by the desire of organized Jewish labor to encourage agriculture and create an ethnically segregated labor market (see chapter 4), Zionism did not view the allocation of public financial funds to support private enterprise (by grants or subsidized credit for capital investments) as sufficient for carrying out the task. The realization of national economic objectives, according to the prevailing Zionist attitudes, called for more direct collective action, which in the absence of Jewish sovereignty could not be achieved by coercive regulations, only by economic means.

Prime among these means was Zionist (national) ownership of Jewish land, an expression of Jewish collective rights in Palestine (as distinct from individual property rights). Nationalized land was to be leased to private or collective would-be settlers at preferential terms, which were expected to guarantee agricultural settlement according to national-spatial considerations. Furthermore, making national land available for private use was to be conditional upon adherence to the requirements of in-residence cultivation and the exclusion of non-Jewish hired labor. It thus follows that the Zionist quasi-government could have wielded certain power over all economic activities undertaken on national land, including those that were to be privately and independently financed (see chapter 4). By the end of the Mandate, national (mostly rural) land owned by the JNF amounted to about 47 percent of all Jewish land holdings in Palestine (Reichman, 1979, p. 79; chapter 4), making it quite a potent instrument for collective action (Metzer, 1978).

Another consideration advocating the promotion of Jewish economic development by collective action early on in the British Mandate was the strong sense of urgency prevailing in Zionism at the time. All Zionist factions accepted the notion that obstructive objections to the Zionist endeavor would be put forward (particularly by Arabs); this made it politically imperative to hasten the Jewish buildup, necessitating immediate public investment in less-than-profitable projects (even if these might, at some later date, be deemed profitable and privately undertaken: Metzer, 1978). Note that even Justice Louis Brandeis, the liberal leader of the American Zionist Organization up to 1921, and in principle a strong advocate of private initiative in realizing the Zionist national plan, argued:

The present unremunerative character of these needed investments of capital is intensified by the present high cost of construction, – yet we cannot wait until prices fall. Their need is urgent. The expenditure must be made immediately like a war expenditure regardless of cost because speed in settlement is indispensable. For the same reason we cannot, as in the case of other colonial development, leave would-be settlers to work out problems slowly and painfully through successive failure to ultimate success. We must succeed reasonably soon in effecting the settlement, partly because others will intervene; partly because our effort will be ever on general exhibition and subject to hostile criticism. (Brandeis, 1921, p. 52)

Notwithstanding this and the other arguments, discussed above, that were raised in support of the public component in the public-private mix of the Jewish economy, the liberal leadership of the Zionist Organization in the 1920s viewed, *ceteris paribus*, a private enterprise regime as a national objective in itself. Underlying this viewpoint was the (proven) hypothesis that while a substantial number of prospective immigrants would be young Jewish socialists in need of public assistance to finance their immigration and absorption, the main reservoir of manpower and capital for Jewish colonization in Palestine was concentrated in the petit bourgeois and middle classes of Diaspora Jewry. These potential immigrants required a free-market environment in order to be attracted to and commit their resources to the Zionist cause.

The design resulting from these and other, often conflicting, considerations was one of a mixed economy in which collective action – designed to ensure the realization of national and social objectives – was to be undertaken by public sectors in amicable coexistence with a private sector in an essentially market environment. From the 1930s onward, the Zionist Organization was controlled by the labor movement. Although this movement held the market's allocative and distributional mechanism in mistrust, and attempted to increase the weight of collective action and non-market mechanisms in economic life, the labor-dominated Zionist leadership did not attempt to alter the basic nature of the Jewish community as a mixed economy (Metzer, 1978).

A major institutional and economic instrument to facilitate collective action in the Jewish economy, besides nationally owned land and public funds placed at the disposal of the Zionist executive, was the growing role of the *Histadrut* – the dominant Jewish labor organization – as a major provider of health and social insurance, and a labor-owned productive sector composed of communal settlements, transportation cooperatives, and large construction, manufacturing, and marketing establishments.

During the period under review (especially from the 1930s onward) a certain division of labor was worked out between the national institutions (namely the Jewish Agency and the *va'ad leumi*) and the *Histadrut* as regards performing public economic functions. The former concentrated primarily on setting priorities and providing allocative guidance within the Jewish economy, and the latter was largely the economic executor of collective functions as determined by the (labor) leadership of the Zionist Organization and by organized labor.[14]

The hegemony of labor Zionism in the Mandatory Jewish community from the mid-1930s (and for the first twenty-nine years of Israel's statehood) did not, however, turn the Jewish community into an economy dominated by agricultural (or other material) production relying exclusively on Jewish labor (see chapters 4 and 5), nor did it lead to the concentration of economic activity in the non-private sector. Throughout the entire Mandate period (and in the Israeli economy as well: see Barkai, 1964), the share of the non-private labor economy (including communal and smallholder settlements [*kibbutzim* and *moshavim*]; producers' cooperatives; *Histadrut*-owned banks, insurance companies, production and marketing companies, and sick fund) probably did not exceed 20 percent of Jewish NDP.[15] Note, too, that from the employment point of view, 14,000 people were estimated to have been employed in 1944 in

---

[14] For more elaborate discussions and a variety of general viewpoints on the subject see Muenzner (1945); Horowitz and Lissak (1978); Greenberg (1987); Kleiman (1987); Barkai (1989a, 1989b); Grinberg (1991); Shalev (1992); Plessner (1994); and Sternhell (1995).

[15] This conjecture is based on the orders of magnitude suggested by Muenzner (1945, p. 14), and on Barkai's (1964) estimates for 1953. See also Metzer (1978).

Histadrut economic establishments and sick fund, with another 26,000 employed in communal and smallholder settlements (Muenzner, 1945, p. 13), totaling only about 18 percent of all Jewish employed persons (222,000) in Palestine at the time.

Nonetheless, the political and economic leadership of labor Zionism certainly did define the general contours of the distinct economic regime of the Jewish community, thereby contributing to the separation of the Jewish economy from its Arab counterpart and, in addition, providing a legacy for the institutional structure and the substantial public involvement in the Israeli economy for years to come (see also Ben-Porath, 1986b; and Plessner, 1994).

Postscript: some observations on economic
coexistence in ethno-national adversity
The area of Mandatory Palestine, past and present

As suggested in the introductory chapter and demonstrated by the
detailed accounts in the rest of the book, the economic fabric of
Mandatory Palestine can best be fathomed in the context of a "dual
economy" approach. The basic ingredients, broadly defined, of economic
dualism were all shown to be major attributes of Palestine's ethno-nationally divided economy. To recapitulate, these are: persistent socio-economic gaps between the economy's advanced sector and its relatively
traditional one; divergent developmental regimes within which each
sector conducts its separate economic life; bilateral trade in production
factors, goods, and services, whose composition is largely determined by
inter-sectoral differences in endowments of physical and human
resources and by disparities in production technology and in market
structure. It has also been stressed that the effective constraints on inter-
sectoral socio-economic convergence and market unification, necessary
to sustain economic dualism, may have reflected ethnic (or other) segmentation, institutional rigidities, market imperfections (including discriminatory market behavior), and, in certain instances, deliberate
policies of exclusion.

A well-known example of economic dualism that exhibits these
entwined factors evolved in the (primarily) African settlement colonies.
European settlers, whose economic activity was concentrated in labor-
intensive plantations and crop farming, mining, and to a lesser extent
manufacturing, were sharply distinguished from the indigenous nomadic
herdsmen and peasants. However, in his study of the economic history of
Kenya and Southern Rhodesia, Paul Mosley (1983) showed that the
mark of a "settler economy" is not necessarily any specific economic
structure, but rather a distinctive mechanism of "extra-market operations" and intervention by the colonial administration.

The colonial administrations typically used their power of coercion to
legislate and enforce property rights in land and to regulate key aspects of
the land and labor markets, including a racial division of land ownership
backed by bans on inter-ethnic transactions in land and by restricting the

mobility of indigenous workers. The result was a supply of cheap (often free) land for settlers and a relatively elastic supply of (indigenous) low-wage labor, secured by fiat. In addition, various regulatory means were used in the settlement colonies to prevent indigenous farmers from competing with settlers in export markets. In actively pursuing such discriminatory policies, suppressing natives, and promoting the interests of the European settlers, the colonial administrations obviously reinforced the developmental cleavage and the exceedingly unequal income distribution between the two population segments.[1]

The economic story of Palestine, where mostly European Jewish immigrants established a modern economic entity under the Mandatory umbrella, separate from the indigenous Arab population, has often been branded in the (primarily sociological) literature with the characteristics of a settlement colony.[2] But such an attribution fails to draw a crucial difference between the two cases. Unlike the colonial settler economy, in which government-imposed allocations and administrative constraints were essential in facilitating and maintaining the settlers' economic superiority, the territorial buildup and economic edge of the Jewish settlers in Palestine stemmed from their *own* comparative advantage in material, human, and technological resources, and from the Jewish community's institutional structure and organizations, which were far better developed than those of the indigenous Arab community.

Consider, for example, the mechanism of Jewish land acquisition and retention. As pointed out, Jews could – and did – acquire land from non-Jews only by paying its full market price to free, willing sellers. But retaining the land in Jewish hands required keeping such transactions unidirectional. The responsibility for land retention was undertaken primarily by the Zionist national institutions, who performed 60 percent of the Jewish land purchases from non-Jews in the Mandatory period, holding their landed property in perpetuity, and leasing it only to Jewish users. Private Jewish landowners followed suit voluntarily and generally refrained from selling land to non-Jews.

However, although Zionist land policy, unlike typical settlers' economies, depended on the availability of an unregulated land market, it generated some effects that resembled the outcomes of the policies implemented by colonial administrations in order to promote settlers' agricul-

---

[1] Examples of settler economies include British Rhodesia, Kenya, South Africa, and French Algeria. Extensive and illuminating discussions on their workings appear, among others, in Albertini (1982), covering the European colonial rule at large between 1880 and 1940; Mosley (1983) for the economic history of Kenya and Southern Rhodesia; and Worden (1994) for the history of modern South Africa.

[2] See discussions in Robinson (1973); Zureik (1979); Kimmerling (1983a, b); Shafir (1989, 1993); Kamen (1991); Ram (1993); Smith (1993); Aaronsohn (1996).

ture. For example, the incentives for settlement created by the Zionist institutions, who leased the land they purchased to Jewish settlers, and at preferred terms, were analogous to similar incentives generated by governments that were interested in promoting private exploitation of public domains – notably the incentives provided by colonial governments in allocating free or generously cheap crown lands to European settlers. Likewise, it could be argued that the effect on Arab tenant-cultivators, who were involuntarily dispossessed from the land they farmed as a result of it being sold (not exclusively, but mainly) to Jews, was qualitatively similar to (though quantitatively much smaller than) the consequences of various "land alienation" schemes for natives who lost their (primarily communal) grazing rights and other rural possessions in settlement colonies.

On the labor scene, the largely futile efforts of labor Zionism to exclude Arab labor from the Jewish (especially private-farm) economy differed completely from the colonial regulatory mechanism of supplying European employers with cheap indigenous labor in settlement colonies. As already emphasized, one of the ideological arguments put forward in Zionism in justification of labor segregation according to ethno-national criteria was precisely the need to prevent Jewish farmers from becoming colonial-type planters who employ natives at low wages.

Nonetheless, both practices are analogous in being manifestations of external intervention, drawing an ethno-national distinction in the workings of the labor market.[3] Moreover, to the extent that the Zionist attempts at segregating the labor market (by means such as the contract-enforcing capacity of the national land-owning institutions on lessees, the organizational power of the *Histadrut* in the Jewish labor market, and public-opinion formation and persuasion) did contribute to the persistence of wage differentials between Arab and Jewish (unskilled) workers, they were comparable to some of the wage effects of the coercive labor policies observed in colonial settler economies.

It is evident from these remarks and from references to Palestine's government's attitudes and policies in previous chapters that the Mandatory government played a distinct economic role in Palestine. Unlike the typically one-sided active involvement of the colonial administrations in settlement colonies, the government of Palestine, while attempting to

---

[3] Institutional imposition of ethnic distinction on the operation of the labor markets is obviously not confined to colonial settings; it can be found in other instances of labor discrimination and segregation along ethnic lines as well. See, for example, Becker's (1971) treatise on the economics of discrimination and Stanley Greenberg's (1980) comparative account concerning issues of race and ethnic domination in the economic lives of South Africa, Alabama USA, Northern Ireland, Mandatory Palestine, and Israel.

fulfill its dual obligation to the Zionist cause and to the well-being of the Arab population, provided a legal framework for mostly unregulated economic activity (a notable exception was the series of attempts to regulate and restrict intercommunal transactions in land in order to protect Arab tenants and peasants from their land-alienation outcomes: see chapter 4). Furthermore, in the domestic economic scene, the government enabled both Jews and Arabs to pursue their different economic agendas, thereby reinforcing Jewish-Arab economic separatism (see also Smith, 1993).

More specifically, and notwithstanding the purportedly economic constraints on Jewish immigration, the generally free-market environment maintained by the Mandatory government prior to World War II became a supportive setting for the mobilization of Jewish settlers' financial, physical, and human resources for the purpose of forming and nurturing their thriving economy. Moreover, the Mandatory government's non-interventionist economic policy went beyond the constitution of a domestic free-market regime. Guided by its general "hands off" attitude, the government did not intervene even when ethno-national rivalry motivated Arabs and Jews to disrupt free economic activity as, for example, in attempts by both sides to limit (even boycott) bilateral trade, or in the efforts of labor Zionism to keep the Jewish economy labor-self-sufficient at high wages.

The discussion so far has emphasized, on the one hand, the structural and functional economic differences between Mandatory Palestine and typical settlement colonies, and, on the other, the similar effects that some of the two systems' operational mechanisms had. As such, it serves to underline the complexity involved in comparing the two ostensibly analogous types of dual economies, and to highlight, with reference to the settlers' colonies, the distinctive features of Palestine's ethno-nationally divided economy.[4]

Another absorbing issue in this comparative context is whether, and to what extent, aggregate economic performance at the sectoral level (especially of the indigenous sector) was affected by ethno-national economic divisions. As regards settler economies, Mosley's (1983) fragmentary estimates seem to indicate that the indigenous peasants in Kenya and Southern Rhodesia responded rationally to the exogenous constraints imposed (and opportunities offered) by the dominating white settlers. For example, the peasants' dynamic adjustment to the declining land-labor ratio included, besides exit from agriculture, the adoption of technological improvements in traditional farming, such as

---

[4] For an illuminating discussion of the merits and limitations of the colonial postulate as a framework for analyzing the political economy of Mandatory Palestine see Kamen (1991), chap. 4.

intensification of husbandry and changes in crop mix and in production methods. Although Mosley was unable to provide a comprehensive picture of aggregate economic activity, it is quite clear that in the colonies he studied the discriminatory restrictions were effective enough to prevent the indigenous sector from achieving "first-best" levels and growth rates of production, even if they did not cause an absolute decline in the economic conditions of the African peasantry.

In Mandatory Palestine, the existing evidence implies not only a rise in the productivity of the indigenous (Arab) agricultural industry and a relative decline in its labor share (and, up to World War II, in its output share as well), but a substantial increase in the area cultivated by Arab peasants in response to the expanding market (of about 40 percent between the early 1920s and the mid-1930s). In other words, unlike Mosley's findings for colonial settler economies, the indigenous farm sector in Mandatory Palestine seems to have experienced considerable extensive expansion, not merely intensive growth.

Similarly, the impressive growth of per capita income, in both the Arab and the Jewish economies, suggests that whatever the ethno-national features of economic domination and discrimination in Palestine may have been, they did not have a significant adverse affect on overall economic performance in either sector, certainly not before the Arab revolt and its subsequent economic disruptions in the second half of the 1930s, or during World War II.

These hypotheses are supported by our findings that each community utilized its primary factors of production mainly in its own domestic economy (note that 95 percent of all Arab labor was gainfully employed within the Arab economy, which, by the end of the period under discussion, produced no less than 40 percent of the country's annual output), and that the bilateral merchandise trade between Arabs and Jews suffered relatively little (barring years of high tension, such as 1936–39) from tendencies of economic separatism on either side.

Moreover, although a more appropriate counterfactual that would allow us reliably to examine the effect of Jewish economic activity on the Arab community is extremely difficult to construct, it may be deduced from our quantitative account that in strict aggregate economic terms (at least as measured by total and per capita income), the Jewish buildup in Palestine is likely, on average, to have benefited both Arabs and Jews. This, however, should not be construed as an assertion that the peoples of Palestine, mainly the Arab community, did not have to bear any material costs (in income forgone) for the ethno-nationally motivated constraints imposed on their economic lives and interactions. Nor is it postulated that these costs were uniformly distributed. Furthermore, I would submit that even if each and every one of Palestine's inhabitants had benefited materially from the Zionist enterprise, the success of the Jewish National Home had imposed sufficient non-material costs on the Arab community, by menacing its standing as a distinct, self-determining, ethno-national entity in Palestine, to render the overall effect of the Zionist endeavor on the Arabs definitely negative.

The economic story of Mandatory Palestine closes with the end of the British rule. The ensuing rapid changes, marked by the establishment of the state of Israel and the war of 1948, by the mass – largely involuntary – departure of Arabs from areas now controlled by the new Jewish state and by mass Jewish immigration (in 1948–51), completely transformed the population mix and the economic fabric of the country.

Due to the emigration of refugees, primarily to Jordan and Lebanon, the Arab population within the boundaries of what had been Mandatory Palestine declined from 1.34 million in 1947 to 1.19 million in 1952. Of these, slightly over 1 million (85 percent of the total), many of whom were refugees, relocated in parts of Palestine not included in Israel (the West Bank and the Gaza strip). Only 179,000 (15 percent), mostly rural, remained by 1952 in Israel, whose territory following the armistice agreements of 1949 covered about 76 percent of the area of Mandatory Palestine.

On the other hand, the massive inflow of immigrants caused the Jewish population of Israel to more than double during the first three years of statehood: from 650,000 (in all of Palestine) in 1947 to 1.45 million in 1952. The proportion of Jews in Israel's population thus rose to 89 percent (versus 32 percent in Palestine by the end of the Mandate). Over the years, the faster natural increase of Israeli Arabs and the sharp fluctuations in net Jewish immigration have reduced this percentage, and nowadays (1995) Jews constitute 81 percent of Israel's population (Ben-Porath, 1966; Metzer, 1992).

The extreme changes in regime and in the ethno-national composition of the population are, no doubt, key elements of discontinuity, clearly distinguishing the ethno-nationally divided economy of Mandatory Palestine from that of Israel. Nonetheless, some components of continuity (at least as far as the Jewish economy is concerned) can be detected in Israel's major attributes of economic structure and dynamics. For example, in the association between patterns of economic growth and of capital imports and immigration; in the important role of the import surplus in resources and domestic uses; in the industrial structure of production and employment; and in the role of public-sector involvement in economic life. All these closely resemble the characteristics of the

Mandatory Jewish economy, and draw a kind of continuum from the pre-statehood *yishuv* to the state of Israel (Ben-Porath, 1986a, b; Syrquin, 1986; Plessner, 1994).

Considering the ethno-national aspects of the economic scene, the transfer of sovereignty from the British Mandate to the state of Israel, in combination with the enormous changes in the Arab-Jewish demographic makeup, obviously formed a new setting for the economic coexistence of the two peoples.[5] On the one hand, Israel's formal identity as a Jewish state, which fully and declaratively subscribed to the Zionist ideology of encouraging immigration and (mainly rural) settlement of Diaspora Jews, and, on the other hand, the persistent uncertainty regarding the attitude of Israel's Arab citizens *vis-à-vis* the unsettled conflict with the Arab world, put the Arab minority of Israel in a disadvantaged position despite the declared, and formally maintained, civil and legal equality which all the citizens of the newly established state were supposed to enjoy.

In practice, various regulatory (but short-lived) attempts were made in the early years to keep trade in agricultural produce segregated. Moreover, in the 1950s the Arab population of Israel was formally under military rule (officially abolished only in the mid-1960s), which restricted the free movement of Arabs, partly for security reasons and partly in order to prevent Arabs from competing with newly arrived Jewish immigrants for employment in a unified labor market. Consequently, the first decade of statehood was, in essence, a continuation and an intensification of the Mandatory pattern of economic separation between Jews and Arabs, with one major difference – it was now enforced by the state.

Toward the end of the 1950s things started to turn around. The rapidly growing Arab population and its declining land area – not least because of extensive expropriation, primarily of property owned by refugees and by broadly defined Arab absentees, some of whom lived in Israel at the time – resulted in a rising supply of Arab labor, which, following the slowdown of Jewish immigration, the upward labor mobility of previous immigrants, and the acceleration of economic activity, met increasing Jewish demand for manual labor. In 1959 an Employment Service Law was enacted, requiring that all employment services be allocated by state-operated labor exchanges on a nondiscriminatory basis. This law effectively lifted the regulatory barriers to Arab labor mobility and Arab workers were accepted by the *Histadrut* as full members. These developments marked the onset of a new phase of incorporation into the large and rapidly

---

[5] The discussion on the Arab minority in the Israeli economy draws on the following studies: Ben-Porath (1966, 1984); Klinov (1990, 1996); Lewin-Epstein and Semyonov (1992, 1993); Rosenhek (1995); Schnell, Sofer, and Drori (1995).

growing Israeli economy, which has since characterized the economic life of the Arabs in Israel.

However, since Arabs continued to live largely in separate (mostly rural) localities, their economic integration was effected primarily by more and more of their wage-earners commuting to their work places (at least half of all Arab employed persons have been employed by Jews since the early 1960s). In addition, the dynamics of integration, while reflected, *inter alia*, in some convergence of the Arab and Jewish industrial structures of employment, and by a narrowing of disparities in socio-economic indicators such as infant mortality, life expectancy, and school attainment, did not altogether remove ethno-national distinctions from the economic scene. On the contrary, by suffering from relatively low levels of municipal expenditure and from an uneven allocation of government resources (mainly, but not exclusively, allocations based on criteria such as military service or on officially designated preferred regions, localities, and industries), Arabs were at a comparative disadvantage as far as ownership of physical and human capital and receipt of public services and transfer payments were concerned. Furthermore, various forms of discrimination in the provision of residential services and effective barriers limiting entry (partly for security reasons) to a good number of employment categories have left notable aspects of ethno-national segregation in the labor market intact, with general factors of "organizational dualism" constraining the access of Arabs to the organized capital market and marginalizing their manufacturing industry.

All told, the above observations suggest that the evolving economic coexistence of Israeli Jews and Arabs can best be characterized as "compartmentalized integration." This process has made the Arab ethno-national minority a partcipant in, and beneficiary of, the long-term rise in production and standard of living in Israel, but has nonetheless left it in an economically disadvantaged position *vis-à-vis* the Jewish majority.

The war of 1967 resulted in the West Bank and the Gaza Strip coming under Israeli control, thereby bringing, for the following quarter of a century (up to the Oslo Agreement), the territory of Mandatory Palestine under a single military and civil administration. This marked another critical turning-point in the complex record of troubled economic coexistence in the area.[6] Interestingly enough, the available estimates and data suggest that in terms of population and volume of aggregate economic activity, the combined territories of the West Bank (excluding annexed

---

[6] The following discussion draws on Ben-Porath (1984), Metzer (1988, 1992), and Kleiman (1993).

East Jerusalem) and the Gaza Strip (hereafter "the territories") were comparable in size in the late 1960s and early 1970s to Palestine's Arab sector in 1947 more than twenty years earlier. It may thus be inferred that continuing emigration (mainly from the West Bank), which intensified in the two years following the 1967 war, caused the Arab community and economy within the boundaries of former Mandatory Palestine – excluding the Arab community of Israel – to contract substantially between the end of the British mandate and the aftermath of the 1967 war.

The contraction of the Palestinian Arab sector on the one hand, and the extremely fast growth of the Israeli economy (whose GNP in real terms was in 1970 twenty times larger than the total product of the Jewish sector in 1947) on the other, held down the combined national product of the West Bank and the Gaza Strip to no more than 7 percent of the area's (Israel and the territories') total product. This relative size was obviously a far cry from that of the Mandate-era Arab economy, whose production never fell below 40 percent of Palestine's total output.

The simple fact that the territories were economic lightweights meant that they stood to be the main beneficiary of the bilateral economic relations with Israel, which dominated their external trade. These relations were conducted under the control of the occupational administration, within a regime of a common currency (Israeli currency was legal tender in the territories), allowing the territories' inhabitants practically unrestricted access to the Israeli labor market, and maintaining custom-free bilateral trade in goods and services, subject to Israel's protective regulations, primarily those governing the entry of agricultural produce.

To get some idea of the orders of magnitude involved, note that in the mid-1980s the volume of the territories' total exports to Israel (accounting for about three-quarters of all their exports) accounted for 38 percent of their GNP, but for only 3 percent of Israel's GNP. No less than 65 percent of all sales to Israel consisted of labor services; another 30 percent were manufactured goods, primarily furniture, textiles, and leather products, produced mainly in cottage-type industries on a "farming out" basis for Israeli manufactures; the remaining 5 percent were farm products and various services. The territories' imports from Israel – 70 percent manufactured goods, 13 percent agricultural product, and the remaining 17 percent services – accounted for 82 percent of their total imports and as much as 55 percent of their GNP, compared to a mere 3 percent of Israel's GNP.

Given such different orders of magnitude it is not surprising to find (as economic theory would predict) that in the first two decades of Israeli administration (1968–87), prior to the outbreak of the *intifada*, GNP growth in the territories (8.6 percent per annum) was much faster than in

Israel (5.0 percent); the growth rates of GNP per capita (6.3 percent versus 2.6 percent) were even more disparate, narrowing the Israel-territories gap in income per capita from a factor of 7.3 in 1970 to a factor of 4.4 in 1987.

A major factor contributing to the extremely rapid growth of total and per capita income in the territories was their export of manual labor services, primarily to Israel. Since about a quarter of the territories' GNP in 1968–87 was generated by income of factor services received abroad (of which about 80 percent were incomes of workers employed in Israel), their domestic product was only about three-quarters the size of their national product.

Moreover, if the export of labor services is treated as part of total employment, one observes that in the mid-1980s no less than 37 percent of the territories' work force was employed in Israel (about half of them in construction, 18 percent in manufacturing, and 14 percent in agriculture), compared with at most 5 percent of the Arab labor force who were employed by Jews in the Mandate period. On the other hand, whereas Arab workers may have constituted as much as 10 percent of all the employed persons in the Jewish economy of the 1930s, the comparable percentage of workers from the territories did not exceed 6 percent of all the persons employed in Israel. These dissimilarities are a clear reflection of the differences in the relative sizes of the economies concerned, contributing (together with Israel's control over the territories) to the sharp increase in the territories' dependence on the Israeli economy – compared with the relative lack of dependence of the Arab sector on the Jewish sector under the Mandate. They also provide an indication of the changes in the prevailing approach (mainly on the Jewish-Israeli side) toward the economic aspects of the ethno-national coexistence – shifting from the Mandatory postulate of separation to one of economic union with the occupied territories.

The very nature of economic dependence and the implied characteristics of the territories' economic growth prevented the impressive rise in their national product from generating a structural transformation of their domestic economies. Despite indications of socio-economic advance, such as rising school enrollment and declining death rates, the territories remained rather underdeveloped economically, primarily insofar as investments in infrastructure and in a sustained industrial base are concerned. For example, although the territories' rising rate of capital formation (excluding investments within Jewish settlements) did match the predicted rate of investment (25 percent of GNP) by their level of income per capita in the mid-1980s (according to the internationally comparative study by Chenery and Syrquin, 1975), it was channeled mainly to residential housing (about 70 to 80 percent of fixed-capital formation in the 1980s). At the same time, infrastructure investments in the territories by the Israeli government – including those made in the service of Jewish settlements – did not exceed 2 to 4 percent of the territories' GNP.

Likewise, the proportion of manufacturing in the (Palestinian) domestic economy of the territories, about 8 percent of GDP, was only about half the percentage predicted by the Chenery-Syrquin study for their level of income per capita in the 1980s. This proportion was even lower than the output share of manufacturing in the Mandatory Arab economy of the 1930s (which was about 10 percent of domestic production). As regards employment, the size of the average industrial establishment in the territories of the mid-1980s was no larger than that of the Arab establishment in Palestine of 1927 (4.2 workers).

In part, the pattern of growth without industrialization was an expected outcome of the economic union between the territories and Israel. Once this dual-economy-type union was established, disparities in labor endowments and productivity, the implied wage differentials, and considerations of comparative advantage could not fail to induce the territories to export large amounts of manual labor services to Israel in exchange for manufactured goods. In part, however, the situation reflected political and administrative constraints: the Jordanian ban on imports of manufactured goods produced in plants established in the territories after 1967, and various administrative restrictions imposed by the Israeli administration on industrialization in the territories, largely in order to avoid competition with Israel's own manufacturing industry.

Another factor that inhibited industrialization was the lack of adequate financial instruments for channeling savings to productive investments. This deficiency, and the political uncertainty and instability of the area, may have deterred the investment of Israeli private capital in the territories' manufacturing industry, and at the same time directed a disproportionally large amount of domestic funds to residential construction.

The above remarks imply that the territories' status of "occupied areas" was instrumental in shaping the economic lives of their Palestinian inhabitants alongside the Israeli economy, putting them in an inferior legal, institutional, and economic position within the evolving economic union with Israel. For example, although workers from the territories did benefit from superior earning opportunities in Israel, they were certainly at a disadvantage, compared to their local counterparts (Jews and Arabs alike), in the Israeli labor market because they lacked trade-union protection and were subject to restricting security regulations. Moreover, the frequent closures imposed by Israel on the territories for security reasons, during the Gulf war and following terrorist attacks on Israeli civilians, often prevented Palestinian workers from entering Israel altogether. The closures introduced an additional element of uncertainty into the picture, inducing Israeli employers to seek alternative sources of labor supply, such as foreign workers, whose numbers have grown steadily in the 1990s. It follows that apart from the short-term economic hardship caused by the temporary loss of employment during closures, the resultant decline in Israel's demand for Palestinian labor (or at least its slower growth) has critically demonstrated a need for the development of a healthy productive base within the territories, including an effective private capital market and banking system, that would reduce their dependence on the Israeli economy.

Another area in which the state of the occupied territories was clearly evident is land and settlement. In securing possession of all the state-owned land in the territories and attempting to extend their area to the possible legal limits (at times even at the expense of local Arab claimants), the Israeli government has utilized the land under its control primarily for encouraging and supporting Jewish settlements in the West Bank and, to some extent, in the Gaza Strip as well. Although state land placed at the disposal of Jewish settlers was usually unsettled and uncultivated, the notion that such lands in the territories should in the long run serve the needs of the Palestinian population has not become a binding allocative consideration of the Israeli authorities. In this respect, Israel's economic (and national) penetration into the occupied territories by way of settlement, backed – before or after the fact – by the official Israeli authorities, resembles, more than any other facet in the history of Arab-Jewish economic coexistence, the economic dynamics observed in the European settlement colonies (see also Shafir, 1993).

Finally, the present volatile state of affairs following the turmoil of the *intifada*, the interim Israeli-Palestinian agreements that reaffirmed the free-trade regime governing relations between the two entities, the transfer of some (primarily urban) areas to the control of the newly instituted Palestinian Authority, and the generally acknowledged need for the formation of a balanced economic base within the area under the Palestinian Authority's control may all become a prelude to yet another major, possibly *the* major, turning-point in the ethno-nationally complex economic history of the area.

Does all this lead to a steady state that will, if and when achieved, provide for a healthy, developing Palestinian economy, converging on the

212   The divided economy of Mandatory Palestine

Israeli economy, or will the dualistic relations of highly asymmetric economic dependency prevail? Will the ethno-national economic coexistence in the area be part of a mutually beneficial and cherished Israeli-Palestinian equilibrium, or will it continue to be a case of economic coexistence in adversity? At the present stage the best we can offer is questions – not answers.

Appendix

A. DEMOGRAPHIC AND ECONOMIC STATISTICS OF MANDATORY PALESTINE

This appendix provides quantitative documentation of the basic patterns of demographic change and economic activity in Mandatory Palestine's Arab and Jewish communities and in the country as a whole. Its objective is twofold: to present the evidence underlying a good part of the observations and analyses offered in the main text, and to serve as a convenient quantitative reference source for readers interested in the economic history of Palestine in the twentieth century. The areas covered are: population and labor (tables A.1–A.5); output and value added by industry (tables A.6–A.18); domestic and national product (tables A.19–A.22); and investment and capital (tables A.23–A.26).

Prime sources for the material collected here are the compilations of demographic and economic figures that were collected, constructed, and published by the major "producers" of statistics in the Mandate period: the government, the Jewish Agency, the *Histadrut*, and also individual statisticians and economists affiliated with these institutions. Other essential building-blocks are provided by a number of later studies including, among others, Sicron (1957a, b), Szereszewski (1968), and Bachi (1977), which contain systematic estimates of demographic and (mainly Jewish) economic measurements.

Some of the following tables, particularly in the demographic area, bring together data – at times slightly amended – that were scattered in various primary and secondary sources. But the major part of this appendix, namely the output, value added, and investment figures, consist of newly constructed estimates for the Arab economy, which are incorporated with analogous estimates for the Jewish economy (mostly revisions of Szereszewski's [1968] series) and for the government, into a consistent system of ethno-nationally divided accounts of production and investment for Mandatory Palestine. Most of these accounts are included in a technical monograph in Hebrew (Metzer and Kaplan, 1990), containing detailed descriptions of the estimation procedures, on which this appendix draws heavily and to which it refers extensively.

Population

Cols. 1 and 2 of table A.1 present Bachi's annual, end-of-year estimates of Palestine's total population by religious group, excluding the British army (Bachi, 1977, appendix 6, tables A12, A13). The Arab population (col. 1) is taken to be equal to that of all the non-Jewish groups – Muslims, Christians, and others – combined (see the discussion in chapter 1). The yearly figures for the nomadic population (Bedouins) in col. 2 were constructed from Bachi's estimates for three benchmark years (1922, 1931, 1947) and from the derived annual rates of growth, assumed to have been constant, between 1922 and 1931 and between 1931 and 1947 (Bachi, 1977, appendix 6, section 6.3).

The average (or mid-year) estimates of the Arab population in col. 5 were calculated for 1922–31 and for 1946–47 from Bachi's revised end-of-year figures (col. 1), and for 1931–45 from the government's official data of the average annual settled population (*Vital Statistics*, 1947, table A-2), to which the estimates of the nomadic population were added. The Jewish figures in col. 6 were derived for 1922 from the end-of-year estimates of col. 4, and for 1923–31 they are the government's official mid-year estimates (*Vital Statistics*, 1947, table A-2). Note that contrary to Bachi's revision of the official end-of-year figures of the Arab population in the 1920s, the government end-of-year estimates of the Jewish population were adopted by him without change (Bachi, 1977, appendix 6, section 6.7). The average Jewish population figures for 1932–47 were taken from Sicron and Gill (1955, table 3).

In tables A.2 and A.3 the growth of the Arab (settled) and the Jewish populations is divided into a natural increase component and a residual component which serves as a proxy for net migratory changes (see also the discussion in chapter 2). Table A.3 adds (col. 6) the best available estimates of annual Jewish (gross) immigration (Sicron, 1957b, table A1). The annual total growth figures in both tables were calculated from the totals of table A.1 (cols. 3 and 4, respectively), and the natural increase estimates are those of *Vital Statistics* (1947, tables A14, A26) as revised by Bachi (1977, appendix 6, section 6.4). Note that the large residual of Arab population growth in 1923 largely reflects the transfer of population due to the changes in the borders of Mandated Palestine in 1922–23 (Bachi, 1977, appendix 6, section 6.6).

Table A.1. *Estimates of Palestine's Arab and Jewish populations, 1921–47*

	population at end of year				average (or mid-year) population ('000)	
	Arabs			Jews		
	all (1)	nomads (2)	settled ([1]-[2]) (3)	(4)	Arabs (5)	Jews (6)
1921	666,061	62,065	603,996	74,703		
1922	682,840	62,500	620,340	85,400	674.5	80.1
1923	707,850	62,938	644,912	92,300	695.3	89.7
1924	725,400	63,379	662,021	108,330	716.6	94.9
1925	740,950	63,823	677,127	135,610	733.2	121.7
1926	761,470	64,270	697,200	149,640	751.2	149.5
1927	777,260	64,720	712,540	150,720	769.4	149.8
1928	795,260	65,174	730,086	154,070	786.4	151.7
1929	814,320	65,630	748,690	160,640	804.8	156.5
1930	838,100	66,090	772,010	168,410	826.2	164.8
1931	861,291	66,553	794,738	175,138	849.7	172.0
1932	883,445	67,323	816,122	192,137	872.6	181.7
1933	909,403	68,102	841,301	234,967	896.6	210.7
1934	932,691	68,890	863,801	282,975	919.6	255.5
1935	959,760	69,686	890,074	355,157	943.7	322.0
1936	987,620	70,493	917,127	384,078	970.5	371.0
1937	1,009,174	71,308	937,866	395,836	1,000.4	389.0
1938	1,025,498	72,133	953,365	412,722	1,021.5	403.0
1939	1,055,705	72,967	982,738	449,457	1,048.1	432.4
1940	1,082,198	73,811	1,008,387	467,535	1,078.6	460.1
1941	1,114,349	74,665	1,039,684	478,602	1,105.0	474.2
1942	1,140,305	75,529	1,064,776	489,408	1,135.3	483.6
1943	1,176,454	76,403	1,100,051	509,412	1,166.3	498.7
1944	1,211,816	77,287	1,134,529	536,202	1,207.2	522.6
1945	1,254,708	78,181	1,176,527	563,829	1,245.4	549.0
1946	1,301,205	79,085	1,222,120	593,827	1,290.0	579.1
1947	1,340,345	80,000	1,260,345	630,019	1,333.8	609.0

Labor

Table A.4 reports labor force estimates by community as constructed by Metzer and Kaplan (1990) for Arabs, and by BMZ, who revised Szereszewski's (1968) series (utilizing Metzer and Kaplan's corrections), for Jews. Unfortunately, data constraints limit the estimates for the Arab sector to five selected years (col. 1). These were generated for 1931 from

Table A.2. *Sources of growth of settled Arab population, absolute numbers, 1922–45*

	total growth (1)	births (2)	deaths (3)	natural increase ([2]-[3]) (4)	"residual" ([1]-[4]) (5)
1922	16,344	27,259	11,375	15,884	460
1923	24,572	29,999	15,624	14,375	10,197
1924	17,109	32,977	16,598	16,379	730
1925	15,106	32,500	17,791	14,709	397
1926	20,073	36,800	16,848	19,952	121
1927	15,340	34,347	19,816	14,531	809
1928	17,546	37,943	21,234	16,709	837
1929	18,604	36,813	19,813	17,000	1,604
1930	23,320	39,508	17,954	21,554	1,766
1931	22,728	41,051	19,483	21,568	1,160
1932	21,384	38,256	20,212	18,044	3,340
1933	25,179	39,976	18,927	21,049	4,130
1934	22,500	38,271	21,716	16,555	5,945
1935	26,273	44,073	19,501	24,572	1,701
1936	27,053	45,984	21,824	24,160	2,893
1937	20,739	44,452	21,989	22,463	−1,724
1938	15,499	43,367	21,682	21,685	−6,186
1939	29,373	43,465	20,909	22,556	6,817
1940	25,649	45,754	23,289	22,465	3,184
1941	31,297	48,165	20,775	27,390	3,907
1942	25,092	45,531	20,045	25,486	−394
1943	35,275	54,503	23,394	31,109	4,166
1944	34,478	57,472	22,265	35,207	−729
1945	41,998	60,196	21,826	38,370	3,628

the detailed population census taken in that year (*Census of Palestine*, 1933), and for 1935 from Gaathon's (1978, p. 373) figures. To generate the 1922, 1939, and 1945 estimates we applied to Bachi's percentage age distributions of 1926 (1931 for Christians), 1940, and 1944 (Bachi, 1977, pp. 280–81) the implied participation rates of the over-fifteen age group: 45 percent in 1931, 47 percent in 1935, and (assumed) 50 percent in 1945 (for further details of the derivation of the estimates and their plausibility, see Metzer and Kaplan, 1990, pp. 108–109, 152–53). The series of the Jewish labor force (col. 4) was taken without any change from BMZ (table A2). The population shares of labor reported in cols. 2 and 4

Table A.3. *Sources of Jewish population growth (1922–45) and Jewish immigration (1919–47), in absolute numbers*

	total growth (1)	births (2)	deaths (3)	natural growth ([2]-[3]) (4)	"residual" ([1]-[4]) (5)	immigrants (6)
1919						1,806
1920						8,223
1921						8,294
1922	10,697	2,875	970	1,905	8,792	8,685
1923	6,900	3,728	1,318	2,410	4,490	8,175
1924	16,030	3,913	1,201	2,712	13,318	13,892
1925	27,280	4,225	1,812	2,413	24,867	34,386
1926	14,030	5,489	1,783	3,706	10,324	13,855
1927	1,080	5,344	1,987	3,357	−2,277	3,034
1928	3,350	5,298	1,806	3,492	−142	2,178
1929	6,570	5,263	1,815	3,448	3,122	5,249
1930	7,770	5,434	1,558	3,876	3,894	4,944
1931	6,728	5,540	1,649	3,891	2,837	4,075
1932	16,999	5,282	1,746	3,536	13,463	12,553
1933	42,830	6,113	1,939	4,174	38,656	37,337
1934	48,008	7,671	2,420	5,251	42,757	45,267
1935	72,182	9,867	2,748	7,119	65,063	66,472
1936	28,921	11,009	3,271	7,738	21,183	29,595
1937	11,758	10,297	3,003	7,294	4,464	10,629
1938	16,886	10,563	3,262	7,301	9,585	14,675
1939	36,735	9,888	3,251	6,637	30,098	31,195
1940	18,078	10,817	3,730	7,087	10,991	10,643
1941	11,067	9,714	3,710	6,004	5,063	4,592
1942	10,806	10,884	4,119	6,765	4,041	4,206
1943	20,004	14,317	3,808	10,509	9,495	10,063
1944	26,790	15,583	3,681	11,902	14,888	15,552
1945	27,627	16,358	3,595	12,763	14,864	15,259
1946						18,760
1947						22,098

are based on the average (or mid-year) Arab and Jewish populations of table A.1, cols. 5 and 6.

In table A.5 the compositions of the Arab and the Jewish labor forces by industry are presented for five selected years. They were derived from Metzer and Kaplan (1990), in which the sources for and the procedures of the construction of the industrial distributions of labor are carefully

Table A.4. *Labor force 1922–47*

	Arab labor force		Jewish labor force	
	size ('000) (1)	% of population (2)	size ('000) (3)	% of population (4)
1922	194.0	28.8	26.6	33.2
1923			30.1	33.6
1924			32.7	34.5
1925			44.2	36.3
1926			56.5	37.8
1927			55.9	37.3
1928			56.6	37.3
1929			58.6	37.4
1930			62.0	37.6
1931	227.0	26.7	65.0	37.8
1932			67.9	37.4
1933			77.4	36.7
1934			99.5	38.9
1935	255.0	27.0	130.1	40.4
1936			156.5	42.2
1937			163.3	42.0
1938			168.8	41.9
1939	280.0	26.7	182.0	42.1
1940			195.0	42.4
1941			201.0	42.4
1942			207.1	42.8
1943			211.0	42.3
1944			220.4	42.2
1945	345.0	27.7	233.2	42.5
1946			243.1	42.0
1947			253.0	41.5

outlined (pp. 109–19, 149–53). Here I shall only point to their main building-blocks, which include the census of 1931, Gaathon's estimates of national income accounts for 1935–36 (Gaathon, 1941, 1978), and those of Loftus (the government statistician) for 1944 and 1945 (Loftus, 1946, 1948). The major anchor for estimating the industrial structure of labor was provided, naturally, by the occupational breakdown in the 1931 census of "earners" and "workers-dependents," from which the composition of labor by industry in 1931 was extracted for both Arabs and Jews (*Census of Palestine*, 1933, vol. II, table XVI).

Students of the Jewish economy also benefit from periodic surveys and

Table A.5. *Composition of labor by industry in selected years (ʼ000)*

	1922	1931	1935	1939	1945
A Arab labor force					
employed by Arabs and by the government					
agriculture	124.3	139.0	137.9	163.0	186.0
manufacturing	9.1	18.0	18.1	21.0	30.0
construction	3.1	5.1	12.0	3.9	17.0
all material production	136.5	162.1	168.0	187.9	233.0
services	53.3	57.9	75.0	92.1	108.0
all	189.8	220.0	243.0	280.0	341.0
employed by Jews					
agriculture		5.2	7.0		
manufacturing		0.5	1.8		
construction		0.6	1.8		3.0
all material production	3.8	6.3	10.6		3.0
services	0.4	0.7	1.4		1.0
all	4.2	7.0	12.0		4.0
total Arab labor force	*194.0*	*227.0*	*255.0*	*280.0*	*345.0*
B Jewish labor force					
agriculture	5.3	13.5	28.4	40.4	31.3
manufacturing	4.9	14.0	26.8	41.5	72.5
construction	3.8	5.3	12.5	5.5	7.2
all material production	14.0	32.8	67.7	87.4	111.0
services	12.6	32.2	62.4	94.6	122.2
total Jewish labor force	*26.6*	*65.0*	*130.1*	*182.0*	*233.2*

censuses that were conducted for specific industries by the Jewish Agency and the *Histadrut*, thus enabling, for example, Ofer (1967) and Szereszewski (1968) to construct the composition of Jewish labor for a good number of years. These distributions were adjusted in line with the above-mentioned revisions of Szereszewski's labor-force series (BMZ, table A2) and with the need to correct the upward-biased estimates of employment in construction in 1939–45 (Metzer and Kaplan, 1990, pp. 109–11, 149–50).

For the industrial composition of Arab labor in the inter-war period, however, the 1931 census remains the only solid source (Gaathon, too, relied on it partly). Consequently, in order to construct the industrial compositions of Arab labor in 1922, 1935, and 1939, a number of assumptions were made. One such assumption links employment in agriculture to the size of the Arab rural population (suggesting that output per worker in manufacturing did not change in the 1920s), and deriving employment in manufacturing and in construction from the presumed stability of labor productivity in manufacturing relative to all material production in the 1930s, and of product per worker in construction throughout the period (for further discussions of the soundness of these assumptions and of their derived estimates, see Metzer and Kaplan, 1990, pp. 117–19). The labor composition of 1945 was generated from Loftus (1948), corrected for his underestimation of Arab employment in that year (Metzer and Kaplan, 1990, pp. 152–53).

The estimates of Arabs employed by Jews and their industrial compositions, as reported in table A.5, were gathered by Metzer and Kaplan (1990, pp. 111–12, 149–50) from several contemporary sources (such as *Census of Jewish Workers*, 1926, 1937; *Sikumim*; Becker, 1930; Hoofien, 1930; Ater, 1937; Bonne, 1938; *Censuses of Workers in Groves*, 1939; Gaathon, 1941, 1978; Abramowitz and Guelfat, 1944), and from more recent studies (chiefly Sussman, 1973), and offered as likely orders of magnitude.

OUTPUT AND VALUE ADDED BY INDUSTRY IN THE INTER-WAR PERIOD

This section presents annual series of production by industry for the Arab and Jewish sectors in the inter-war period. The estimates of material production (in agriculture, manufacturing, and construction) are reported in producers' prices of both output and net product. The former quantity stands for the total value of the goods (or structures) produced annually in each industry, either for the producers' own use or for the market; the latter stands for the industries' value added, namely the value of output net of raw materials and intermediate inputs purchased from other industries and used in the production process. The overall production of services is estimated in terms of value added only.

Agriculture

Relatively speaking, agriculture was the most "data abundant" industry, and within agriculture, citrus – its single largest branch in value terms, and the country's major source of export revenue – was the most widely reported productive activity. It is against this background, and for the purpose of documenting in detail the patterns of citrus production, that the farm output and product estimates are designed separately for citrus and for a composite "rest of the industry" branch, and then combined into aggregate quantities for all of agriculture in each sector.

Basic data for the inter-war citrus industry are put together in table A.6. The series of planted groves in dunams (col. 1) was generated from the *Statistical Handbook* (1947, p. 179), assuming that the planted areas in

Table A.6. *Palestine's inter-war citrus industry – basic data*

	area of groves ('000 dunams, beginning of year) (1)	all citrus crops ('000 cases)			exported crops ('000 cases) (5)	export prices (P£ per case) (6)
		Arabs (2)	Jews (3)	total (4)		
1921	29.0	872.5	512.5	1,385.0	831.0	0.605
1922	29.0	972.0	570.9	1,542.9	1,234.3	0.585
1923	29.0	1,075.3	631.6	1,706.9	1,365.5	0.465
1924	29.5	1,251.6	735.0	1,986.6	1,589.3	0.568
1925	30.0	1,690.4	992.7	2,683.1	2,146.5	0.468
1926	30.5	1,196.0	702.4	1,898.4	1,518.7	0.615
1927	38.5	1,867.8	1,097.0	2,964.8	2,668.3	0.562
1928	56.0	1,554.3	912.8	2,467.1	2,220.4	0.535
1929	67.0	1,261.8	741.0	2,002.8	1,802.5	0.555
1930	87.0	1,827.1	1,073.1	2,900.2	2,610.2	0.499
1931	106.5	1,646.6	1,097.7	2,744.3	2,469.9	0.527
1932	121.5	2,301.3	1,808.1	4,109.4	3,698.5	0.483
1933	156.5	2,653.4	2,449.3	5,102.7	4,490.4	0.467
1934	200.0	3,189.8	3,320.0	6,509.8	5,533.3	0.476
1935	250.0	3,624.0	5,004.6	8,628.6	7,334.3	0.461
1936	278.0	2,770.1	4,155.1	6,925.2	5,886.4	0.431
1937	298.0	4,907.2	7,360.9	12,268.1	10,795.9	0.359
1938	298.0	5,202.0	7,803.0	13,005.0	11,444.4	0.339
1939	298.0	5,936.3	11,024.6	16,960.9	15,264.8	0.285
1940	299.5					

1921 and 1922 were the same as in 1923, and that no new groves were planted in 1937 and in 1938. The crop and export figures in cases (cols. 2–5) and the f.o.b. export prices (col. 6) are Metzer and Kaplan's estimates (1990, pp. 31–32), derived from a variety of contemporary reports and studies, quoting annual figures of volume and prices (notably, Viteles, 1928; Hazen, 1938; *SAP*, 1940; *Statistical Handbook*, 1947; Horowitz, 1948).

The above-mentioned sources, combined with additional ones providing information and assessments of the cost of planting, cultivation, production, and marketing (for example, Clark-Powell, 1928; Poshter, 1939; Gaathon, 1941, 1978; Nathan, Gass, and Creamer, 1946; Szereszewski, 1968), enabled the construction of Arab and Jewish annual output and value added estimates of citrus crops at the "grove gate," as

Table A.7. *Citrus crop output, 1921–39*

| | price index of citrus crops (1936=100) (1) | crop output (P£ '000) | | | | | |
| | | current prices | | | 1936 prices | | |
		Arabs (2)	Jews (3)	total (4)	Arabs (5)	Jews (6)	total (7)
1921	140.4	338	198	536	241	142	383
1922	135.7	409	240	649	302	177	479
1923	107.2	358	210	568	334	196	530
1924	131.8	512	301	813	388	228	616
1925	108.6	570	334	904	525	308	833
1926	142.7	530	311	841	371	218	589
1927	130.4	798	468	1,266	612	359	971
1928	124.1	632	371	1,003	509	299	808
1929	128.8	532	313	845	413	243	656
1930	115.8	693	407	1,100	598	352	950
1931	122.3	659	440	1,099	539	359	898
1932	112.1	845	664	1,509	754	592	1,346
1933	108.4	932	860	1,792	860	794	1,654
1934	110.4	1,124	1,182	2,306	1,018	1,071	2,089
1935	107.0	1,212	1,686	2,898	1,133	1,576	2,709
1936	100.0	885	1,295	2,180	885	1,295	2,180
1937	83.3	1,305	1,916	3,221	1,566	2,301	3,867
1938	78.7	1,301	1,905	3,206	1,653	2,421	4,074
1939	66.1	1,270	2,302	3,572	1,921	3,483	5,404

well as of their respective components of capital formation, embodied in the planting, caring for, and maturing of young trees (see Metzer and Kaplan, 1990, pp. 33–43, and the discussion there). These estimates are presented in tables A.7–A.9, and A.13, which also report the price indices of citrus crops and investment, respectively. The crop price index (table A.7, col. 1) was calculated directly from the series of f.o.b. prices in table A.6, and the index of citrus investment cost (table A.8, col. 1) was taken from Szereszewski (1968, p. 77).

The procedures for estimating the output and product figures of non-citrus farming, reported in tables A.10 and A.13, are carefully outlined and their source material thoroughly discussed in Metzer and Kaplan (1990, pp. 19–30). The documentation there elaborates on the derivation of the annual output series from estimates for five benchmark years (1921, 1927, 1931, 1935, 1939), whose selection (following and revising

Table A.8. *Investment in citrus groves, 1922–39*

	price index of investment in citrus (1936=100) (1)	investment (P£ '000)					
		current prices			1936 prices		
		Arabs (2)	Jews (3)	total (4)	Arabs (5)	Jews (6)	total (7)
1922	111.5						
1923	98.7		16	16		16	16
1924	102.2		22	22		22	22
1925	106.5		29	29		28	28
1926	97.7	52	191	243	53	196	249
1927	92.5	222	283	505	240	306	546
1928	96.5	175	368	543	181	381	562
1929	97.5	232	700	932	238	718	956
1930	99.4	292	848	1,140	294	853	1,147
1931	94.6	300	795	1,095	317	841	1,158
1932	95.6	476	1,161	1,637	498	1,215	1,713
1933	100.0	536	1,692	2,228	536	1,692	2,228
1934	107.1	907	1,846	2,753	847	1,723	2,570
1935	105.3	942	1,373	2,315	895	1,304	2,199
1936	100.0	982	1,093	2,075	982	1,093	2,075
1937	99.1	647	856	1,503	653	864	1,517
1938	97.2	548	538	1,086	564	553	1,117
1939	105.2	429	268	697	408	255	663

Szereszewski) was largely led by the availability of detailed reports of the government's Department of Agriculture (particularly Sawer, 1923, for 1921, and later annual reports) and of comprehensive surveys of Jewish agriculture (summarized in Gurevich and Gertz, 1938, 1947). Note, however, that various adjustments had to be made in the officially quoted raw production figures before they could be taken to represent likely output aggregates. This refers particularly to rural underreporting of production, while the Ottoman gross output tax was still in effect (see chapter 6 in this volume, and Metzer and Kaplan, 1990, pp. 19–22).

A large number of general and specific sources were consulted for estimating the benchmark output figures in value terms (for the country as a whole, for Jewish farming, and, as a residual, for Arab agriculture), and for constructing "non-citrus" indices of prices (table A.10, col. 1) and quantities. Together with Szereszewski's revised output series for Jewish farming, these indices served to turn the five base-year estimates into

Table A.9. *Total citrus output (crops and investments), 1921–39 (P£ '000)*

	current prices			1936 prices		
	Arabs (1)	Jews (2)	total (3)	Arabs (4)	Jews (5)	total (6)
1921	338	198	536	241	142	383
1922	409	240	649	302	177	479
1923	358	226	584	334	212	546
1924	512	323	835	388	250	638
1925	570	363	933	525	336	861
1926	582	502	1,084	424	414	838
1927	1,020	751	1,771	852	665	1,517
1928	807	739	1,546	690	680	1,370
1929	764	1,013	1,777	651	961	1,612
1930	985	1,255	2,240	892	1,205	2,097
1931	959	1,235	2,194	856	1,200	2,056
1932	1,321	1,825	3,146	1,252	1,807	3,059
1933	1,468	2,552	4,020	1,396	2,486	3,882
1934	2,031	3,028	5,059	1,865	2,794	4,659
1935	2,154	3,059	5,213	2,028	2,880	4,908
1936	1,867	2,388	4,255	1,867	2,388	4,255
1937	1,952	2,772	4,724	2,219	3,165	5,384
1938	1,849	2,443	4,292	2,217	2,974	5,191
1939	1,699	2,570	4,269	2,329	3,738	6,067

continuous annual output series in current and constant prices (table A.10, cols. 2–7).

A list of the sources containing data and assessments of farm output in physical terms, of prices, and of cost of production, used by Metzer and Kaplan in generating the output and value added estimates (tables A.10 and A.13, cols. 3 and 4), consists, in addition to the sources mentioned above and to general statistical compilations and periodic reports (for example, the *Commercial Bulletin; Statistical Abstract of Palestine 1929; Agricultural Supplement; SAP; Statistical Handbook, 1947*), also of a number of monographic studies. These include the comprehensive treatise on the economy of Palestine edited by Himadeh (1938); contemporary surveys of economic activity in the early 1920s (Harary, 1922; Southard, 1922); specific studies concerning agricultural production, such as Viteles (1927), Pinner (1930), Hirsch (1933), and Samuel (1946, 1947); and analyses of the structure and operation of the (Arab) farm economy (Johnson and Crosbie, 1930; Volcani, 1930).

Table A.10. *Non-citrus farm output, 1921–39*

	price index of non-citrus output (1936=100) (1)	non-citrus output (P£ '000)					
		current prices			1936 prices		
		Arabs (2)	Jews (3)	total (4)	Arabs (5)	Jews (6)	total (7)
1921	204.3	6,021	394	6,415	2,947	193	3,140
1922	159.6	5,272	389	5,661	3,303	244	3,547
1923	131.3	4,223	357	4,580	3,216	272	3,488
1924	141.6	5,184	496	5,680	3,661	350	4,011
1925	165.5	5,908	657	6,565	3,570	397	3,967
1926	142.0	5,373	686	6,059	3,784	483	4,267
1927	134.6	5,141	771	5,912	3,819	573	4,392
1928	147.7	4,579	768	5,347	3,100	520	3,620
1929	120.2	4,396	734	5,130	3,657	611	4,268
1930	91.3	3,283	579	3,862	3,596	634	4,230
1931	85.0	3,092	574	3,666	3,637	675	4,312
1932	98.4	3,098	658	3,756	3,148	669	3,817
1933	96.9	2,764	684	3,448	2,852	706	3,558
1934	94.4	3,705	878	4,583	3,925	930	4,855
1935	90.8	4,454	1,040	5,494	4,906	1,145	6,051
1936	100.0	4,579	1,174	5,753	4,579	1,174	5,753
1937	98.1	5,975	1,404	7,379	6,092	1,433	7,525
1938	91.9	4,780	1,287	6,067	5,199	1,400	6,599
1939	87.7	4,768	1,330	6,098	5,436	1,517	6,953

Manufacturing

Unlike agriculture, which "gained" from rich quantitative documentation of its country-wide activity, the manufacturing industry of Palestine suffers from partial, uneven, and rather fragmented data coverage. Only one broad census, reporting employment, capital, itemized cost of production, and output in Arab and Jewish manufacturing, was taken during the inter-war period. This was the government's *First Census of Industries* of 1928, summarizing the state of the industry by the end of 1927 (see Eliachar, 1979; Gross, 1979, and the discussion in chapter 5 in this volume). While Jewish manufacturing was covered reasonably well in a number of additional surveys that Szereszewski used in constructing his series of manufacturing output and product ("Current Topics," 1926; Kruglak, 1934; Gurevich, 1931, 1939), the 1928 census is the only source of systematic information on Arab manufacturing in the inter-war years.

Table A.11. *Total agricultural output (citrus and non-citrus combined), 1921–39 (P£ '000)*

	current prices			1936 prices		
	Arabs (1)	Jews (2)	total (3)	Arabs (4)	Jews (5)	total (6)
1921	6,359	592	6,951	3,188	335	3,523
1922	5,681	629	6,310	3,605	421	4,026
1923	4,581	583	5,164	3,550	484	4,034
1924	5,696	819	6,515	4,049	600	4,649
1925	6,478	1,020	7,498	4,095	733	4,828
1926	5,955	1,188	7,143	4,208	897	5,105
1927	6,161	1,522	7,683	4,671	1,238	5,909
1928	5,386	1,507	6,893	3,790	1,200	4,990
1929	5,160	1,747	6,907	4,308	1,572	5,880
1930	4,268	1,834	6,102	4,488	1,839	6,327
1931	4,051	1,809	5,860	4,493	1,875	6,368
1932	4,419	2,483	6,902	4,400	2,476	6,876
1933	4,232	3,236	7,468	4,248	3,192	7,440
1934	5,736	3,906	9,642	5,790	3,724	9,514
1935	6,608	4,099	10,707	6,934	4,025	10,959
1936	6,446	3,562	10,008	6,446	3,562	10,008
1937	7,927	4,176	12,103	8,311	4,598	12,909
1938	6,629	3,730	10,359	7,416	4,374	11,790
1939	6,467	3,900	10,367	7,765	5,255	13,020

As such, it naturally provided the basis for estimating Arab manufacturing output and value added, and also for revising Szereszewski's output and product figures for Jewish manufacturing (which he constructed before the ethno-nationally disaggregated data of the census were available). The newly estimated and revised series of output and product are displayed in tables A.14 and A.15 in current prices; the output figures are shown in constant prices, as well, with the government's wholesale price index (reported in *SAP*, 1944–45, p. 110, and reproduced below in table A.21, col. 5) being used for the conversion.

The entire estimation procedure is described in detail in Metzer and Kaplan (1990, pp. 54–73), and its main components are summarized here. The government industrial census of 1928, comprehensive though it was intended to be, suffered from widely recognized undercoverage due to the exclusion of home industries, custom-made production, and repair work, as well as from underreporting, probably for fear of using the

Table A.12. *Relative weight of citrus in Arab, Jewish, and total farm output, 1921–39 (% of output in current prices)*

	Arabs (1)	Jews (2)	total (3)
1921	5.3	33.4	7.7
1922	7.2	38.2	10.3
1923	7.8	38.8	11.3
1924	9.0	39.4	12.8
1925	8.8	35.6	12.4
1926	9.8	42.4	15.3
1927	16.6	49.3	23.1
1928	15.0	49.0	22.4
1929	14.8	58.0	25.7
1930	23.1	68.4	36.7
1931	23.7	68.3	37.4
1932	29.9	73.5	45.6
1933	34.7	78.9	53.8
1934	35.4	77.5	52.5
1935	32.6	74.6	48.7
1936	29.0	67.0	42.5
1937	24.6	66.4	39.0
1938	27.9	65.5	41.4
1939	26.3	65.9	41.2

census information for taxation purposes (see Gross, 1979; and chapter 5 in this volume). Consequently a substantial part of the estimation effort of Metzer and Kaplan concentrated on attempting to correct the downward-biased output figures in the census (1990, pp. 55–59). This task was carried out in two stages. In the first stage, the employment figures of the industrial census were corrected upward on the basis of the distributions of labor by industry in 1931; these were derived from the 1931 population census (see table A.5), and adjusted to the conjectured changes in industrial employment between 1927 and 1931, assumed to be generated by the rise in the labor force and by the decline in unemployment between these two years.

The resulting adjustment of the 1927 employment figures was considerable: a 38 percent increase in Jewish and a 117 percent rise in Arab employment in manufacturing. Nonetheless, because the assumptions used in the process were aimed at minimizing the extent of the corrections, the (substantially) revised numbers should be regarded a lower

Table A.13. *Agricultural product (value added), 1921–39 (P£ '000, current prices)*

| | citrus | | non-citrus | | all agricultural product | | |
| | | | | | Arabs (1)+(3) | Jews (2)+(4) | total (5)+(6) |
	Arabs (1)	Jews (2)	Arabs (3)	Jews (4)	(5)	(6)	(7)
1921	67	42	4,388	218	4,455	260	4,715
1922	175	107	3,921	216	4,096	323	4,419
1923	163	107	3,112	196	3,275	303	3,578
1924	314	189	3,914	274	4,228	463	4,691
1925	318	197	4,419	361	4,737	558	5,295
1926	375	294	4,023	373	4,398	667	5,065
1927	637	449	3,871	422	4,508	871	5,379
1928	471	403	3,288	412	3,759	815	4,574
1929	435	528	3,253	396	3,688	924	4,612
1930	562	657	2,409	311	2,971	968	3,939
1931	551	658	2,269	308	2,820	966	3,786
1932	754	965	2,202	343	2,956	1,308	4,264
1933	775	1,323	1,923	350	2,698	1,673	4,371
1934	1,088	1,603	2,716	457	3,804	2,060	5,864
1935	1,138	1,643	3,372	543	4,510	2,186	6,696
1936	913	1,091	3,356	608	4,269	1,699	5,968
1937	947	1,321	4,597	740	5,544	2,061	7,605
1938	802	993	3,498	667	4,300	1,660	5,960
1939	643	928	3,476	689	4,119	1,617	5,736

bound of the "true" adjustments called for, particularly in the Arab sector. In the second stage the estimates of labor productivity by industrial branch, which were deduced from the 1928 industrial census, were applied to the adjusted employment data, so as to correct the 1927 output figures, from P£2.153 million to P£2.752 million and from P£1.734 million to P£2.075 million in Arab and Jewish manufacturing, respectively (Metzer and Kaplan, 1990, p. 57, and the corrected figures in table A.14, cols. 1 and 2).

The industrial census reveals that in 1927 80 percent of Arab manufacturing output consisted of: flour milling (36 percent); tobacco and cigarettes (22 percent); soap (15 percent); and oil (7 percent). Assuming that these branches, combined, constituted a similar proportion (about 80 percent) of Arab manufacturing output in the early 1920s, the output of 1921 was estimated from the available production figures of the agricul-

Table A.14. *Output of manufacturing, 1922–39 (P£ '000)*

	current prices			1936 prices		
	Arabs (1)	Jews (2)	total (3)	Arabs (4)	Jews (5)	total (6)
1922	1,974	1,039	3,013	1,254	660	1,914
1923	1,848	1,087	2,935	1,392	819	2,211
1924	2,071	1,408	3,479	1,546	1,051	2,597
1925	2,465	1,928	4,393	1,716	1,343	3,059
1926	2,601	2,019	4,620	1,905	1,479	3,384
1927	2,752	2,075	4,827	2,116	1,595	3,711
1928	2,719	2,256	4,975	2,148	1,782	3,930
1929	2,778	2,511	5,289	2,362	2,135	4,497
1930	2,387	2,859	5,246	2,402	2,876	5,278
1931	2,338	3,133	5,471	2,578	3,454	6,032
1932	2,476	3,451	5,927	2,524	3,518	6,042
1933	2,598	5,352	7,950	2,693	5,546	8,239
1934	2,904	7,104	10,008	3,019	7,385	10,404
1935	3,367	8,593	11,960	3,489	8,905	12,394
1936	3,342	9,109	12,451	3,342	9,109	12,451
1937	3,780	8,500	12,280	3,519	7,914	11,433
1938	3,402	8,915	12,317	3,369	8,827	12,196
1939	3,410	9,481	12,891	3,400	9,453	12,853

ture-originated raw materials (grains, tobacco, and oil), supported by various consumption surveys ("Report on Investigation of Cost of Living," 1922; Kligler et al., 1931), foreign trade statistics (found mainly in various issues of the *Commercial Bulletin*), and a number of assumptions regarding Jewish production of these goods (Metzer and Kaplan, 1990, pp. 64–67).

Arab manufacturing output in constant prices was assumed to grow at a constant annual rate between 1921 and 1927. To construct the output estimates for Arab manufacturing in the rest of the inter-war period, a number of linkages between the output of Arab manufacturing by product group (in constant prices) and related demographic and economic parameters, for which annual data are available, were assumed, and utilized as a basis for the yearly output figures of 1928–39.

Note that the empirical likelihood of this procedure is confirmed by the closeness of its derived, end-of-period, Arab manufacturing output (P£3.410 million in 1939, table A.14, col. 1) to an alternative independent estimate of the same quantity, amounting to P£3.430 million.

Table A.15. *Product (value added) of manufacturing,*
1922–39 (P£ '000, current prices)

	Arabs (1)	Jews (2)	total (3)
1922	539	491	1,030
1923	534	514	1,048
1924	634	663	1,297
1925	794	904	1,698
1926	879	941	1,820
1927	975	901	1,876
1928	968	979	1,947
1929	1,022	1,091	2,113
1930	883	1,241	2,124
1931	891	1,416	2,307
1932	936	1,560	2,496
1933	1,006	2,419	3,425
1934	1,179	3,211	4,390
1935	1,459	3,884	5,343
1936	1,447	3,862	5,309
1937	1,637	3,604	5,241
1938	1,473	3,780	5,253
1939	1,476	4,020	5,496

The latter estimate was derived by subtracting Jewish product from the country's overall manufacturing product (originally estimated by Wood, 1943, as part of his construction of the country-wide national accounts for 1939, and revised in Metzer and Kaplan, 1990, p. 71), and then dividing the result by the product-output ratio in Arab manufacturing for that year.

The Arab product-output ratios for 1939 and for all other inter-war years were deduced with various adjustments from the 1928 census. They were applied to the output series, turning it into a manufacturing value added series. Further elaborations on the estimation methods are provided in Metzer and Kaplan (1990, pp. 68–73).

Construction
The output and product series for the construction industry reported in tables A.16 and A.17 reflect the productive activity of Jewish and Arab construction firms within their respective communities or as sub-contractors for the central and local government, and that of self-construction by and within households, especially in the rural Arab community.

Table A.16. *Output of construction, 1922–39*

| | index of construction costs (1936=100) (1) | construction output (P£ '000) | | | | | |
| | | current prices | | | 1936 prices | | |
		Arabs (2)	Jews (3)	total (4)	Arabs (5)	Jews (6)	total (7)
1922	128.0	406	625	1,031	317	488	805
1923	108.6	380	359	739	350	331	681
1924	110.9	382	668	1,050	344	602	946
1925	121.7	430	1,834	2,264	353	1,507	1,860
1926	112.0	541	759	1,300	483	678	1,161
1927	110.3	571	332	903	518	301	819
1928	105.7	514	306	820	486	289	775
1929	96.1	537	472	1,009	559	491	1,050
1930	92.7	543	826	1,369	585	891	1,476
1931	86.5	595	1,065	1,660	688	1,231	1,919
1932	82.5	657	1,331	1,988	798	1,613	2,411
1933	103.7	994	3,557	4,551	958	3,430	4,388
1934	111.9	1,621	5,895	7,516	1,449	5,268	6,717
1935	102.7	1,760	7,055	8,815	1,714	6,870	8,584
1936	100.0	1,330	5,325	6,655	1,330	5,325	6,655
1937	102.9	744	2,976	3,720	723	2,892	3,615
1938	98.0	470	1,881	2,351	480	1,919	2,399
1939	94.1	381	1,524	1,905	405	1,620	2,025

The constant price estimates are derived from the cost-of-construction index devised by Szereszewski (1968, pp. 76–77) and reproduced in table A.16, col. 1. Note, however, that the part of government construction which was not sub-contracted but was directly executed by the government itself, using its own Arab and Jewish employees, is included in the output of the two ethno-national sectors' service industries, not in the output of the construction industry (see the discussion in the next section below, outlining the conceptual and empirical framework for our national accounting).

Productive activity in the construction industry (primarily in urban localities), like that of agriculture, is also rather well documented. The major sources for data on the volume of construction and its composition were the report on Jewish and non-Jewish urban construction in 1924–1935 (*Aliya*, 1936, pp. 20–29), and the official statistics of urban construction by localities from 1930 onward (*SAP*, 1936–1944/45). In addition, extremely useful information on the inputs used and the extent

Table A.17. *Product (value added) of construction,*
1922–39 (P£ '000, current prices)

	Arabs (1)	Jews (2)	total (3)
1922	183	313	496
1923	171	162	333
1924	172	281	453
1925	193	770	963
1926	243	319	562
1927	257	139	396
1928	231	129	360
1929	242	198	440
1930	244	347	591
1931	268	447	715
1932	296	559	855
1933	447	1,494	1,941
1934	729	2,476	3,205
1935	792	2,963	3,755
1936	599	2,236	2,835
1937	335	1,250	1,585
1938	212	790	1,002
1939	171	640	811

of activity in Jewish construction is contained in a number of general and specific surveys and studies (Viteles, 1929; Gaathon, 1941, 1978; Schlesinger, 1944; Karpman, 1946; Ettinger, 1947; Horowitz, 1948), and in statistics of wages (*MBS*, 1936–39; *Meshek Leumi*, 1936–41) and employment periodically published by the Jewish Agency and the Histadrut (*Bulletin of the Economic Research Institute*; *Statistical Bulletin*; *Sikumim*).

Careful scrutiny of these sources by Metzer and Kaplan (1990, pp. 76–82) led to some corrections of Szereszewski's (1968) output and value added series of Jewish construction (notably, a downward revision of his figures for the depression years of the second half of the 1930s), and to the estimation of the output of Arab annual construction in urban localities. However, estimating the output of Arab construction in villages was a more difficult procedure, due to the absence of statistical coverage. It was approached indirectly, by using information on the value of construction permits in small localities (*SAP*, various years) as a basis for estimating the value of the per capita stock of dwelling in the rural areas. Making some assumptions regarding the patterns of change in the per capita stock of rural dwellings, and utilizing benchmark estimates of the size of the Arab rural population (Bachi, 1977, table 1.2), the stock figures were turned into flow estimates of output. On the basis of the information of the cost of production in the industry, a value-added-to-output ratio of 45 percent was used to derive the product series for all of Arab construction in 1922–39 (Metzer and Kaplan, 1990, pp. 82–84).

Services

The value added of services produced by each of the two ethno-national sectors consists of the product generated by the following branches and economic activities: transportation and commerce; other private and public business and personal services (including the product generated by public employees who were engaged in material production, see above); and the export of factor services. Since the paucity of data precludes the estimation of separate value added series for the different components of services, estimates of the aggregate product of all the domestically produced services, including governmental employment (see the discussion in the next section, below), were constructed for Arabs and – largely by revising Szereszewski's series – for Jews. In addition, the value of the annual flow of factor services (labor and rented structures) exported by Arabs to Jews, which was naturally part of Jewish, but not of Arab, domestically produced services, was estimated separately (the export of similar services by Jews to Arabs was assumed, according to the information available, to be negligible). All these series are reported in table A.18.

The construction of the series presented in table A.18 and its underlying methodological and empirical considerations are thoroughly outlined in Metzer and Kaplan (1990, pp. 120–33). Here we highlight only the main points. Following Szereszewski's procedures, the basic method utilized for constructing the product-of-services estimates was to turn the figures of employment in the industry in 1931 and in other benchmark years into value added quantities, from which annual series of product were derived by assuming some systematic links between material and service production.

The adjustment of Szereszewski's labor-force series (see table A.4 and the discussion in the population and labour section above), the exclusion of Arabs employed by Jews from his industrial distributions of labor in the Jewish domestic economy, and the inclusion of dwellings in his labor-productivity-derived numbers called for substantial revisions of his figures of Jewish domestic production of services. This was done by separating housing and other structures (whose services were independently estimated: see below) from the rest of the industry. Accordingly,

Table A.18. *Product (value added) of services, 1922–39 (P£ '000, current prices)*

| | | Arabs | | | | |
| | | factor services exported to Jews | | | | |
	domestically produced services[a] (1)	labor (2)	rented structures (3)	total (4)	Jews[a] (5)	total (1)+(5) (6)
1922	5,581	196	68	264	1,370	6,951
1923	4,497	164	66	230	1,336	5,833
1924	5,321	199	80	279	1,775	7,096
1925	6,002	279	130	409	2,520	8,522
1926	5,710	251	105	356	2,587	8,297
1927	5,877	283	82	365	2,698	8,575
1928	5,433	287	81	368	2,718	8,151
1929	5,246	279	91	370	3,062	8,308
1930	4,425	255	104	359	3,426	7,851
1931	4,343	238	122	360	3,798	8,141
1932	4,825	329	156	485	4,646	9,471
1933	5,048	444	237	681	6,647	11,695
1934	6,704	525	318	843	9,062	15,766
1935	8,285	540	388	928	10,680	18,965
1936	8,734	282	250	532	10,199	18,933
1937	10,088	186	228	414	10,296	20,384
1938	8,252	300	221	521	9,878	18,130
1939	7,897		225	225	10,314	18,211

Note:
[a] Including government employment.

Szereszewski's base figures for 1931 and 1936 were adjusted to provide net-of-structures estimates. The Arab-inclusive industrial distributions of employment in the Jewish economy in 1931 and 1936 were then applied to the 1931 and 1936 figures of relative labor productivity in services to derive the product of net-of-structures services in 1922 and 1927 and in 1935 and 1939, respectively.

Following Szereszewski's assumption concerning the inverse relationship between the employment and product shares of services and those of construction in 1922–39, it was assumed that in the intervals between any two consecutive base years the employment share of services varied in the same direction and relative intensity as that of the composite share of agriculture and manufacturing in material product. Based on this assumption, an annual series of the employment share of services was constructed, to which the relative labor productivity in services of 1931 was applied to deduce the product of services in 1922–32 and that in 1936 for the remainder of the inter-war period.

The annual series of value added generated by residential and productive uses of structures in the Jewish sector (including those that were rented from Arab landlords) were constructed on the basis of Gaathon's (1941, 1978) figures of capital stock, rates of return, and rental costs for 1936, and the adjusted annual index of rental cost which Szereszewski (1968) constructed as part of his cost of living index (see Metzer and Kaplan, 1990, pp. 120–27, 175–78). The value added figures for the services of structures were then combined with those of all other services into an all-industry product series for the Jewish domestic economy as reported in col. 5 of table A.18.

As for the Arab sector, the product of the domestically produced services was divided for estimation purposes into two components: dwellings and all the rest. The value added of dwellings was obtained from the estimate of the product per capita of residential services in 1936 which, in turn, was derived from Gaathon's (1941, 1978) data, adjusted by the estimates of the rural stock of housing per capita (see the discussion of Arab construction above). Assuming that product per capita of dwelling services grew between 1922 and 1936 at the same rate as that of material product per head, and that it remained unchanged in the depression years of 1936–39, an annual series of the product per capita of housing services for the entire period was generated.

The basis for the product of Arab non-dwelling domestic services was provided by the detailed estimate constructed for 1931. A transportation and commerce component was calculated by applying Gaathon's (1941, 1978) ratio of the value added of these two branches to total Arab material product in 1936, to the combined value added of material production in 1931. The product of the rest of the non-dwelling service industry for that year was generated from the number of employed persons in services, net of transportation and commerce, extracted from the 1931 population census, and from estimates of their average product which were derived from various wage quotations (for example, Ben-Zvi, 1930; *Wage Rate Statistics Bulletin*; *SAP*).

Utilizing the industrial distributions of employment (table A.5), these two components were combined to obtain an estimate of relative labor productivity in all Arab domestic non-dwelling services in 1931. This was then applied, with minor adjustments, to the Arab employment by industry distributions of 1921, 1936, and 1939, to derive estimates of the value added of Arab domestic services in these base years. In view of the very large share of transportation and commerce in the value added of Arab domestic services in 1931 (73 percent), it is assumed that the scale of activity in the industry was highly dependent on that of material production. Hence, the product of services in the "in-between" years was estimated on the presumption that it varied in direction and relative intensity together with the annual variation of the value added of material output. The product of Arab domestic services was converted from constant to current prices (table A.18, col. 1) by using the implicit deflator of Arab material output (table A.21, col. 1), which was calculated from the ratio of material output in current prices to that of constant (1936) prices (tables A.11, A.14, A.16), with the extension to 1940–47 being facilitated by the application of the percentage annual changes of the Jewish cost-of-living index in these years to its value in 1939. Further elaborations on the estimation process are found in Metzer and Kaplan (1990, pp. 128–31).

To complete the picture of the Arab service industry, we estimated the annual income generated by the export of factor services to the Jewish sector. The yearly rental income in current prices (table A.18, col. 3) was calculated on the basis of its share in the overall product of structure services in the Jewish sector in the mid-1930s, coupled with some assumptions on the changes in this share over time (Metzer and Kaplan, 1990, pp. 125–27).

The annual series of income derived from employment in the Jewish economy (table A.18, col. 2) was constructed from the employment figures for 1922, 1931, and 1935 (table A.5) and from corresponding wage data (*Blue Book*, 1929–35; Ben-Zvi, 1930; Ater, 1937; Gaathon, 1941, 1978). The figures for 1922–30 and 1932–34 were generated under the assumption that in each of the intervals the income from the export of labor services varied in the same direction and relative intensity as a composite measure of Jewish productive activity made up of total Jewish product and the output of citrus weighted by the share of agriculture in Arab employment in the Jewish economy. In 1936–39, the period of relative economic disengagement between the two communities, direct estimates based on various accounts of contemporaries regarding changes in the volume of Arab employment in the Jewish sector (*Censuses of Workers in Groves*, 1939; Gaathon, 1941, 1978; Duesterwald, 1945) have been worked out.

PALESTINE'S PRODUCT BY ETHNO-NATIONAL SECTOR, 1922–1947

According to the conceptual foundations and the standard methodology of national income accounts, the "national" economies of the Arab and the Jewish communities of Palestine are composed of all the productive units owned by their respective members, with their bilateral trade in goods and services (including factor services) being considered as foreign trade for each one of them. At the all-country level this trade was obviously part of domestic commerce.

Assuming that foreign trade in factor services, other than bilaterally, was negligible, and that no such services were sold by Jews to Arabs, the following distinction between "domestic" and "national" product is made for each of the two ethno-national economies: Jewish net domestic product (NDP_J) is identified as comprising the value added of all the economic establishments operating in the Jewish economy, including the wage component paid by Jewish employers to their Arab employees and the rents received by Arab landlords from Jewish tenants and other property users. Subtracting these payments from NDP_J turns it into Jewish net national product (NNP_J). By inverse symmetry, the income generated by Arab labor and rental services "exported" to Jews is part of the net national product of the Arab economy (NNP_A), but not of its net domestic product (NDP_A), which, analogously, sums up the value added of all the productive activities undertaken within the Arab economy.

To be consistent with these criteria, the government, too, should have been treated as a separate economic unit, and the wages it paid to its Arab and Jewish employees (i.e., the value added derived from the government's productive activity) should have been taken to be part of the "national," but not of the "domestic," products of the respective communities. However, the lack of appropriate data makes it impossible to construct an ethno-nationally disaggregate series of government wage payments, and the income derived from government employment of Arabs and Jews is considered (adopting Szereszewski's [1968] approach) part of the national and domestic product of each community respectively. Furthermore, it is assumed that all of the government's wage bill (estimated by Gaathon, 1941, to comprise no more than 1.5 percent of the country's national income) is included in the service products of the two ethno-national sectors. In the present context this is not an unreasonable assumption as the Arab labor-force figures underlying the estimated product of services in the Arab economy were, in fact, derived from data pertaining to all non-Jews (of whom the Arabs comprised about 98 percent), and the product of Arab services therefore includes the value added of the government economic activity due to the employment of non-Arab (and non-Jewish) public employees.

It thus follows that Palestine's net domestic product (NDP_P), which is identical in our system to its net national product (NNP_P), is given in current prices by:

$$NDP_P = NDP_A + NDP_J = NNP_A + NNP_J = NNP_P.$$

Note, though, that since a number of foreign companies (non-Arab and non-Jewish) operated in Palestine during the Mandate period, the all-country domestic product (NDP_P) may have been somewhat larger than the sum total of the two sectors' domestic (or national) products, and hence also larger than Palestine's net national product (NNP_P). All the indications, however, are that the extent of the economic activity of foreign companies in Palestine was rather small, so the biases resulting from their exclusion from the product estimates are, most probably, inconsequential.

Based on the framework summarized by the above equation (see Metzer and Kaplan, 1990, pp. 12–16, 137–54 for further discussions), the net product series for Arabs, Jews, and the country as a whole are presented in tables A.19 and A.20 in current prices, and in table A.22 in constant (1936) prices at total and per capita (for Arabs and Jews) levels. The conversion of Arab product in current prices (table A.19, cols. 5 and 6) to constant prices (table A.22, cols. 1, 2) was done by means of the deflator of Arab material output, discussed above (table A.21, col. 1), which was assumed to represent the changes in the prices of Arab aggregate product better than other aggregate price indices. For the Jewish economy this conversion (from cols. 5 and 6 of table A.20 to cols. 4 and 5 of table A.22, respectively) was done by using the Jewish cost-of-living index (table A.21, col. 4), originally devised by Szereszewski (1968) and revised, on the basis of a newly constructed rental price index, by Metzer and Kaplan (1990, pp. 175–78).

The domestic product figures in current prices were derived for the inter-war period (1922–39) by annually aggregating the industrial value added estimates in each sector (cols. 1–4 in tables A.19 and A.20, for Arabs and Jews respectively), and the corresponding quantities of national product were calculated by adding to the domestic product (for Arabs) and subtracting from it (for Jews) the bilateral flow of factor services (table A.18, col. 4). Interestingly, it turns out that our country-wide product estimate in current prices for 1939 ($NDP_P = NNP_P = P£30.254$ million) is practically identical to the official national income estimate for the country as a whole in 1939 (P£30.242 million; Wood, 1943). Because of many offsetting differences between the two sets of estimates at the industry level (these are discussed at length in Metzer and Kaplan, 1990), their matching at the aggregate level may certainly reflect, in part, sheer coincidence. Nonetheless, since our sector-based approach to the estimation procedure is substantially different from Wood's consolidated method, the observed closeness of

Table A.19. *Arab net product by industry, 1922–47 (P£ '000, current prices)*

	agriculture (1)	manu- facturing (2)	construction (3)	services (4)	net domestic product (NDP$_A$) (5)	net national product (NNP$_A$) (6)
1922	4,096	539	183	5,581	10,399	10,663
1923	3,275	534	171	4,497	8,477	8,707
1924	4,228	634	172	5,321	10,355	10,634
1925	4,737	794	193	6,002	11,726	12,135
1926	4,398	879	243	5,710	11,230	11,586
1927	4,508	975	257	5,877	11,617	11,982
1928	3,759	968	231	5,433	10,391	10,759
1929	3,688	1,022	242	5,246	10,198	10,568
1930	2,971	883	244	4,425	8,523	8,882
1931	2,820	891	268	4,343	8,322	8,682
1932	2,956	936	296	4,825	9,013	9,498
1933	2,698	1,006	447	5,048	9,199	9,880
1934	3,804	1,179	729	6,704	12,416	13,259
1935	4,510	1,459	792	8,285	15,046	15,974
1936	4,269	1,447	599	8,734	15,049	15,581
1937	5,544	1,637	335	10,088	17,604	18,018
1938	4,300	1,473	212	8,252	14,237	14,758
1939	4,119	1,476	171	7,897	13,663	13,888
1940					17,321	17,667
1941					23,887	24,365
1942	14,700	4,500	1,955	19,269	40,424	41,232
1943					51,953	52,992
1944	21,870	6,300	1,807	26,155	56,132	57,255
1945	25,400	6,700	1,559	31,554	65,213	66,517
1946					79,486	81,076
1947					88,367	90,134

outcomes implies that the order of magnitude of our all-country product figures is empirically sound.

Unlike the inter-war period, the World War II years were relatively rich in estimates of national income accounts whose foundations were laid down by the Department of Statistics of the Mandatory government. It was in this context that Wood, the government statistician in 1938–45, constructed industry-based national income estimates for the country as a whole for 1942 and 1943, supplementing his work for 1939 (Wood, 1943, 1944). Loftus, Wood's successor, carried on the work by producing

Table A.20. *Jewish net product by industry, 1922–47 (P£ '000, current prices)*

	agriculture (1)	manu-facturing (2)	construction (3)	services (4)	net domestic product (NDP$_J$) (5)	net national product (NNP$_J$) (6)
1922	323	491	313	1,370	2,497	2,233
1923	303	514	162	1,336	2,315	2,085
1924	463	663	281	1,775	3,182	2,903
1925	558	904	770	2,520	4,752	4,343
1926	667	941	319	2,587	4,514	4,158
1927	871	901	139	2,698	4,609	4,244
1928	815	979	129	2,718	4,641	4,273
1929	924	1,091	198	3,062	5,275	4,905
1930	968	1,241	347	3,426	5,982	5,623
1931	966	1,416	447	3,798	6,627	6,267
1932	1,308	1,560	559	4,646	8,073	7,588
1933	1,673	2,419	1,494	6,647	12,233	11,552
1934	2,060	3,211	2,476	9,062	16,809	15,966
1935	2,186	3,884	2,963	10,680	19,713	18,785
1936	1,699	3,862	2,236	10,199	17,996	17,464
1937	2,061	3,604	1,250	10,296	17,211	16,797
1938	1,660	3,780	790	9,878	16,108	15,587
1939	1,617	4,020	640	10,314	16,591	16,366
1940	1,639	5,500	1,150	13,185	21,474	21,128
1941	2,016	8,800	1,590	18,302	30,708	30,230
1942	3,810	16,000	3,866	30,627	54,303	53,495
1943	5,824	21,950	4,076	38,928	70,778	69,739
1944	7,617	25,000	3,828	41,071	77,516	76,393
1945	9,600	29,800	5,408	45,248	90,056	88,752
1946	11,574	33,287	7,168	57,737	109,766	108,176
1947	14,180	31,618	10,580	65,652	122,030	120,263

national income and employment estimates by industry for 1944 and 1945, which he divided into their Arab and Jewish sectoral origins (Loftus, 1946, 1948). In addition, Ettinger (1947) constructed independent estimates of the product of Arab manufacturing in 1942, and Szereszewski (1968) had already utilized, among other sources, the official national income figures in extending to 1947 his annual series of product accounts by industry for the Jewish economy.

Naturally, the derivation of the various product figures for 1940–47, reported in tables A.19, A.20, and A.22, relies heavily on the sources

Table A.21. *Aggregate price indices (1936=100)*

	deflator of Arab material output (1)	index of the cost of Arab capital formation (2)	deflator of Jewish capital formation (3)	Jewish cost-of-living index (4)	wholesale price index (5)
1922	156.9	128.1	121.1	144.2	157.4
1923	129.2	108.6	114.0	126.1	132.7
1924	137.9	111.0	108.4	132.7	134.0
1925	155.8	121.8	113.8	144.7	143.6
1926	139.2	110.6	104.5	132.3	136.5
1927	131.0	104.6	99.9	122.3	130.1
1928	137.3	103.3	100.1	111.3	126.6
1929	118.1	96.5	98.3	108.0	117.6
1930	95.4	95.0	97.3	98.4	99.4
1931	89.4	89.1	92.0	92.7	90.7
1932	98.3	87.4	91.0	93.0	98.1
1933	99.0	102.4	102.9	102.6	96.5
1934	99.3	110.1	107.6	104.9	96.2
1935	95.7	103.6	102.5	102.6	96.5
1936	100.0	100.0	100.0	100.0	100.0
1937	98.7	101.1	102.5	103.7	107.4
1938	93.0	97.5	99.4	101.6	101.0
1939	89.1	99.6	106.7	103.3	100.3
1940	107.0	97.4	104.3	124.1	124.4
1941	132.2	126.1	135.1	153.2	169.9
1942	191.9	145.3	155.6	222.5	247.8
1943	233.1	194.5	208.3	270.3	302.2
1944	237.3	228.6	244.8	275.2	319.2
1945	255.1	250.8	268.6	295.8	319.4
1946	269.7	253.7	271.7	312.7	332.2
1947	273.2	282.2	302.2	316.7	

mentioned, adjusting their numbers to assure the consistency of the product series for the entire Mandate period. Two main adjustments were called for. One was to revise (upward) Loftus' figures for Arab manufacturing which were based on the highly selective 1942 census of manufacturing, enumerating only establishments whose lines of production could be related to the war effort (see chapter 5 in this volume). The second correction was to raise Szereszewski's value added estimates for the Jewish wartime construction industry, which did not include a significant part of the work done by Jewish contractors for the Allied forces in

Table A.22. *Palestine's net product by ethno-national sector, 1922–47 (1936 prices)*

	Arabs			Jews			total net domestic product (NDP$_P$) of Palestine (P£ '000) (1)+(4) (7)
	P£ '000			P£ '000			
	net domestic product (NDP$_A$) (1)	net national product (NNP$_A$) (2)	P£ NNP$_A$ per capita (3)	net domestic product (NDP$_J$) (4)	net national product (NNP$_J$) (5)	P£ NNP$_J$ per capita (6)	
1922	6,628	6,796	10.1	1,732	1,549	19.3	8,360
1923	6,561	6,739	9.7	1,836	1,653	18.4	8,397
1924	7,509	7,711	10.8	2,398	2,188	23.1	9,907
1925	7,527	7,789	10.6	3,284	3,001	24.7	10,811
1926	8,067	8,323	11.1	3,412	3,143	21.0	11,479
1927	8,868	9,147	11.9	3,769	3,470	23.2	12,637
1928	7,567	7,835	10.0	4,170	3,839	25.3	11,737
1929	8,635	8,948	11.1	4,884	4,542	29.0	13,519
1930	8,934	9,310	11.3	6,079	5,714	34.7	15,013
1931	9,307	9,709	11.4	7,149	6,761	39.3	16,456
1932	9,169	9,663	11.1	8,681	8,159	44.9	17,850
1933	9,291	9,978	11.1	11,923	11,259	53.4	21,214
1934	12,505	13,354	14.5	16,024	15,220	59.6	28,529
1935	15,725	16,694	17.7	19,213	18,309	56.9	34,938
1936	15,049	15,581	16.1	17,996	17,464	47.1	33,045
1937	17,833	18,252	18.2	16,597	16,198	41.6	34,430
1938	15,307	15,868	15.5	15,854	15,342	38.1	31,161
1939	15,331	15,584	14.9	16,061	15,843	36.6	31,392
1940	16,188	16,511	15.3	17,304	17,025	37.0	33,492
1941	18,069	18,430	16.7	20,044	19,732	41.6	38,113
1942	21,065	21,486	18.9	24,406	24,043	49.7	45,471
1943	22,288	22,734	19.5	26,185	25,801	51.7	48,473
1944	23,654	24,128	20.0	28,167	27,759	53.1	51,822
1945	25,564	26,075	20.9	30,445	30,004	54.7	56,009
1946	29,472	30,062	23.3	35,103	34,594	59.7	64,575
1947	32,345	32,992	24.7	38,532	37,974	62.4	70,877

neighboring countries. These and some additional adjustments, including the extension of Arab domestic product figures to 1947 (by assuming that its relative share in the all-country product remained as in 1945), conclude the estimation of the sector-based domestic product series (Metzer and Kaplan, 1990, pp. 143–54).

The domestic product of Arabs and Jews in 1940–47 was turned into national product (cols. 5 and 6 in tables A.19 and A.20) by assuming that in the Arab sector national product exceeded domestic product by 2 percent, and that Jewish domestic product was larger than its national product by 1.5 percent; these were approximately the respective differentials found for 1939. Finally, the 1940–47 Arab and Jewish product figures in current prices were transformed into constant price figures – as for the inter-war years – by using the deflator of Arab material output and the Jewish cost-of-living index, respectively.

INVESTMENT AND CAPITAL, 1922–1947

Tables A.23 and A.24 report Jewish investment, capital imports, and capital stock figures annually in current and constant prices. The disaggregate gross investment series in current prices (table A.23, cols. 1–5), which were originally constructed by Szereszewski (1968), and revised by Metzer and Kaplan (1990), were taken from BMZ, table A3, and from table A.8 above. Their aggregate total was converted into constant price figures (table A.23, col. 6) by the derived deflator of Jewish capital formation (table A.21, col. 3: see BMZ, table A7). The same deflator is used for transforming the Jewish capital import figures of table A.24, cols. 1–4, from current to constant prices (BMZ, table A3). Szereszewski's revised net investment and capital stock estimates (BMZ, tables A3 and A4) are shown in table A.24, cols. 5 and 6.

The results of the attempted estimates of Arab annual capital and investment figures are presented in table A.25. The basis for the estimation is provided by the gross investment series in constant (1936) prices of col. 2, which was derived from the data on investments in citrus (table A.8, col. 5) and in construction (table A.16, col. 5), assuming that these two items combined constituted 70 percent of fixed gross capital formation in the Arab domestic economy over the entire inter-war period. The gross investment figures were turned into net investment (table A.25, col. 3) by assuming an annual discard of 20 percent of gross capital formation.

Multiplying the Jewish capital stock of 1922 (P£5.056 million, table A.24, col. 6) by 4.4 (the Arab-Jewish capital ratio calculated from Duesterwald's [1957] capital stock estimates for 1920–22), a suggested figure for Arab net capital of P£22.246 million (in 1936 prices) was generated for 1922. Adding to this base-year stock figure the annual net investments of col. 3, a yearly series of Arab net fixed reproducible capital for 1922–40 was derived (table A.25, col. 4). Another benchmark capital stock figure was that of 1945 (P£53.057 million, table A.25, col. 4). It was

Table A.23. *Jewish gross investments in fixed reproducible capital, 1922–47* (*P£ '000*)

| | investments by type in current prices | | | | | total gross investment (1936 prices) |
	structures (1)	citrus (2)	non-citrus agriculture (3)	others (4)	total (5)	(6)
1922	625		101	490	1,216	1,004
1923	359	16	103	498	976	856
1924	668	22	123	639	1,452	1,339
1925	1,834	29	143	853	2,859	2,512
1926	759	191	145	603	1,698	1,625
1927	332	283	163	397	1,175	1,176
1928	306	368	89	404	1,167	1,166
1929	472	700	83	530	1,785	1,816
1930	826	848	113	644	2,431	2,498
1931	1,065	795	113	542	2,515	2,734
1932	1,331	1,161	67	449	3,008	3,307
1933	3,557	1,692	117	970	6,336	6,156
1934	5,895	1,846	83	2,074	9,898	9,198
1935	7,055	1,373	93	2,060	10,581	10,327
1936	5,325	1,093	167	1,339	7,924	7,924
1937	2,976	856	167	1,611	5,610	5,474
1938	1,881	538	267	1,471	4,157	4,180
1939	1,524	268	300	1,592	3,684	3,453
1940	2,500		252	1,039	3,791	3,634
1941	1,500		222	735	2,457	1,819
1942	3,647		320	1,154	5,121	3,291
1943	3,846		578	1,088	5,512	2,646
1944	5,000		909	1,745	7,654	3,126
1945	7,358	100	833	1,513	9,804	3,650
1946	15,373	200	1,000	5,300	21,873	8,051
1947	22,146		1,158	7,839	31,143	10,304

estimated from the change of NDP_A in constant prices in 1940–45, assuming that the observed elasticity of NDP_A with respect to capital in 1939–45 was the same as in 1930–36. The cogency of this assumption rests on the close similarity between the increase of NDP_A over these two time intervals. The derived (constant) yearly growth rate of capital in 1940–45 was assumed to hold for 1940–47 as well, thus allowing for the extension of the annual net capital stock and of net and gross investment series (table A.25, cols. 4, 3, and 2) to the end of the Mandate period. The

Table A.24. *Jewish capital import, net investment, and fixed reproducible capital stock, 1922–47 (P£ '000)*

	capital import				net fixed reproducible capital in 1936 prices	
	current prices			1936 prices (all)	investment in year	stock of capital, beginning of year
	private (1)	public (2)	all (3)	(4)	(5)	(6)
1922	3,000	821	3,821	3,155	796	5,056
1923	3,251	896	4,147	3,638	679	5,852
1924	4,502	1,020	5,522	5,094	1,062	6,531
1925	5,626	1,136	6,762	5,942	1,992	7,593
1926	3,750	1,263	5,013	4,797	1,289	9,585
1927	1,500	1,417	2,917	2,920	933	10,874
1928	1,625	1,266	2,891	2,888	925	11,807
1929	2,125	1,298	3,423	3,482	1,440	12,732
1930	2,375	1,308	3,683	3,785	1,981	14,172
1931	2,250	975	3,225	3,505	2,168	16,153
1932	3,748	821	4,569	5,021	2,622	18,321
1933	7,002	679	7,681	7,465	4,882	20,943
1934	10,251	842	11,093	10,310	7,295	25,825
1935	9,871	965	10,836	10,572	8,191	33,120
1936	5,875	1,204	7,079	7,079	6,285	41,311
1937	4,124	1,417	5,541	5,406	4,959	47,596
1938	4,752	1,636	6,388	6,427	3,526	52,555
1939	4,875	1,993	6,868	6,437	2,712	56,081
1940	2,876	1,948	4,824	4,625	3,053	58,793
1941	2,500	1,996	4,496	3,328	1,145	61,846
1942	3,000	2,408	5,408	3,476	2,204	62,991
1943	4,500	3,738	8,238	3,955	1,528	65,195
1944	4,626	5,605	10,231	4,179	1,981	66,723
1945	5,648	6,132	11,780	4,381	2,536	68,704
1946	7,060	7,650	14,710	5,414	6,745	71,240
1947	4,683	5,072	9,755	3,228	8,791	77,985

gross investment figures in current prices (table A.25, col. 1) were generated by applying the index of the cost of Arab capital formation (table A.21, col. 2) to the series of gross investment in constant prices. The former was calculated for 1922–39 as the implicit price index of investment in citrus and construction combined; it was extended to 1947 by imposing on its value in 1939 the percentage change per annum of the cost of Jewish investment cost (table A.21, col. 3).

Table A.25. *Arab fixed reproducible capital, investment, and stock, 1922–47* (P£ '000)

	current prices	1936 prices		
	gross investment (1)	gross investment (2)	net investment (3)	net capital stock (beginning of year) (4)
1922	580	453	362	22,246
1923	543	500	400	22,608
1924	546	491	393	23,008
1925	614	504	403	23,401
1926	847	766	613	23,804
1927	1,133	1,083	866	24,417
1928	984	953	762	25,283
1929	1,099	1,139	911	26,045
1930	1,193	1,256	1,005	26,956
1931	1,279	1,436	1,149	27,961
1932	1,619	1,851	1,481	29,110
1933	2,186	2,134	1,707	30,591
1934	3,611	3,280	2,624	32,298
1935	3,860	3,727	2,982	34,922
1936	3,303	3,303	2,642	37,904
1937	1,987	1,966	1,573	40,546
1938	1,454	1,491	1,193	42,119
1939	1,157	1,161	929	43,312
1940	1,992	2,046	1,637	44,241
1941	2,678	2,123	1,698	45,878
1942	3,198	2,201	1,761	47,576
1943	4,439	2,283	1,826	49,337
1944	5,412	2,368	1,894	51,163
1945	6,157	2,455	1,964	53,057
1946	6,457	2,545	2,036	55,021
1947				57,057

The annual figures of government investment of table A.26 comprise governmental capital outlays on public works (roads and construction), on communication infrastructure, and on railways (derived from data and estimates contained in various issues of the *Report by the Treasurer*; Gross and Metzer, 1978, table A-4; and Gross, 1984b, tables 1–3, and converted, when necessary, from budgetary to calendar years on a prorated basis). The series of investment in current prices (col. 2) was turned into a constant price series (col. 3), by using the index of government invest-

Table A.26. *Government overhead investments, 1922–46*

| | index of government investment cost (1936=100) (1) | government investment (P£ '000) | |
		current prices (2)	1936 prices (3)
1922	124.6	629	505
1923	111.4	245	220
1924	109.9	82	75
1925	116.6	64	55
1926	108.9	60	55
1927	107.5	208	193
1928	104.2	433	416
1929	97.4	248	255
1930	94.6	451	477
1931	89.7	519	578
1932	89.0	477	536
1933	104.1	576	553
1934	108.3	736	679
1935	102.0	1,296	1,271
1936	100.0	1,135	1,135
1937	103.1	725	703
1938	99.0	823	831
1939	100.8	888	881
1940	104.4	1,591	1,524
1941	134.8	988	733
1942	155.1	687	443
1943	204.7	711	347
1944	248.7	725	292
1945	267.9	616	230
1946	278.4	1,230	442

ment cost (col. 1), which was devised by BMZ, table A7, col. 4 as a weighted average of the index of the cost of construction (reproduced in table A.16, col. 1, above) with a weight of 0.75, and of the cost of industrial machinery and equipment index (Szereszewski, 1968, p. 77), with a weight of 0.25.

B. SOCIO-ECONOMIC INDICATORS BY COUNTRY

Table B.1 presents estimates of country data (pertaining to forty-seven national economies in all) that were used as sources for the comparative examination of Palestine's growth performance, socio-economic attrib-

Table B.1. *Socio-economic indicators by country, c. 1939*

	index of income per capita (USA=100) (1)	inter-war growth of income per capita (% per annum) (2)	life expectancy at birth (years) (3)	illiteracy (% of population age 10+) (4)	Enrollment in schools (% of 5–19 age group) (5)
Argentina	39.4	2.8			46.4
Australia	72.7	1.0	66.1	2.5	56.7
Austria	30.0	5.1	56.5		60.3
Belgium	47.1	2.3	59.1	4.5	66.1
Brazil	15.3	2.4	36.7	56.7	
Bulgaria	19.7	3.1		31.4	38.6
Canada	70.2	2.3	64.6	3.2	
Chile	39.3	4.7	38.1	28.2	43.0
China	5.2	0.0			
Colombia	17.4	2.4	36.0	44.1	24.4
Cuba	17.7			22.1	42.8
Czechoslovakia	24.2	5.2	56.8	3.6	68.7
Denmark	61.0	2.8	66.3	1.5	70.8
Dom. Republic	9.2		29.9		
Egypt	11.8	0.2	38.6	84.9	23.3
El Salvador	8.1			72.8	
Finland	33.2	5.1	57.4	8.8	47.8
France	63.1	5.3	58.8	3.8	49.5
Germany	70.9	4.6	61.3		77.3
Greece	28.6	1.2	54.4	34.4	37.5
Guatemala	8.7		30.4	65.4	
Honduras	8.1		37.5	66.4	
Hungary	22.6	4.2	56.6	6.0	58.8
India	6.1	−0.3	32.3	86.5	11.9
Ireland	44.8	0.9	60.0	1.5	60.4
Italy	44.7	1.3	56.4	21.6	39.3
Japan	46.5	3.3	49.1		50.3
Luxembourg	51.3		60.1	4.4	
Mexico	13.5	−0.4	38.8	51.5	29.9
Netherlands	61.0	3.3	65.4	1.5	64.4
New Zealand	71.5	2.1	67.0	1.5	
Nicaragua	9.0		34.5	63.0	
Norway	50.4	2.7	65.9		57.4
Palestine: Arabs	7.2	3.6	47.8	81.4	24.6
Jews*	19.2 (27.7)	4.8	63.4	14.1	75.9
Panama	12.8		42.4	35.3	
Peru	13.0	2.1	36.5	56.4	22.2
Philippines	14.4	0.6	46.3	37.8	32.3
Puerto Rico	26.7		46.1	31.5	
Romania	15.5	0.9		23.1	39.0

Table B.1. (*cont.*)

	index of income per capita (USA=100) (1)	inter-war growth of income per capita (% per annum) (2)	life expectancy at birth (years) (3)	illiteracy (% of population age 10+) (4)	Enrollment in schools (% of 5–19 age group) (5)
Sweden	78.7	3.8	66.6	0.1	66.0
Switzerland	80.3	4.5	64.9	1.5	56.5
Taiwan	23.0	2.4	47.8		
Thailand	8.3	0.5	40.0	46.3	25.5
Turkey	13.3	4.1	33.9	79.1	16.2
United Kingdom	81.7	1.3	61.6	1.5	64.3
United States	100.0	2.0	63.7	4.2	81.4
Venezuela	32.6	7.3	39.9	56.5	22.0
Yugoslavia	18.4	2.9		45.2	33.7

Note:
* The index number in parentheses stands for Jewish resources (composed of Jewish national income and net capital import, combined) per capita.

utes, and the state of the human development index (figures 1.1, 2.5, 2.7, 2.8, and table 2.8 of the main text).

Column 1 of the table reports an index of income per capita by country relative to that of the United States, in about 1939. It was derived for most economies (thirty out of the forty-seven reported) from internationally comparative figures of income per capita on the eve of World War II (1939) compiled by the American Department of State and quoted in American dollars of 1939 (*Point Four*, 1950, appendix C-1). Maddison (1970, table I-1) provides a source of per capita income (in 1965 American dollars) for an additional thirteen countries in 1938 (Brazil, Chile, Colombia, Egypt, France, Greece, Italy, Japan, Mexico, Turkey, the UK, Venezuela, and Taiwan). The income figure for Romania was obtained in 1938–40 American dollars from "Current Items" (1947, p. 101), and those for Luxembourg in 1939, Puerto Rico in 1938–40, and Thailand in 1939, quoted in 1970 American dollars, from Preston (1980, table 5.A.1). Note that all these sources present income per capita figures for the USA, quoted in the (dollar) prices of their respective compilations. This enabled the construction of the index of relative (to the USA) income per capita for each country, irrespective of the different prices used in the various sources.

The index of relative Jewish and Arab income was devised by turning the average level of income per capita (for 1935–39) in 1936 P£ prices (see table A.22 above) into 1970 American dollars. The first step in this procedure was to transform the figure of Jewish income, from 1936 prices in P£ to 1970 prices in Israeli currency (I£ at the time). This was done by multiplying the former quantity by 21.7 – the ratio of the 1970 to the 1936 price level (see table A.21; *Statistical Abstract of Israel*, 1957/58, p. 285 and 1975, table X/2). The income figure in 1970 I£ was then converted into dollars by dividing it by 3.206 (the conversion rate was derived from the *World Bank Atlas*, 1972 and the *Statistical Abstract of Israel*, 1975, table VI/2). The index of Jewish resources per capita was calculated by applying to the index of income per capita the ratio of resources (NNP$_J$+capital import: see table A.24, col. 4) to NNP$_J$ in the relevant years. Similarly, the index of Arab relative income per capita was derived by multiplying the Jewish quantity by the Arab-Jewish ratio of (national) product per capita in 1935–39.

The annual growth rates of income per capita reported in table B.1, col. 2 were generated from Maddison (1995, tables D-1a to D-1f). For most countries the presented rates are the higher decadal average between the two inter-war decades (1919–29 and 1929–39). The exceptions are: (a) countries for which the reported growth rates were calculated for a nine-year span: 1920–29 for Czechoslovakia, Hungary, Yugoslavia, and 1929–38 for China, Ireland, Romania, Thailand; (b) countries for which the rates cover longer periods: 1913–29 for the Philippines and Venezuela, and 1913–50 for Egypt.

The estimates of life expectancy at birth (col. 3) were taken for Arabs and Jews in 1939–41 from table 2.5 of the main text; for Austria in 1930–33, France in 1933–38, Germany in 1932–34; and Norway in 1931–41 from *Age and Sex Patterns of Mortality* (1955, pp. 32–35); for the Dominican Republic in 1935 and for Italy in 1935–36 from Preston (1975, table A-2). The life-expectancy figures for all other countries, estimated for the late 1930s and/or the early 1940s, are quoted in Preston (1980, table 5.A.1), which reports also the exact year of estimate for each one of them.

The sources for the illiteracy rates (col. 4) are: the *Census of Palestine* (1933, table IX[A]) for Arabs and Jews in 1931; the *Demographic Yearbook 1948*, table 7 for Brazil in 1940, Bulgaria in 1934, Cuba in 1943, El Salvador in 1930, France in 1936, Italy in 1931, Romania in 1948, and Yugoslavia in 1943; Preston (1980, table 5.A.1) for all other countries, with the exact year of estimate between 1937 and 1948 specified there.

The enrollment figures of col. 5 were derived from the estimates of the proportion of school enrollment in the entire population (in 1928 for the USA and the European countries and in 1938 for all other countries) that

Easterlin prepared (1965, pp. 422–29). They were turned into percentages of the five-to-nineteen age groups by means of the age compositions of population for the various countries between 1930 and 1947 reported in the *Demographic Yearbook 1948*, table 4, and in *The Aging of Populations* (1956, table III).

References

Aaronsohn, Ran (1996). "Settling Eretz-Israel – A Colonial Enterprise?" In
 Pinhas Ginossar and Avi Bareli (eds.), *Zionism: A Contemporary Controversy:
 Reasearch Trends and Ideological Approaches*. Beersheba: Ben-Gurion
 University of the Negev Press, pp. 340–54 (in Hebrew).
Abcarius, Michael F. (1946). *Palestine through the Fog of Propaganda*. London:
 Hutchinson.
Abramowitz, Ze'ev (1935). "National Economies – A Country Economy?"
 Ha'Meshek Ha'Shitufi (The Cooperative Economy), 3 (nos. 3, 4, 8, 9, 10):
 40–43, 129–34, 158–63 (in Hebrew).
 (1945). "Wartime Development of Arab Economy in Palestine," *The Palestine
 Year Book*, 1: 130–44.
Abramowitz, Ze'ev and Isaac Guelfat (1944). *The Arab Economy in Palestine and in
 the Middle-Eastern Countries*. Tel Aviv: HaKibbutz HaMeuhad (in Hebrew).
Age and Sex Patterns of Mortality (1955). New York: United Nations, Department
 of Social Affairs, Population Branch.
The Aging of Populations and its Economic and Social Implications (1956). New York:
 United Nations, Department of Economic and Social Affairs.
Agricultural Supplement (monthly issues 1936–39). *Official Gazette of the
 Government of Palestine, Agricultural Supplement*. Jerusalem: Government
 Printer.
Albertini, Rudolf von (1982). *European Colonial Rule, 1880–1940*. Oxford: Clio
 Press.
Ali, Anwar (1957–58). "Banking in the Middle East," *International Monetary
 Fund Staff Papers*, 6: 51–79.
Aliya (1936), No. 4. Jerusalem: Jewish Agency, Immigration Department (in
 Hebrew).
Anand, Sudhir and Martin Ravallion (1993). "Human Development in Poor
 Countries: On the Role of Private Incomes and Public Services," *The Journal
 of Economic Perspectives*, 7 (no. 1): 133–50.
Asfour, J. (1945). "Arab Labor in Palestine," *Royal Central Asian Society Journal*,
 32: 201–205.
Ater [Ettinger], M. (1937). "The Balance of Payment between Jews and Arabs,"
 Haaretz (daily), January 5 and 12 (in Hebrew); appeared also as M. Ettinger,
 "Die jüdische-arabische Zahlungsbilanz," in *Palästina*, 20: 1–7 (in German).
Aturupane, Horsha, Paul Glewwe, and Paul Isenman (1994). "Poverty, Human
 Development, and Growth: An Emerging Consensus," *American Economic
 Review*, 84 (no. 2): 244–49.

Bachi, Roberto (1977). *The Population of Israel*. Jerusalem: Institute of Contemporary Jewry, the Hebrew University of Jerusalem, and Demographic Center, the Prime Minister's Office.

Baer, Gabriel (1980). "The Village Mukhtar." In Joel S. Migdal et al., *Palestinian Society and Politics*. Princeton: Princeton University Press, pp. 103–23.

Baines, Dudley (1991). *Emigration from Europe 1815–1930*. London: Macmillan.

Barkai, Haim (1964). "The Public, Histadrut, and Private Sectors in the Israeli Economy." In *Sixth Report 1961–1963*. Jerusalem: Falk Project for Economic Research in Israel.

(1989a). "Economic Democracy and the Origins of the Israeli Labor Economy," *The Jerusalem Quarterly*, no. 49: 17–39.

(1989b). "Fifty Years of Labor Economy: Growth, Performance, and the Present Challenge," *The Jerusalem Quarterly*, no. 50: 81–109.

Barron, J. B.: see *Census* (1922).

Becker, A. (1930). "Is There an Arab Unemployment Problem in Palestine?" *Palestine and Near East Economic Magazine*, 5 (nos. 12–13): 233–36.

Becker, Gary S. (1971). *The Economics of Discrimination*. Chicago and London: University of Chicago Press.

Beenstock, Michael, Jacob Metzer, and Sanny Ziv (1995) (BMZ). "Immigration and the Jewish Economy in Mandatory Palestine," *Research in Economic History*, 15: 149–213.

Bell, Clive (1988). "Credit Markets and Interlinked Transactions." In Chenery and Srinivasan, *Handbook of Development Economics*, vol. I, pp. 763–830.

Ben-Porath, Yoram (1966). *The Arab Labor Force in Israel*. Jerusalem: Maurice Falk Institute for Economic Research in Israel.

(1984). "Israeli Dilemmas: Economic Relations between Jews and Arabs," *Dissent*, Fall: 459–67.

(1986a). "The Entwined Growth of Population and Product 1922–1982." In Yoram Ben-Porath (ed.), *The Israeli Economy: Maturing through Crises*. Cambridge, MA and London: Harvard University Press, pp. 27–41.

(1986b). "Patterns and Peculiarities of Economic Growth and Structure," *The Jerusalem Quarterly*, no. 38: 43–63.

Ben-Zvi, I. (1930). "The Findings of the Wage Commission, a Shelved Report," *Palestine and Near East Economic Magazine*, 5 (nos. 12–13): 237–38.

Bernstein, Deborah (1996). "The Palestine Labor League and the 'Hebrew Labor' Policy Trap," *Megamot*, 37 (no. 3): 229–53 (in Hebrew).

Biger, Gideon (1983). *Crown Colony or National Homeland? British Influence upon Palestine, 1917–1930*. Jerusalem: Yad Izhak Ben-Zvi (in Hebrew).

Blue Book (annual issues, 1926–38). Alexandria, Jerusalem, and London: Government of Palestine.

BMZ: see Beenstock et al.

Boeke, J. H. (1953). *Economics and Economic Policy of Dual Societies*. New York: Institute of Pacific Relations.

Bonne, Alfred (1938). *Palestine Land and Economy*. Tel Aviv: Dvir (in Hebrew).

Brandeis, Louis D. (1921). "The Zeeland Memorandum." In *Statement to the Delegates of the Twelfth Zionist Congress on Behalf of the Former Administration of the Zionist Organization of America*. New York: Commanday-Roth, pp. 51–57.

Breton, Albert (1964). "The Economics of Nationalism," *Journal of Political Economy*, 72 (no. 4): 376–86.

Breton, Albert and Margot Breton (1995). "Nationalism Revisited." In Albert Breton, Gianluigi Galeotti, Pierre Salmon, and Ronald Wintrobe (eds.), *Nationalism and Rationality*. Cambridge: Cambridge University Press, pp. 98–115.

Bulletin of the Economic Research Institute (periodical, 1937–48). Tel Aviv: Jewish Agency for Palestine.

Carmel, Alex (1975). "The German Settlers in Palestine and their Relations with the Local Arab Population and the Jewish Community." In Moshe Ma'oz (ed.), *Studies on Palestine during the Ottoman Period*. Jerusalem: Magnes Press, the Hebrew University Institute of Asian and African Studies, and Yad Izhak Ben-Zvi, pp. 442–65.

Census (1922). J. B. Barron, *Report and General Abstract on the Census of 1922*. Jerusalem: Government Printer.

Census of Jewish Workers (1926). *The Second Census of the Jewish Workers in Palestine* (September 1, 1926). Tel Aviv: General Federation of Jewish Labor in Eretz-Israel (in Hebrew).

Census of Jewish Workers (1937). *The General Census of the Jewish Workers in Palestine* (March 2, 1937). Tel Aviv: General Federation of Jewish Labor in Eretz-Israel (in Hebrew).

Census of Palestine (1933). E. Mills, *Census of Palestine 1931*, vol. II, *Tables*. Alexandria: Government of Palestine.

Censuses of Workers in (Moshavot) Groves (1939). Jerusalem: Jewish Agency, Departments of Labor and Statistics (in Hebrew).

Chenery, Hollis (1986). "Growth and Transformation." In H. Chenery, S. Robinson, and M. Syrquin, *Industrialization and Growth*. New York: Oxford University Press, pp. 13–36.

Chenery, Hollis and T. N. Srinivasan (eds.) (1988). *Handbook of Development Economies*, 2 vols. Amsterdam: North Holland.

Chenery, Hollis and M. Syrquin (1975). *Patterns of Development, 1950–1970*. London: Oxford University Press.

Clark-Powell, H. (1928). "The Citrus Industry in Palestine," *Agricultural Leaflets*, series 4, Horticulture, no. 9. Jerusalem: Government of Palestine, Department of Agriculture and Forests.

Commercial Bulletin (periodical, 1922–38). Jerusalem: Government of Palestine, Department of Commerce and Industry.

"Current Items" (1947). *Population Index*, 13 (no. 2): 88–106.

"Current Topics – Census of Jewish Industry" (1926). *Palestine and Near East Economic Magazine*, 1 (no. 8): 227.

CZA: Central Zionist Archive (various files).

Demographic Yearbook 1948. New York: Statistical Office of the United Nations.

The Determinants and Consequences of Population Trends (1953 and 1973), vols. I–II. New York: United Nations, Department of Social Affairs, Population Division.

Dickens, William T. and Kevin Lang (1992). "Labor Market Segmentation Theory: Reconsidering the Evidence." Cambridge, MA: National Bureau of Economic Research, Working Paper No. 4087.

Duesterwald, A. W. (1945). "Indications on Arab Jewish Balance of Payments," Jewish Agency for Palestine, Economic Department, December 19. CZA/S/2510233 (mimeo).

(1957). "The National Wealth," *Encyclopedia Hebraica*, vol. VI. Jerusalem and Tel Aviv: Encyclopedia Publishing Co. Ltd., pp. 740–44 (in Hebrew).

Durand, John D. (1953). "Population Structure as a Factor in Manpower and Dependency Problems of Underdeveloped Countries," *Population Bulletin of the United Nations*, no. 3: 1–16.

Easterlin, Richard A. (1965). "A Note on the Evidence of History." In C. Arnold Anderson and Mary Jean Bowman (eds.), *Education and Economic Development*. Chicago: Aldine, pp. 422–29.

(1978). "The Economics and Sociology of Fertility: A Synthesis." In Charles Tilly (ed.), *Historical Studies of Fertility*. Princeton: Princeton University Press, pp. 57–133.

(1982). "Economics and Social Characteristics of Immigrants." In Richard A. Easterlin, David Ward, William S. Bernard, and Reed Ueda, *Immigration*. Cambridge, MA: Belknap Press of Harvard University Press, pp. 1–34.

Easterlin, Richard A. and Eileen M. Crimmins (1985). *The Fertility Revolution: A Supply-Demand Analysis*. Chicago: University of Chicago Press.

El-Badry, M. A. (1965). "Trends in the Components of Population Growth in the Arab Countries of the Middle East: A Survey of Recent Information," *Demography*, 2 (no. 1): 140–86.

El-Erian, Mohamed A. and Stanley Fischer (1996). "Is the Middle East and North Africa (MENA) a Region? The Scope for Regional Integration." IMF Working Paper 96/30.

Eliachar, Elie (1979). "The Government's Census of Industry, 1928," *Economic Quarterly*, 26 (nos. 101–102): 257–62 (in Hebrew).

Ettinger (Ater), M. (ed.) (1947). *Book of the Economy of the Yishuv*. Tel Aviv: Vaad Leumi (in Hebrew).

Ferenczi, Imre (compiler and author) and Walter Willcox (ed.) (1929). *International Migrations*, vol. I. New York: National Bureau of Economic Research Inc.

Firestone, Ya'akov (1981). "Land Equalization and Factor Scarcities: Holding Size and the Burden of Impositions in Imperial Central Russia and the Late Ottoman Levant," *The Journal of Economic History*, 41 (no. 4): 813–33.

(1990). "The Land-Equalizing Musha' Village: A Reassessment." In Gad G. Gilbar (ed.), *Ottoman Palestine 1800–1914*. Leiden: E. J. Brill.

Fischer, Stanley (1993). "Prospects for Regional Integration in the Middle East." In Jaime De Melo and Arvind Panagariya (eds.), *New Dimensions in Regional Integration*. Cambridge: Cambridge University Press.

Fischer, Stanley, Rudiger Dornbusch, and Richard Schmalensee (1988). *Economics*, 2nd ed. New York: McGraw-Hill.

Flapan, Simha (1979). *Zionism and the Palestinians*. London: Croom Helm.

Fraenkel, Daniel (1994). *On The Edge of the Abyss: Zionist Policy and the Plight of the German Jews, 1933–1938*. Jerusalem: Magnes Press, the Hebrew University, and Leo Baeck Institute (in Hebrew).

Friedlander, Dov and Calvin Goldscheider (1979). *The Population of Israel*. New York: Columbia University Press.

Fry, Maxwell, J. (1988). *Money, Interest, and Banking in Economic Development.* Baltimore and London: Johns Hopkins University Press.

Gaathon [Gruenbaum], A. L. (1978). *National Income and Outlay in Palestine, 1936,* 2nd (enlarged) ed. Jerusalem: Bank of Israel (1st ed., 1941, Jewish Agency for Palestine).

Gelber, Yoav (1979). *Jewish Palestinian Volunteering in the British Army during the Second World War,* vol. I, *Volunteering and its Role in Zionist Policy 1939–1942.* Jerusalem: Yad Izhak Ben-Zvi (in Hebrew).

(1981). *Jewish Palestinian Volunteering in the British Army during the Second World War,* vol. II, *The Struggle for a Jewish Army.* Jerusalem: Yad Izhak Ben-Zvi (in Hebrew).

(1990). *New Homeland: Immigration and Absorption of Central European Jews 1933–1948.* Jerusalem: Leo Baeck Institute and Yad Izhak Ben-Zvi (in Hebrew).

Gemery, Henry A. (1994). "Immigrants and Emigrants: International Migration and the US Labor Market in the Great Depression." In Timothy J. Hatton and Jeffrey G. Williamson (eds.), *Migration and the International Labor Market 1850–1939.* London and New York: Routledge, pp. 175–99.

General Monthly Bulletin of Current Statistics of Palestine (MBS) (monthly issues), 1936–47. Jerusalem: Office of Statistics.

Gertz, Aaron (1945). *Jewish Agricultural Settlement in Numbers.* Jerusalem: Jewish Agency for Palestine, Department of Statistics (in Hebrew).

GGB: see Gurevich, Gertz, and Bachi (1944).

Giladi, Dan (1973). *Jewish Palestine during the Fourth Aliya Period (1924–29): Economic and Social Aspects.* Tel Aviv: Am Oved (in Hebrew).

(1982). "From Aliya to Aliya." In Yehoshua Porath and Ya'acov Shavit (eds.), *The History of Eretz Israel – The British Mandate and the Jewish National Home.* Jerusalem: Keter, pp. 161–73 (in Hebrew).

Gilbar, Gad G. (1987). "Trends in the Demographic Development of Palestinian Arabs 1870–1948," *Cathedra,* 12 (no. 45): 42–56 (in Hebrew).

(1990). *The Economic Development of the Middle East in Modern Times.* Tel Aviv: Ministry of Defense Publishing House (in Hebrew).

Gorny, Yosef (1985). *The Arab Question and the Jewish Problem.* Tel Aviv: Am Oved (in Hebrew).

Gottheil, Fred M. (1973). "Arab Immigration into Pre-State Israel: 1922–1931," *Middle Eastern Studies,* 9 (no. 3): 315–24.

Granott [Granovsky], Avraham (1952). *The Land System in Palestine.* London: Eyre & Spottiswoode.

Granovsky, Avraham (1938). *Jewish Land Policy in Palestine.* Jerusalem: Rubin Mass (in Hebrew).

Greenberg, Stanley (1980). *Race and State in Capitalist Development: South Africa in Comparative Perspective.* New Haven: Yale University Press.

Greenberg, Yitzhak (1987). *From Workers' Society to Workers' Economy: Evolution of the Hevrat Ha'ovdim Idea, 1920–1929.* Tel Aviv: Papirus (in Hebrew).

Grinberg, Lev (1991). *Split Corporatism in Israel.* Albany: State University of New York Press.

Gross, Nachum T. (1977). "Economic Changes in Eretz Israel at the End of the Ottoman Period," *Cathedra,* 1 (no. 2): 109–25 (in Hebrew).

(1979). "Then and Now: Comments on the Palestine Census of Industry, 1928," *Economic Quarterly*, 26 (nos. 101–102): 257–62 (in Hebrew).

(1981). "A Note on the Periodization of the Yishuv's History during the Mandatory Period," *Cathedra*, 5 (no. 18): 174–77 (in Hebrew).

(1984a). "The Development of Agricultural Techniques in the Jewish Economy in Mandatory Palestine." In Heral Winkel and Klaus Herrmann (eds.), *The Development of Agricultural Technology in the 19th and 20th Centuries*. Ostfildern: Scripta Mercaturae Verlag, pp. 157–68.

(1984b). "The Economic Policy of the Mandatory Government in Palestine," *Research in Economic History*, 9: 143–85.

Gross, Nachum T. and Yitzhak Greenberg (1994). *Bank Ha'poalim: The First 50 Years 1921–1971*. Tel Aviv: Am Oved (in Hebrew).

Gross, Nachum T. and Jacob Metzer (1978). "Public Finance in the Jewish Economy of the Mandatory Government in Palestine," *Research in Economic History*, 3: 87–159.

(1993). "Palestine in World War Two: Some Economic Aspects." In Geofrey T. Mills and Hugh Rockoff (eds.), *The Sinews of War*. Iowa City: University of Iowa Press, pp. 59–82.

Gruenbaum (1941): see Gaathon (1978).

Grunwald, Kurt (1932). "The Trade-Cycle in Palestine," *Palestine and Near East Economic Magazine*, 7 (nos. 8–9): 249–52.

Gurevich, David (1931). *Report and General Abstract of the Censuses of Jewish Agriculture, Industry and Handicrafts and Labour*. Jerusalem: Jewish Agency for Palestine, Department of Statistics (text in Hebrew, tables in English and Hebrew).

(1936). "Taxation of the Jewish Community, 1934/35." Jerusalem: Jewish Agency for Palestine, Economic Research Institute (mimeo).

(1939). *Jewish Manufacturing, Transportation and Commerce, Report and Statistical Abstracts of the Censuses Taken in 1937*. Jerusalem: Jewish Agency for Palestine, Department of Commerce and Industry (text in Hebrew, tables in English and Hebrew).

Gurevich, David and Aaron Gertz (1938). *Jewish Agricultural Settlement in Palestine*. Jerusalem: Jewish Agency for Palestine, Department of Statistics (text in Hebrew, tables in English and Hebrew).

(1947). *Agriculture and Jewish Agricultural Settlement in Palestine*. Jerusalem: Jewish Agency for Palestine, Department of Statistics (text in Hebrew, tables in English and Hebrew).

Gurevich, David, Aaron Gertz, and Roberto Bachi (1944) (GGB). *The Jewish Population of Palestine*. Jerusalem: Jewish Agency for Palestine, Department of Statistics (text in Hebrew, tables in English and Hebrew).

Hadawi, Sami (1957). *Land Ownership in Palestine*. New York: Palestine Arab Refugee Office.

Haines, Michael R. (1994). "The Population of the United States, 1790–1920." NBER Working Paper Series on Historical Factors in Long Run Growth, No. 56. Cambridge, MA: National Bureau of Economic Research.

Halevi, Nadav (1977). *Banker for a Renewed Nation: The History of Bank Leumi Le'Israel*, part 2. Ramat Gan: Massada Ltd. (in Hebrew).

(1979). "The Economic Development of The Jewish Community in Palestine

1917–1947." Jerusalem: Maurice Falk Institute for Economic Research in
Israel, Discussion Paper No. 7914 (in Hebrew).

(1983). "The Political Economy of Absorptive Capacity; Growth and Cycles in
Jewish Palestine under the British Mandate," *Middle Eastern Studies*, 19 (no.
4): 456–69.

Halevi, Nadav and Ruth Klinov-Malul (1968). *The Economic Development of Israel*.
New York: Praeger.

Halperin, Asher (1954). "Palestine's Balance of Payments, 1932–1946."
Unpublished Ph.D. dissertation, Princeton University.

Harary, R. (1922). *Report on the Economic and Commercial Situation in Palestine to
March 31st 1921*. Jerusalem: Government of Palestine, Department of
Commerce and Industry.

Harris, J. R. and M. P. Todaro (1970). "Migration Unemployment and
Development: A Two-Sector Analysis," *American Economic Review*, 60 (no.
1): 126–42.

Hattis-Rolef, Shila (1979). "Sir Herbert Samuel's Policy of Economic
Development 1920–21," *Cathedra*, 3 (no. 12): 70–90 (in Hebrew).

Hatton, Timothy J. and Jeffrey G. Williamson (1994). "International Migration
1850–1939: An Economic Survey." In Timothy J. Hatton and Jeffrey G.
Williamson (eds.), *Migration and the International Labor Market 1850–1939*.
London and New York: Routledge, pp. 3–32.

Hazen, William N. (1938). *The Citrus Industry in Palestine*. Washington, DC:
United States Department of Agriculture, Bureau of Agricultural
Economics.

Himadeh, Said B. (ed.) (1938). *Economic Organization of Palestine*. Beirut:
American University of Beirut Publications of the Faculty of Arts and
Sciences, Social Science Series No. 11.

Hinrichs, Hanley H. (1966). *A General Theory of Tax Structure Change during
Economic Development*. Cambridge, MA: Harvard Law School.

Hirsch, S. (1933). "Sheep and Goats in Palestine," *Bulletin of the Palestine
Economic Society*, 6 (no.2).

Historical Statistics of the United States: Colonial Times to 1970, 1975, parts 1 and 2.
Washington, DC: US Department of Commerce, Bureau of the Census.

Hoofien, E. S. (1930). "The Blessing of Immigration," *Commerce and Industry*, 8:
86–108 (in Hebrew).

Horowitz, Dan and Moshe Lissak (1978). *Origins of Israeli Polity: Palestine under
the Mandate*. Chicago: University of Chicago Press.

Horowitz, David (1948). *The Economy of Palestine and its Development*, 2nd ed. Tel
Aviv: Dvir (in Hebrew).

Horowitz, David and Rita Hinden (1938). *Economic Survey of Palestine*. Tel Aviv:
Jewish Agency for Palestine, Economic Research Institute.

Hull, Terence H. and Gavin Jones (1986). "Introduction: International Mortality
Trends and Differentials." In *Consequences of Mortality Trends and
Differentials*. New York: United Nations, Department of International
Economic and Social Affairs, pp. 1–9.

Human Development Report (annual issues). New York: United Nations
Development Programme.

Issawi, Charles (1982). *An Economic History of the Middle East and North Africa.* New York: Columbia University Press.

Johnson, W. J. and R. E. H. Crosbie (1930). *Report of a Committee on the Economic Condition of Agriculturists in Palestine and the Fiscal Measures of Government in Relation Thereto.* Jerusalem: Government of Palestine.

Kamen, Charles S. (1991). *Little Common Ground: Arab Agriculture and Jewish Settlement in Palestine 1920–1948.* Pittsburgh: University of Pittsburgh Press.

Karlinsky, Nahum (1995). "Private Entrepreneurship in Eretz Yisrael during the Period of the British Mandate: The Citrus Industry 1920–1939." Unpublished Ph.D. dissertation, the Hebrew University of Jerusalem (in Hebrew with summary in English).

Karpman, I. J. (1946). *Housing and Mortgage Credit in Palestine.* Tel Aviv: Tversky (in Hebrew).

Kayyali, Abd al-Wahhab (1979). *Zionism, Imperialism and Racism.* London: Croom Helm.

Keysar, Ariela, Eitan F. Sabatello, Ronny Shtarkshall, Ilana Ziegler, Shlomo Kupinsky, and Eric Peritz (1992). "Fertility and Modernization in the Moslem Population of Israel." In Eric Peritz and Mario Baras (eds.), *Studies in the Fertility of Israel.* Jerusalem: Institute of Contemporary Jewry, the Hebrew University of Jerusalem, Jewish Population Studies no. 24, pp. 97–132.

Kimmerling, Baruch (1983a). *Zionism and Economy.* Cambridge, MA: Schenkman.

(1983b). *Zionism and Territory: The Socio-Territorial Dimensions of Zionist Politics.* Berkeley: Institute of International Studies, University of California.

Kirk, Dudley (1946). *Europe's Population in the Interwar Years.* Geneva: League of Nations.

(1966). "Factors Affecting Moslem Natality." In Bernard Berelson et al. (eds.), *Family Planning and Population Programs.* Chicago: University of Chicago Press, pp. 561–79.

(1969). "Natality in the Developing Countries: Recent Trends and Prospects." In S. J. Behrman, Leslie Corsa, and Ronald Freedman (eds.), *Fertility and Family Planning: A World View.* Ann Arbor: University of Michigan Press, pp. 75–98.

Kleiman, Ephraim (1987). "The Histadrut Economy of Israel: In Search of Criteria," *The Jerusalem Quarterly,* no. 41: 77–94.

(1993). "Some Basic Problems of the Economic Relationships between Israel and the West Bank and Gaza." In Stanley Fischer, Dani Rodrik, and Elias Tuma (eds.), *The Economy of Middle East Peace: Views from the Region.* Cambridge, MA: MIT Press, pp. 305–33.

Kligler, I. J., A. Greiger, S. Broomberg, and D. Gurevich (1931). "An Inquiry into the Diets of Various Sections of the Urban and Rural Population of Palestine," *Bulletin of the Palestine Economic Society,* 5 (no. 3).

Klinov, Ruth (1990). "Arabs and Jews in the Israeli Labor Force." In Michael L. Wyzan (ed.), *The Political Economy of Ethnic Discrimination and Affirmative Action.* New York: Praeger, pp. 1–24.

(1996). "Changes in School Enrollment Patterns in Israel: A Comparison between Two Disadvantaged Groups," *Economics of Education Review*, 15 (no. 3): 289–301.

Kruglak, P. (1934). *Directory of Jewish Industry and Handicrafts in Palestine*. Tel Aviv: Jewish Agency for Palestine (in Hebrew; an English summary appears in Himadeh [1938], pp. 242–43).

Kuznets, Simon (1973). "Modern Economic Growth: Findings and Reflections," *American Economic Review*, 113 (no. 3): 247–58.

(1975). "Immigration of Russian Jews to the United States: Background and Structure," *Perspectives in American History*, 9: 35–124.

Lavsky, Hagit (1980). *The Foundations of Zionist Financial Policy: The Zionist Commission, 1918–1921*. Jerusalem: Yad Izhak Ben-Zvi (in Hebrew).

Lestschinsky, Jacob (1965). *Jewish Migration in Recent Generations*. Tel Aviv: Aleph (in Hebrew).

Levels and Trends of Mortality since 1950 (1982). New York: United Nations, Department of International Economic and Social Affairs.

Lewin-Epstein, Noah and Moshe Semyonov (1992). "Local Labor Markets, Ethnic Segregation, and Income Inequality," *Social Forces*, 70 (no. 4): 1101–19.

(1993). *The Arab Minority in Israel's Economy: Patterns of Ethnic Inequality*. Boulder: Westview Press.

Lewis, Arthur W. (1979). "The Dual Economy Revisited," *The Manchester School*, 37: 212–17.

Lockman, Zachary (1996). *Comrades and Enemies: Arab and Jewish Workers in Palestine, 1906–1948*. Berkeley and Los Angeles: University of California Press.

Loftus, P. J. (1946). *National Income of Palestine 1944*. Jerusalem: Government Printer.

(1948). *National Income of Palestine 1945*. Jerusalem: Government Printer.

Maddison, Angus (1962). "Growth and Fluctuation in the World Economy, 1870–1960," *Banca Nazionale Del Lavoro Quarterly Review*, 15 (no. 61): 127–95.

(1970). *Economic Progress and Policy in Developing Countries*. New York: W. W. Norton.

(1987). "Growth and Slowdown in Advanced Capitalist Economies: Techniques of Quantitative Assessment," *Journal of Economic Literature*, 25 (no. 2): 649–98.

(1991). *Dynamic Forces in Capitalist Development: A Long-run Comparative View*. Oxford and New York: Oxford University Press.

(1995). *Monitoring the World Economy*. Paris: OECD.

Makover, Rachela (1988). *Government and Administration of Palestine 1917–1925*. Jerusalem: Yad Izhak Ben-Zvi (in Hebrew).

MBS: see *General Monthly Bulletin of Current Statistics*.

McCarthy, Justin (1990). *The Population of Palestine: Population History and Statistics of the Late Ottoman Period and the Mandate*. New York: Columbia University Press.

Meier, Gerald M. (1989). *Leading Issues in Economic Development*, 5th ed. New York and Oxford: Oxford University Press.

Memoranda (1937). *Palestine Royal Commission, Memoranda Prepared by the Government of Palestine,* Colonial No. 133. London: HMSO.

Memorandum (1947). Government of Palestine, *Memorandum on the Administration of Palestine under the Mandate.* Jerusalem: Government Printer.

Meredith, David (1975). "The British Government and Colonial Economic Policy, 1919–39," *Economic History Review,* 28 (no. 4): 484–99.

Meshek Leumi (periodical, 1936–41). Tel Aviv (in Hebrew).

Metzer, Jacob (1977). "The Concept of National Capital in Zionist Thought 1918–1921," *Asian and African Studies,* 11 (no. 3): 305–36.

   (1978). "Economic Structure and National Goals – Jewish National Home in Interwar Palestine," *The Journal of Economic History,* 38 (no. 1): 101–19.

   (1979). *National Capital for a National Home.* Jerusalem: Yad Izhak Ben-Zvi (in Hebrew).

   (1982). "Fiscal Incidence and Resource Transfer between Jews and Arabs in Mandatory Palestine," *Research in Economic History,* 7: 87–132.

   (1988). "Growth and Structure of the Arab Economy in Palestine – An Historical Perspective," *Economic Quarterly,* 39 (no. 137): 129–45 (in Hebrew).

   (1992). "What Kind of Growth? A Comparative Look at the Arab Economies in Mandatory Palestine and in the Administered Territories," *Economic Development and Cultural Change,* 40 (no. 4): 843–65.

Metzer, Jacob and Oded Kaplan (1985). "Jointly but Severally: Arab-Jewish Dualism and Economic Growth in Mandatory Palestine," *Journal of Economic History,* 95 (no. 2): 327–45.

   (1990). *The Jewish and the Arab Economy in Mandatory Palestine: Product, Employment and Growth.* Jerusalem: Maurice Falk Institute for Economic Research in Israel (in Hebrew).

Michaelis, Dolf (1986). "One Hundred Years of Banking and Currency in Palestine," *Research in Economic History,* 10: 155–97.

Michaely, Michael (1963). *Foreign Trade and Capital Imports in Israel.* Tel Aviv: Am Oved (in Hebrew).

Miller, Ylana N. (1985). *Government and Society in Rural Palestine: The Impact of British Norms on Arab Community Life, 1920–1948.* Austin: University of Texas Press.

Mills, E. (1933): see *Census of Palestine* (1933).

Mitchell, B. R. (1982). *International Historical Statistics: Africa and Asia.* London: Macmillan.

   (1992). *International Historical Statistics: Europe 1750–1988,* 3rd ed. London: Macmillan.

   (1993). *International Historical Statistics: The Americas 1750–1988,* 2nd ed. London: Macmillan.

Morag, Amotz (1967). *Public Finance in Israel: Problems and Development.* Jerusalem: Magnes Press (in Hebrew).

Mosley, Paul (1983). *The Settler Economies: Studies in the Economic History of Kenya and Southern Rhodesia 1900–1963.* Cambridge: Cambridge University Press.

Muenzner, Gerhard (1945). *Jewish Labour Economy in Palestine.* London: Victor Gollancz.

Myint, Hla (1985). "Organizational Dualism and Economic Development," *Asian Development Review,* 3 (no. 1): 25–42.

Nathan, Robert R., Oscar Gass, and Daniel Creamer (1946). *Palestine: Problem and Promise.* Washington, DC: Public Affairs Press of the American Council on Public Affairs.

"New Growth Theory" Symposium (1994). *The Journal of Economic Perspectives,* 8 (no. 1): 3–72.

Niederland, Doron (1996). *German Jews, Emigrants or Refugees? Emigration Patterns between the Two World Wars.* Jerusalem: Magnes Press (in Hebrew).

North, Douglass C. (1981). *Structure and Change in Economic History.* New York and London: W. W. Norton.

"Occupational Structure of the Jewish Population" (1946). *Alon Statisti* (Statistical Bulletin), 1 (nos. 1–6): 16–52.

Ofer, Gur (1967). *The Service Industries in a Developing Economy: Israel as a Case Study.* New York: Praeger.

Ottensooser, Robert David (1955). *The Palestine Pound and the Israel Pound: Transition from a Colonial to an Independent Currency.* Geneva: Librairie E. Droz.

Owen, Roger (1982). "Introduction." In Roger Owen (ed.), *Studies in the Economic and Social History of Palestine in the Nineteenth and Twentieth Centuries.* London and Oxford: Macmillan Press Ltd. and St. Antony's College, pp. 1–9.

(1988). "Economic Development in Mandatory Palestine 1918–1948." In George T. Abed (ed.), *The Palestinian Economy.* London and New York: Routledge, pp. 13–35.

(1993). *The Middle East in the World Economy.* London and New York: I. B. Tauris (1st ed. Methuen, 1981).

Palestine Facts and Figures (1947). Jerusalem: Jewish Agency for Palestine, Economic Department.

Palestine Royal Commission Report (RCR) (1937). London: HMSO.

Peters, Joan (1984). *From Time Immemorial: The Origin of the Arab-Jewish Conflict over Palestine.* New York: Harper & Row.

Pinner, L. (1930). "Wheat Culture in Palestine 1930," *Bulletin of the Palestine Economic Society,* 5 (no. 2).

Plessner, Yakir (1994). *The Political Economy of Israel: From Ideology to Stagnation.* Albany: State University of New York Press.

Point Four (1950). *Point Four: Cooperative Program for Aid in the Development of Economically Underdeveloped Areas.* Washington, DC: Department of State Publication 3719.

"Population." (1971). *Encyclopedia Judaica,* vol. XIII. Jerusalem: Keter, pp. 866–903.

Porath, Yehoshua (1974). *The Emergence of the Palestinian-Arab National Movement 1918–1929.* London: Frank Cass.

(1977). *From Riots to Rebellion: The Palestinian-Arab National Movement 1929–1939.* London: Frank Cass.

(1986). "Mrs. Peters' Palestine," *The New York Review of Books,* January 16.

Poshter, A. (1939). *The Development of the Citrus Marketing Cooperative Societies in the 1937/38 Season*. Tel Aviv: Anglo-Palestine Bank.

Preston, Samuel H. (1975). "The Changing Relation between Mortality and Level of Economic Development," *Population Studies*, 29 (no. 2): 231–46.

  (1976). *Mortality Patterns in National Populations*. New York: Academic Press.

  (1980). "Causes and Consequences of Mortality Declines in Less Developed Countries during the Twentieth Century." In Richard A. Easterlin (ed.), *Population and Economic Change in Developing Countries*. Chicago: University of Chicago Press.

Preston, Samuel H., Nathan Keyfitz, and Robert Schoen (1972). *Causes of Death: Life Tables for National Populations*. New York and London: Seminar Press.

Ram, Uri (1993). "The Colonization Perspective in Israeli Sociology: Internal and External Comparisons," *Journal of Historical Sociology*, 6 (no. 3): 327–350.

RCR: see *Palestine Royal Commission Report*.

Reichman, Shalom (1971). "The Evolution of Land Transportation in Palestine, 1920–1947," *Jerusalem Studies in Geography*, 2: 55–90.

  (1979). *From Foothold to Settled Territory: The Jewish Settlement, 1918–1948*. Jerusalem: Yad Izhak Ben-Zvi (in Hebrew).

Report (1925). Colonial Office, *Palestine. Report of the High Commissioner on the Administration of Palestine 1920–1925*. Colonial No. 15. London: HMSO.

Report of the Censuses (1931). *Report and General Abstracts of the Censuses of Jewish Agriculture, Industry and Handicrafts and Labor*. Jerusalem: Jewish Agency for Palestine, Department of Statistics.

"Report on Investigation of Cost of Living" (1922). *Commercial Bulletin*, 2 (nos. 23, 24): 504–507, 557–63.

Report by the Treasurer (annual issues). *Report by the Treasurer on the Financial Transactions of the Palestine Government*. Jerusalem: Government Printer.

Reuveny, Jacob (1993). *The Administration of Palestine under the British Mandate 1920–1948*. Ramat Gan: Bar-Ilan University Press (in Hebrew).

Review of World Trade (various years). Geneva: League of Nations.

Robinson, Maxime (1973). *Israel: A Colonial-Settler State?* New York: Pathfinder Press.

Rosenhek, Zeev (1995). "The Origin and Development of a Dualistic Welfare State: The Arab Population in the Israeli Welfare State." Unpublished Ph.D. dissertation, Hebrew University of Jerusalem (in Hebrew).

Ruppin, Arthur (1932). "Income Tax in Palestine," *Palestine and Near East Economic Magazine*, nos. 18–19: 443–45.

Samuel, Ludwig (1946). *Jewish Agriculture in Palestine*. Jerusalem: Jewish Agency for Palestine, Economic Research Institute.

  (1947). "Arab Agriculture and Its Development Between 1931 and 1945," CZA/S90/633 (mimeo).

SAP: see *Statistical Abstract of Palestine*.

Sarnat, Marshall (1966). *The Development of the Securities Market in Israel*. Tübingen: J. C. Mohr (Paul Siebeck).

Sato, Kazuo (1971). "International Variations in the Incremental Capital-Output Ratio," *Economic Development and Cultural Change*, 19 (no. 4): 621–40.

Sawer, E. R. (1923). *A Review of the Agricultural Situation in Palestine.* Jerusalem: Department of Agriculture and Fisheries.

Schlesinger, Yaacov (1944). *The Weight of Wages and Imported Inputs in the Cost of Construction.* Jerusalem: Jewish Agency for Palestine, Economic Research Department (in Hebrew).

Schnell, Izhak, Michael Sofer, and Israel Drori (1995). *Arab Industrialization in Israel: Ethnic Entrepreneurship in the Periphery.* Westport: Praeger.

Schultz, T. Paul (1988). "Education Investments and Returns." In Chenery and Srinivasan, *Handbook of Development Economics*, vol. I, pp. 544–630.

Schultz, Theodore W. (1964). *Transforming Traditional Agriculture.* New Haven: Yale University Press.

(1971). *Investment in Human Capital.* New York: Free Press.

(1981). *Investing in People: The Economics of Population Quality.* Berkeley and Los Angeles: University of California Press.

Sen, Amartya K. (1984). "The Living Standard," *Oxford Economic Papers*, 36 (Supplement): 74–90.

(1985a). *Commodities and Capabilities.* Amsterdam: North Holland.

(1985b). "Well-Being, Agency and Freedom: The Dewey Lectures 1984," *Journal of Philosophy*, 82 (no. 4): 169–221.

(1987a). *The Standard of Living.* Cambridge: Cambridge University Press.

(1987b). *On Ethics and Economics.* Oxford: Basil Blackwell.

Sex and Age of International Migrants, Statistics for 1918–1947 (1953). New York: United Nations, Department of Social Affairs, Population Division.

Shafir, Gershon (1989). *Land, Labor and the Origin of the Israeli-Palestinian Conflict 1882–1914.* Cambridge: Cambridge University Press.

(1993). "Land, Labor and Population in the Zionist Colonization: General and Specific Aspects." In Uri Ram (ed.), *Israeli Society: Critical Perspectives.* Tel Aviv: Breirot, pp. 104–19 (in Hebrew).

Shalev, Michael (1992). *Labour and the Political Economy in Israel.* Oxford: Oxford University Press.

Shapira, Anita (1977). *Futile Struggle: Hebrew Labor, 1929–1939.* Tel Aviv: HaKibbutz HaMeuhad (in Hebrew).

Sicron, Moshe (1957a). *Immigration to Israel 1948–53.* Jerusalem: Falk Project for Economic Research in Israel and Central Bureau of Statistics.

(1957b). *Immigration to Israel 1948–53: Statistical Supplement.* Jerusalem: Falk Project for Economic Research in Israel and Central Bureau of Statistics.

Sicron, Moshe and B. Gill (1955). "The Jewish Population by Sex, Age and Country of Birth (1931–1954)," *Special Series*, no. 37. Jerusalem: Central Bureau of Statistics.

Sikumim (statistical bulletin; various issues, 1930–46). Tel Aviv: General Federation of Jewish Labor in Eretz-Israel, Department of Statistics and Information (in Hebrew).

Smith, Barbara J. (1993). *The Roots of Separatism in Palestine: British Economic Policy 1920–1929.* Syracuse: Syracuse University Press.

Southard, Addison E. (1922). *Palestine, Its Commercial Resources with Particular Reference to American Trade.* Washington, DC: Department of Commerce, Bureau of Foreign and Domestic Commerce, Special Consular Reports, No. 83.

Srinivasan, T. N. (1994). "Human Development: A New Paradigm or Reinvention of the Wheel?" *American Economic Review*, 84 (no. 2): 238–43.

Statistical Abstract of Israel (annual issues). Jerusalem: Central Bureau of Statistics.

Statistical Abstract of Palestine 1929 (1930). Jerusalem: Keren Hayesod.

Statistical Abstract of Palestine (SAP) (annual issues, 1936–45). Jerusalem: Office of Statistics.

Statistical Bulletin (periodical, 1939–44). Tel Aviv: General Federation of Jewish Labor in Eretz-Israel, Department of Statistics and Information (in Hebrew).

Statistical Handbook of Jewish Palestine (1947). Jerusalem: Jewish Agency for Palestine, Department of Statistics.

Statistical Handbook of Middle Eastern Countries (1945). Jerusalem: Jewish Agency for Palestine, Economic Research Institute.

Stein, Kenneth W. (1984). *The Land Question in Palestine, 1917–1939*. Chapel Hill and London: University of North Carolina Press.

Sternhell, Zeev (1995). *Nation-Building or a New Society?: The Zionist Labor Movement (1904–1940) and the Origin of Israel*. Tel Aviv: Am Oved (in Hebrew).

Stiglitz, Joseph E. (1988). "Economic Organization, Information, and Development." In Chenery and Srinivasan, *Handbook of Development Economics*, vol. I, pp. 93–160.

Streeten, Paul (1994). "Human Development: Means and Ends," *American Economic Review*, 84 (no. 2): 232–37.

Supplement to Survey of Palestine (1947). Jerusalem: Government Printer.

Survey, 1946. *A Survey of Palestine*, vols. I-III. Jerusalem: Government Printer.

Sussman, Zvi (1973). "The Determinants of Wages for Unskilled Labor in the Advanced Sector of the Dual Economy of Mandatory Palestine," *Economic Development and Cultural Change*, 22 (no. 1): 95–113.

   (1974). *Wage Differentials and Equality within the Histadrut: The Impact of Egalitarian Ideology and Arab Labor on Jewish Wages in Palestine*. Ramat Gan: Massada Ltd. (in Hebrew).

Syrquin, Moshe (1986). "Economic Growth and Structural Change: An International Perspective." In Yoram Ben-Porath (ed.), *The Israeli Economy: Maturing Through Crises*. Cambridge, MA: Harvard University Press, pp. 42–74.

Szereszewski, Robert (1968). *Essays on the Structure of the Jewish Economy in Palestine and Israel*. Jerusalem: Maurice Falk Institute for Economic Research in Israel.

Taqqu, Rachelle Leah (1977). "Arab Labor in Mandatory Palestine, 1920–1948." Unpublished Ph.D. dissertation, Columbia University.

   (1980). "Peasants into Workmen: Internal Labor Migration and the Arab Village Community under the Mandate." In Joel S. Migdal et al., *Palestinian Society and Politics*. Princeton: Princeton University Press, pp. 261–85.

Taubman, Paul and Michael L. Wachter (1986). "Segmented Labor Markets." In Orley Ashenfelter and Richard Layard (eds.), *Handbook of Labor Economics*, vol. II. Amsterdam: North Holland, pp. 1183–1217.

Taylor, Alan T. (1994). "Mass Migration to Distant Southern Shores: Argentina and Australia, 1870–1939." In Timothy J. Hatton and Jeffrey G. Williamson (eds.), *Migration and the International Labor Market 1850–1939*. London and New York: Routledge, pp. 91–115.

Tel Aviv (1926). *Tel Aviv in View of the Numbers (The Results of the September 1925 Census)*. Tel Aviv: Tel Aviv Municipality (in Hebrew).

Thalman, Naftali (1991). "The Character and Development of the Farm Economy in the Templar Colonies in Palestine, 1869–1939." Unpublished Ph.D. dissertation, the Hebrew University of Jerusalem (in Hebrew).

Tidrick, Gene, M. (1975). "Wage Spillover and Unemployment in a Wage-Gap Economy: The Jamaican Case," *Economic Development and Cultural Change*, 23 (no. 2): 306–24.

Timmer, Peter, C. (1988). "The Agricultural Transformation." In Chenery and Srinivasan, *Handbook of Development Economics*, vol. I, pp. 275–331.

Tun Wai, U. (1956–57). "Interest Rates in the Organized Money Markets of Underdeveloped Countries," *International Monetary Fund Staff Papers*, 5: 249–78.

(1957–58). "Interest Rates outside the Organized Money Markets of Underdeveloped Countries," *International Monetary Fund Staff Papers*, 6: 80–142.

(1977). "A Revisit to Interest Rates outside the Organized Money Markets of Underdeveloped Countries," *Banca Nazionale del Lavoro Quarterly Review*, 31 (no. 2): 291–312.

Twenty Five Years of Service to Arab Economy 1930–1955 (1956). Amman: Arab Bank Ltd.

Village Statistics 1945, A Classification of Land and Area Ownership in Palestine: originally published by the government of Palestine; new edition published in 1970 with explanatory notes by Sami Hadawi. Beirut: Palestine Liberation Organization Research Center.

Vital Statistics Tables 1922–1945 (1947). Jerusalem: Department of Statistics, Palestine Government.

Viteles, H. (1927). *Report on Almond Cultivation in Palestine*. Jerusalem: Central Bank of Co-operative Institutions in Palestine Ltd.

(1928). "Expansion of the Orange Industry in Palestine," *Bulletin of the Palestine Economic Society*, 4 (no. 1).

(1929). "The Jewish Cooperative Movement in Palestine," *Bulletin of the Palestine Economic Society*, 4 (no. 1).

Volcani [Elazary-Volcany], I. (1930). *The Fellah's Farm*. Tel Aviv: Jewish Agency for Palestine, Institute of Agriculture and Natural History.

Wage Rate Statistics Bulletin (various issues, 1937–40). Jerusalem: Government of Palestine, Office of Statistics.

Warriner, Doreen (1948). *Land and Poverty in the Middle East*. Westport: Hyperion Press.

Waschitz, Yosef (1947). *The Arabs in Palestine*. Merhavia: Sifriyat Hapoalim (in Hebrew).

Wasserstein, Bernard (1979). *The British in Palestine: The Mandatory Government and the Arab-Jewish Conflict, 1917–1929*. London: Royal Historical Society.

Willcox, Walter, F. (ed.) (1931). *International Migrations*, vol. II. New York: National Bureau of Economic Research.

Wood, G. E. (1943). *Survey of National Income of Palestine*. Jerusalem: Government Printer.

(1944). "National Income of Palestine," *General Monthly Bulletin of Current Statistics*, 9 (no. 8): 342–45.

Worden, Nigel (1994). *The Making of Modern South Africa*. Oxford: Blackwell.

World Bank Atlas (annual issues). Washington, DC: World Bank.

World Development Report (annual issues). Washington, DC: World Bank.

Ziv, Sanny (1996). "Jewish Welfare Outlays in the Mandatory Period." Unpublished MA thesis, the Hebrew University of Jerusalem (in Hebrew).

Zureik, Elia T. (1979). *The Palestinians in Israel: A Study in Internal Colonialism*. London: Routledge & Kegan Paul.

Index

absentee landlords, 89, 90
absorption, *see* immigration, economic absorption of
absorptive capacity, 66, 74–5, 91, 137
Africa, 35, 59, 159, 165, 200, 202, 204
age structure, 16, 36, 43, 64, 79, 80, 117
  of immigrants, 53, 72, 74, 78–80
agriculture (agricultural), 10, 12–14, 111, 119, 204
  Arab employment in and exit from, 93, 128, 132, 143–4, 219
  citrus, 131, 145–9, 153
  demonstration effects, 140–1
  employment and labor productivity, 127, 142–5, 151, 204
  employment of Arabs in, and exclusion from, Jewish, 128–9, 175
  employment of Palestinians in Israel, 209
  export and trade, 169–75
  in Arab and Jewish aggregate economic activity, 26–7
  in colonial settler economies, 203–4
  land tenure and production, 94–103
  land utilization and investment in, 20, 90, 95, 100, 146, 148, 150–4, 193, 195, 204
  productivity of land in, 100–2
  research and extension services, 140, 150, 152, 189
  settlement in Zionism, 5, 6, 8, 193–6, 198
  statistics (appendix), 220–5
  structure and development, 145–54
  tariff protection of, 183
  taxation, 181–2
  trade between Israel and the territories, 208
  see also cash crops; citrus; export, farming; irrigation; land, nation building; peasant economy; trade; Zionist
Agricultural Mortgage Company, 111
Agudat Israel, 5

Aliya, 65, 72
  3rd, 67, 72, 74, 77, 79
  4th, 68, 72, 77
  5th, 69, 72, 78, 82, 113, 135, 154
Alliance of Palestine Workers, 6
Allied forces, 143, 153, 166, 241
America, 59, 60, 62
  North, 18, 35, 38, 44
  see also US
Anglo Palestine Bank (APB), 112–16
APB *see* Anglo Palestine Bank
Arab Bank, 111
Arab National Bank, 111, 115
Arab revolt, 6, 9, 20, 24, 30, 66, 69, 91, 130, 170, 174, 204
Arabs in the Israeli economy, 205–7
Austria, 19, 24, 45, 60, 78, 250

balance-of-payments, 9, 166
Banco di Roma, 112
Banking Ordinance, 113
banks (banking industry), 109–16, 179, 198
  see also credit; financial institutions, instruments, and markets
Barclays Bank, 111, 112, 178
birth control, 39–42
birth rate, 32–6
  determinants of, 36–43, 61
  see also fertility; life expectancy; natural increase
Britain (British)
  as Mandatory for Palestine (obligations and rule), 1–6, 176–7, 183, 188, 203
  colonial currency system, 178
  colonial empire and administration, 176–8
  government expenditures at home and in the colonies, 179–80, 194
  occupation authorities in Palestine, 14
  war-time logistical strategy, 166
  see also colonial; government; UK

Cambridge Middle East Studies